STAFFORDSHIRE LIBRARY AND INFORMATION SERVICES
Please return or renew by the last date shown

BASW

05. MAR 11		
	20. JAN 16	
	26. MAR 14	
	02. JAN 15	
05. JUL 11	24. MAR 17	
22. MAR 12	30. JUN 18	
08. NOV 12	2 8 NOV 2019	
04. NOV 13	29. FEB 20	
	1 4 MAY 2022	
25. NOV 13	1 5 SEP 2022	
- 8 APR 2015	0 3 NOV 2023	
24	11	23	24 NOV 23	
15	12	23	5	1	2024	

If not required by other readers, this item may be renewed in
person, by post or telephone, online or by email.
To renew, either the book or ticket are required

3

24 HOUR RENEWAL LINE 0845 33 00 740

D1464522

3 8014 07048 7068

Published by:
Travel Publishing Ltd
Airport Business Centre, 10 Thornbury Road,
Estover, Plymouth PL6 7PP

ISBN13 9781904434993

© Travel Publishing Ltd

First Published: 1991   Second Edition: 1994
Third Edition: 1997   Fourth Edition: 1999
Fifth Edition: 2002   Sixth Edition: 2005
Seventh Edition: 2007   Eighth Edition: 2009
Ninth Edition: 2010

Please Note:

All advertisements in this publication have been accepted in
good faith by Travel Publishing.

All information is included by the publishers in good faith and
is believed to be correct at the time of going to press. No
responsibility can be accepted for errors.

Editor: Mike Gerrard

Printing by: Latimer Trend, Plymouth

Location Maps: © Maps in Minutes ™ (2010)
                   © Collins Bartholomews 2010 All rights reserved.

Cover Photo: Stanage Edge, Peak District
                   © James Osmond/Alamy

Text Photos: See page 220

Foreword

This is the 9th edition of the **Hidden Places of the Peak District and Derbyshire** which has an attractive new cover and redesigned page layouts. The changes will significantly improve the usefulness, accessibility and appeal of the guide. We do hope you like the new look.

Editorially, the new style will continue Travel Publishing's commitment to exploring the more interesting, unusual or unique places of interest in The Peak District and Derbyshire. In this respect we would like to thank the Tourist Information Centres who helped us update the editorial content of the book.

The *Peak District National Park* was the very first of Britain's National Parks covering an area of 540 square miles. The *Dark Peak* covering north Derbyshire and small parts of Cheshire and South Yorkshire is an area of windswept moorland, steep river valleys and impressive crags. Futher south is the *White Peak* a limestone-based undulating green landscape criss-crossed by miles of dry stone walls and gently flowing rivers whilst to the west can be found the beautiful valleys and rivers of the *Dales* as well as the *Staffordshire Moorlands*. In contrast the rest of Derbyshire offers the visitor an intriguing mix of villages and towns packed with cultural and industrial heritage and should certainly not be missed.

The Hidden Places of the Peak District and Derbyshire contains a wealth of information on the history, culture and the hundreds of interesting places to be found within the National Park and the county of Derbyshire. But it also promotes the more secluded and little known visitor attractions and advertises places to stay, eat and drink many of which are easy to miss unless you know exactly where you are going. These are cross-referenced to more detailed information contained in a separate, easy-to-use section to the rear of the book. This section is also available as a free supplement from the local Tourist Information Offices.

We include hotels, bed & breakfasts, restaurants, pubs, bars, teashops and cafes as well as historic houses, museums, gardens and many other attractions throughout the Peak District and Derbyshire, all of which are comprehensively indexed. Many places are accompanied by an attractive photograph and are easily located by using the map at the beginning of each chapter. We do not award merit marks or rankings but concentrate on describing the more interesting, unusual or unique features of each place with the aim of making the reader's stay in the local area an enjoyable and stimulating experience.

Whether you are travelling around the Peak District and Derbyshire on business or for pleasure we do hope that you enjoy reading and using this book. We are always interested in what readers think of places covered (or not covered) in our guides so please do not hesitate to use the reader reaction form provided to give us your considered comments. We also welcome any general comments which will help us improve the guides themselves. Finally if you are planning to visit any other corner of the British Isles we would like to refer you to the list of other **Hidden Places** titles to be found to the rear of the book and to the Travel Publishing website.

Travel Publishing

Did you know that you can also search our website for details of thousands of places to see, stay, eat or drink throughout Britain and Ireland? Our site has become increasingly popular and now receives hundreds of thousands of visits. Try it!

website: www.findsomewhere.co.uk

Location Map

Contents

LOCATION MAP

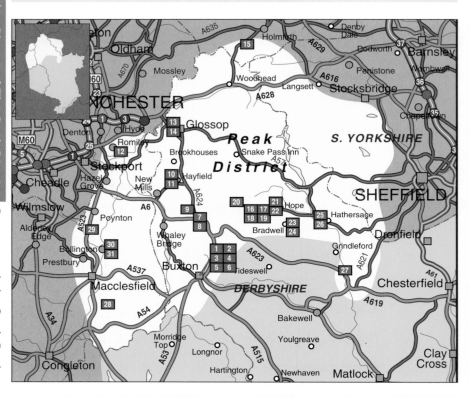

Accommodation

2	The Devonshire Arms, Buxton	*pg 5, 139*
3	Nat's Kitchen, Buxton	*pg 5, 140*
5	Alpine Lodge Guest House, Buxton	*pg 6, 142*
8	The Roebuck Inn, Chapel-en-le-Frith	*pg 9, 143*
10	The Sportsman, Hayfield, High Peak	*pg 13, 145*
13	The Star Inn, Glossop	*pg 14, 147*
16	Ye Olde Cheshire Cheese Inn, Castleton,	
	Hope Valley	*pg 17, 150*
18	Denewood, Castleton, Hope Valley	*pg 18, 152*
19	Causeway House, Castleton, Hope Valley	*pg 18, 153*
21	The Old Hall Hotel, Hope, Hope Valley	*pg 19, 154*
23	Ye Olde Bowling Green Inn, Bradwell,	
	Hope Valley	*pg 20, 155*
24	Stoney Ridge, Bradwell, Hope Valley	*pg 20, 156*
25	Elliotts Coffee Shop & Bistro, Hathersage,	
	Hope Valley	*pg 22, 157*

Accommodation

26	The Little John Inn, Hathersage,	
	Hope Valley	*pg 22, 158*
28	The Ryles Arms, Higher Sutton,	
	Macclesfield	*pg 26, 160*
31	The Church House Inn, Bollington	*pg 28, 162*

Food & Drink

1	Cheshire Cheese, Buxton	*pg 5, 139*
2	The Devonshire Arms, Buxton	*pg 5, 139*
3	Nat's Kitchen, Buxton	*pg 5, 140*
4	The Tradesman's Entrance, Buxton	*pg 5, 141*
7	In a Pickle, Chapel-en-le-Frith	*pg 9, 143*
8	The Roebuck Inn, Chapel-en-le-Frith	*pg 9, 143*
9	The Lamb Inn, Chinley, High Peak	*pg 10, 144*
10	The Sportsman, Hayfield, High Peak	*pg 13, 145*

BUXTON AND THE DARK PEAK

The Peak District is a truly topographically diverse tract of land in the Southern Apennine Range, also known as the 'Backbone of England'. It divides the rugged north from the softer pastoral countryside of the south and lies mostly in the county of Derbyshire but extends its reaches into the neighbouring counties of Staffordshire, Cheshire, South Yorkshire, and as far north as West Yorkshire and Greater Manchester.

At its hub is the Peak District National Park – the first in Britain – covers an area of 555 square miles (1,438-km). The land itself is divided into two distinct regions that take their names from the underlying rocks: the Dark Peak and the White Peak. The contrast could not be more marked, and it gives the Peak District a unique, dual personality which is constantly changing, yet as comfortably enduring as the rocks themselves.

The northern area of the Peak District National Park, known as the Dark Peak or High Peak, is a landscape of moorland and deep valleys edged with escarpments of dark

Pennine Way, Peak District

sandstone and shale. The rugged millstone grit moorland and crags enclose the softer limestone plateau of the White Peak like a horseshoe. The ancient, originally pagan custom of well-dressing and the mysterious Castleton Garlanding Ceremony are found mainly in these limestone areas of Derbyshire, where the streams frequently disappear through the porous rock.

There are spectacular rock formations, picturesque villages and historic churches and

3

castles. The Romans left their roads and the remains of their forts and baths, there are Saxon and Norman churches, and the Civil War raged through the area leaving a trail of destruction. The National Park is scattered with the remains of ancient settlements. Mainly agricultural for hundreds of years, with some coal mining and ironworks, the industrial revolution transformed the place as mills, mines and works sprang up everywhere. As the population of the towns grew, the factory and mine owners built houses for the workforce, churches and grand civic buildings, and left a rich legacy of Victorian architecture.

The Amber Valley, the Erewash and the Trent Valley, to the east and south of Derbyshire, although not part of the National Park, have many pleasant walks and magnificent stately homes for visitors to enjoy. Derbyshire was at the forefront of the Industrial Revolution, and its history is recorded in the Industrial Museum at Derby. It is reflected, too, in many of the villages with their rows of 18th and 19th century workers' cottages. To the northeast of Derbyshire is the heart of the coal-mining area, which prospered during the 19th and early 20th centuries. Sometimes overlooked, this part of Derbyshire is well worth exploring for its industrial architecture alone.

On the southern edge of the Peak District, the undulating pastures and crags of the Staffordshire Moorland are ideal places to walk, cycle or trek. It is a mixture of charming villages, historic market towns, ancient farms and relics of the Industrial Revolution, including the reservoirs of Rudyard and Tittesworth. They were originally the water supply for the Midlands, but are now peaceful havens for wildlife and leisure.

The Dark Peak, or High Peak, is not as forbidding as its name might suggest. These high moors are ripe for exploring on foot, and a walk from the Kinder Reservoir will lead to the western edge of Kinder Scout. This whole area is really a series of plateaux, rather than mountains and valleys, with the highest point on Kinder Scout being some 2,088 feet above sea level. In this remote and wild area the walker can feel a real sense of freedom -

however, it is worth remembering that the moors, with their treacherous peat bogs and unpredictable mists, which can rise quickly even in summer, should not be dismissed as places for a casual ramble.

It was at Kinder Scout, in April 1932, that the single most important action in securing access rights for ordinary people to the English countryside took place. Seventy or so years ago, the unique sense of freedom offered by the beckoning Dark Peak moors was available only to a privileged few, for most of the moorland was the strictly-private game reserve of a handful of wealthy owners. 'Trespassers will be Prosecuted' and 'Keep Out' signs were abound, but these didn't ward off over 400 walkers who took part in what became known as the "Mass Trespass", by walking over the land. Five of the leaders received prison sentences ranging from two and six months, they immediately became martyrs to the cause of free access, and their actions led to legislation which opened up England's countryside to walkers. The Peak District National Park was also formed as a direct result of the trespass, and nowadays the Pennine Way passes directly over Kinder Scout.

To the eastern side of this region are the three reservoirs created by flooding of the upper valley of the River Derwent. Howden, Derwent and Ladybower provide water for the East Midlands but their remote location, along with the many recreational activities found there, make them popular places to visit. The Derwent dam is particularly famous as the site of practice exercises for the Dambusters of the Second World War. Even those who have not visited the area before will be familiar with some of the place names, as they feature heavily in winter weather reports. Snake Pass (the A57), one of the few roads that run through this northern section of the National Park, is often closed during the winter; even in spring, conditions can deteriorate quickly to make driving hazardous.

The Peak District National Park is now one of the most visited areas in the world. There are up to 30 million visits each year - only Mount Fuji National Park in Japan has more visits!

BUXTON

Although not actually situated within the National Park itself, the elegant Georgian town of Buxton is the largest habitation that lies within what is widely know as, "The Peak District", where it is possibly one of the best centres to base a short, or even long term stay within the area. Referred to as the heart of the Peak District, Buxton, like Bakewell, is right on the divide between the Dark Peak and White Peak areas of the National Park. A large part of the White Peak lies between the two towns. The reason why Buxton was excluded from the National Park becomes obvious as you approach it from the south on the A6. As you drop off the limestone plateau, enormous quarry faces open up on your right at Tunstead. Buxton in fact is almost ringed by gigantic quarries, so the Park boundary was drawn neatly around it. At 1,000 feet above sea level, Buxton is also England's second-highest market town (only Alston in Cumbria is higher), and provides a wealth of things to do.

Both the Peak District and the Peak District National Park are filled with much of historical interest, some of which dates back several thousand years. For its gracious architecture, the town of Buxton wears the crown, and can be attributed mainly to the 5th Duke of Devonshire, who hoped to establish a northern spa town that would rival, and possibly surpass, the attractions of Bath. In both locations it was the Romans who first exploited the healing waters of apparently inexhaustible hot springs as a commercial enterprise. They arrived in AD70, and called the place *Aquae Arnemetiae* that translates as "The Spa of the Goddess of the Grove". It is one of only two places in Britain which had the Roman prefix aquae (meaning "waters") - the other being *Aquae Sulis*, or Bath. The waters still bubble up at Buxton, always maintaining a constant temperature of 82°F (28°C). Buxton water is reputed to be particularly pure and especially effective at relieving the symptoms of rheumatism. Countless rheumatism sufferers are on record attesting that Buxton water has helped to soothe their symptoms but it wasn't until the Tudor period that the reputation of the spa waters was enhanced when Mary, Queen of Scotland, under the custodianship of the 6th Earl of Shrewsbury, was given leave to take the waters for her numerous ailments. The Hall, now the Old Hall Hotel was specially built to house her visits between 1573 and 1584. The people of Buxton also say that it makes the best cup of tea possible, and collect bottles of it to take

---

1 CHESHIRE CHEESE

Buxton

This must see public house attracts plenty of customers through its doors to sample home cooked food and real ales.

See entry on page 139

---

2 THE DEVONSHIRE ARMS

Buxton

A warm welcome is guaranteed at this family-run pub on the edge of beautiful Buxton.

See entry on page 139

---

3 NAT'S KITCHEN

Buxton

Award winning food and accommodation come with a warm welcome at this popular restaurant.

See entry on page 140

---

4 THE TRADEMANS ENTRANCE

Buxton

An up and coming place to dine during the day in the Georgian town of Buxton.

See entry on page 141

home. Experts have calculated that the water that bubbles up nowadays fell as rainfall over 5,000 years ago.

In the 18th century, the 5th Duke of Devonshire was inspired to build **The Crescent** and **Great Stables** to ensure that visitors would flock here. Between 1780 and 1811 he was also responsible for the development of the Square, Hall Bank and St John's Church. Built to the designs of John Carr of York, The Crescent was the first 'resort' hotel in Britain and was at the heart of Buxton's aspirations to become a fashionable spa town. The building is similar to the architecture found in Bath and, after suffering from neglect, is being converted into a 5-star luxury spa hotel. Next to The Crescent, the Thermal Baths are now the Cavendish Arcade, and the former town house of Bess of Hardwick and her husband the Earl of Shrewsbury, The Hall, is now the Old Hall Hotel. **Turner's Memorial** stands opposite, and commemorates Samuel Turner, treasurer to the Devonshire Hospital. It was built by Robert Rippon Duke in 1879, a very good friend of Turner. During 1959, a local motorist crashed into the memorial, the choice was made to demolish it at the time. When the area received its pedestrian modernization some years later however, it was repaired and reinstated to its former glory, being part of Buxton's important heritage.

-When the railway first arrived in 1863 it brought even greater numbers of visitors to Buxton to holiday and take the waters. New baths, a Pump Room, churches and hotels were built to accommodate them. The Great Stables were converted into the Royal Devonshire Hospital and had its magnificent slate roof added in 1881. The **Pavilion and Gardens** were laid out and in 1903 the **Opera**

Pavilion Gardens, Buxton

House was opened to much acclaim.

The attractive **Buxton Opera House** was designed by the renowned theatre architect, Frank Matcham. Gertrude Lawrence, Gracie Fields and Hermione Gingold all played here and on one memorable occasion, the famous Hollywood screen stars Douglas Fairbanks and Mary Pickford were in the audience to watch the Russian ballerina, Anna Pavlova. However, in 1932 it became a cinema and, apart from an annual pantomime and a handful of amateur performances, showed films only. In the late 1970s it was restored to its former Edwardian grandeur and was officially opened by Princess Alice in 1979. Today it is one of Britain's leading provincial theatres, practically bursting at the seams with around 450 performances each year including dance, comedy, children's shows, drama, music, pantomime, opera and even shows on ice!

St John the Baptist Church was built in Greek style, with pediment, in 1811 by Sir

---

5   **ALPINE LODGE GUEST HOUSE**

Buxton

Jean welcomes guests into her home with charming hospitality and is known for her delicious home cooked breakfasts.

See entry on page 142

Buxton Opera House

Jeffrey Wyatville. That same year Wyatville laid out The Slopes, the area below the Market Place in Upper Buxton. The grand **Town Hall** was built between 1887 and 1889 and dominates the Market Place. Further down Terrace Road is the **Buxton Museum**, which reveals the long and varied history of the town and its surrounding area. As well as housing an important local archaeology collection, the museum also has a fine collection of Ashford Marble, Blue John ornaments, paintings, prints, pottery and glassware.

It is not known for certain whether well dressing took place in Buxton before 1840. There are stories that Henry VIII put a stop to the practice, but it has certainly been a part of Buxton's cultural calendar since the Duke of Devonshire provided the townsfolk with their first public water supply at **Market Place Fountain**. From then on, High Buxton Well (as the fountain came to be called) and St Anne's Well were decorated sporadically. In 1923 the Town Council set about organising a well-dressing festival and carnival that continues to this day. Every year on the second Wednesday in July, this delightful tradition is enacted.

St Anne's Church, built in 1625, reflects the building work here before Buxton's 18th century heyday when limestone was the most common construction material, rather than the mellow sandstone that dominates today.

Buxton is surrounded by some of the most glorious of the Peak District countryside. These moorlands also provide one of the town's specialties - heather honey. Several varieties of heather grow on the moors: there is ling, or common heather which turns the land purple in late summer; there is bell-heather which grows on dry rocky slopes; and

there is cross-leaved heather which can be found on wet, boggy ground.

The town is also the starting point for both the Brindley Trail and the Monsal Trail. Covering some 61 miles, the **Brindley Trail**, which takes its name from the famous canal engineer, leads southwest to Stoke-on-Trent, while the **Monsal Trail**, beginning just outside Buxton at Blackwell Mill Junction, finishes at Coombs Viaduct near Bakewell, some 8 miles away.

AROUND BUXTON

Less than one mile to the west of the town, on Green Lane, is **Poole's Cavern**. Since the 16th century, the cavern has been known as "the first wonder of the Peak". It is a natural limestone cave, said to be over 2 million years old, which was used by tribes from the Neolithic period onwards. Archaeological digs have discovered Stone Age, Bronze Age and Roman artefacts near the cave entrance. Art Hacker's "Buxton Thro' Other Glasses" (turn of the century) says …

"A kind of abandon-hope-all-ye-who-enter-here sort of feeling assails you as you pass beneath the low arch of rock."

The spectacular natural formations in the cavern include a large stalactite called the 'Flitch of Bacon' and the 'Poached Egg Chamber', with blue grey and orange formations, coloured by manganese and iron soaking down from the lime-tips above.

Axe Edge Moor, which receives an average annual rainfall of over four feet, is strictly for

6 **BUXTON MUSEUM AND ART GALLERY**

Buxton

Explore the history of the area from pre-history to the Victorian era and enjoy displays of art works.

See entry on page 142

Axe Edge Moor, Buxton

hardened walkers. It should come as no surprise that this moor is the source of several rivers which play important roles in the life of the Peak District including the River Dove, River Manifold, River Dane, River Wye and River Goyt. The moor actually spreads over three counties, and at Three Shire's Head, to the south east, the counties of Derbyshire, Staffordshire and Cheshire meet.

The entire length of the River Goyt can be walked, from its source to its confluence with the River Etherow to the north and just outside the boundaries of the National Park. Once marking the boundary between Derbyshire and Cheshire (which now lies just to the west), a walk along the Goyt takes in sections of the riverbank as well as the Errwood and Fernilee reservoirs before leaving Derbyshire just north of New Mills. Although the two reservoirs look well established and very much part of the landscape, they are relatively recent additions: the Fernilee was opened in 1938 while the Errwood was flooded in 1967.

The highest point in this area is **Shining Tor**, overlooking **Errwood Reservoir** and standing some 1,834 feet above sea level. To the north is **Pym Chair**, the point at which an old packhorse road running east to west crosses this gritstone ridge. An old salters' route, it was used for transporting salt from the Cheshire plains across the Peak District moorlands to the industrial and well-populated areas of south and west Yorkshire. Pym Chair is said to be named after a highwayman called Pym, who used to sit here awaiting travellers whom he could rob. During the 19th century the Goyt Valley, with its natural resources of both coal and water,

developed rapidly into one of the nation's major textile production centres. In order to service this growth, the valley also developed an intense system of transport, including canals and railways. The rugged terrain that had to be negotiated has made for some spectacular solutions to major engineering difficulties.

NORTH OF BUXTON

TAXAL

5 miles NW of Buxton off the A5004

Overlooking the Goyt Valley, Taxal is home to the **Church of St James**, the tower of which dates from the 12th century. Inside are a series of fascinating memorials - the earliest to William Jaudrell, who died in 1375, and Roger Jaudrell, a soldier killed at Agincourt in 1415. This is the same family that gave its name to Jodrell Bank, where the radio telescope can be found. An unusual memorial is one dated 1768 to the "Yeoman of the King's Mouth" or "food taster" to George II. West of Taxal are **Windgather Rocks**, a gritstone outcrop popular with trainee rock-climbers. East of the village is the elegant and gracious **Shallcross Hall**, dating back to the 18th century and at one time home of the Shawcross family.

COMBS

3 miles N of Buxton off the A6

Combs Reservoir is situated near to the village, just outside Chapel-en-le-Frith, and is crossed at one end by Dickie's Bridge. 'Dickie' is said to have lived at a farm in Tunstead where he was known as Ned Dixon. Apparently murdered by his cousin, he nevertheless continued his 'working life' as a sort of guard-skull, alerting the household with a series of knockings on the walls whenever strangers drew near. Of course, Dickie's little 'security' alarm was a problem at times; for instance, labourers had to be recruited for harvest time but were unable to sleep with the noises they heard. They left

Errwood Reservoir

Combs Reservoir

very quickly. Strange occurrences are said to have ensued when attempts were made to move the skull.

CHAPEL-EN-LE-FRITH

5 miles N of Buxton off the A6

This charming town stands on a high hill, near the High Peak, adjacent to the Buxton and Whaley-Bridge railway. It sprang from an ancient chapel within the Peak 'frith' or forest when in 1225 the guardians of the High Peak's Royal Forest purchased land from the Crown and built a chapel here, dedicating it to St Thomas à Becket of Canterbury. A century later the chapel was replaced with a more substantial building and further modernisation took place in the early 1700s. The building of the original chapel led to the foundation of the town and also its name, which is Norman French for 'chapel in the forest'. Although the term 'forest' suggests a wooded area, the 'frith' or forest never really existed, but referred to the Royal Forest of the Peak: hunting grounds that extended over much of north Derbyshire during the Middle Ages.

One piece of its heritage is the Peak Forest Tramway. This connected the

limestone quarries around Dove Holes with the canal basin at Buxworth, and provided a further means to getting the stone to market where it was needed.

A great scandal occurred here in 1648, when Cromwell's men used the church as a gaol for 1,500 prisoners of the Scottish Army who had fought at the Battle of Ribbleton Moor. The conditions were appalling, few could even lie down because of the overcrowding and they were left there for 16 days before being released. No fewer than 44 died during this period and another 10 were too weak to survive the forced march back to Scotland. The dead were buried in the churchyard and after that the church became known as 'Derbyshire's Black Hole'.

Chapel Brow is a steep and cobbled street lined with picturesque little cottages leading down from the church onto Market Street and the modern section of the town, and is the true centre of Chapel. Visitors to this part of the town will notice several curious relics from a bygone era, notably the old stocks on the market place, put there by the town elders to meet out justice to wrong doers, and the old market cross. A more recent curio can be seen over the doorway of a premises on the Market Place. A bull's head stares out over the street, and is all that remains of the inn that once stood here in pre-war years.

Looming over the town is the prominent **Eccles Pike** (1,250 feet high) which, every year in August, is the site of the Eccles Pike Fell Race, one of the oldest fell races in the country – renowned for being tough and demanding. The road up to the Eccles Pike from Chapel-en-le-Frith has stunning views of the surrounding valleys and hills. From the top, and from Castle Naze, you can see as far

---

7 IN A PICKLE

Chapel-en-le-Frith

This popular café and delicatessen is run by a charming mother and daughter team who serve up fresh home baked food all day.

See entry on page 143

8 THE ROEBUCK INN

Chapel-en-le-Frith

The perfect welcoming pub, with good food, good ale, and rooms to rent right on the Market Place.

See entry on page 143

Eccles Pike Topograph

as Manchester, 20 miles to the northwest.

On the Castleton Road just a few miles northeast of the village lies the **Chestnut Centre**, a fascinating wildlife and conservation park. It is set in 50 acres of landscaped grounds and home, not only to a unique collection of birds and animals, but to many wild birds and mammals.

CHINLEY

6 miles N of Buxton off the B6062

Chinley is beautifully situated with plenty of walking close at hand, and a walk up **Chinley Churn** or **Cracken Edge** gives an excellent view across the area. This small north Derbyshire village lays claim to the superb **Chinley Viaducts**, a masterpiece of Victorian engineering. Chinley Station was once an important railway junction; from here you would have been able to catch a train to Sheffield, Manchester, Derby or even London. However, the railway is now a shadow of its former self, with the line to London closed since 1968 and the Manchester - Sheffield service much reduced from its heyday. Nonetheless, a legacy of fine railway bridges and viaducts can be seen around Chinley, and

it must have been an amazing sight in the era of the steam engine.

The most important building around Chinley is probably the Elizabethan Hall at nearby Whithough which was built by the Kyrke family in the 16th century but is now the Old Hall Inn.

Another notable residence in the area is **Ford Hall** which was home to Reverend William Bagshawe (known as the "Apostle of the Peak"). He served as vicar of Glossop from 1652 until his ejection in 1662 under the Act of Uniformity. Bagshawe's successor as Nonconformist minister at Chinley, Dr James Clegg, built **Chinley Chapel** in 1711. Chinley Chapel, a simple Georgian building, looks deceptively like an ordinary house from the outside.

BUXWORTH

6 miles N of Buxton off the B6062

The village name has had a chequered history, starting off as Buggesworth in 1222, then Bugsworth in 1625. In the summer of 1929 the villagers had a choice of 'Bugsworth' or 'Buxworth', according to the original petition document, which was rescued from a refuse bin in the late 1980's. There were 365 signatures for 'Buxworth' and only 3 against.

During 1999 there was an attempt to put the 'bug' back in Buxworth, in order to commemorate the Millennium, but villagers voted the idea down, so it remains 'Buxworth' to some and 'Buggy' to others.

Buxworth is the site of the terminal basin for the Peak Forest Canal (see Whaley

9 THE LAMB INN

Chinley

A great country pub renowned in the town for its well stocked bar, fine food and first class service.

See entry on page 144

Bugsworth Basin, Buxworth

Bridge), finished in 1800. It became one of the largest ports on the English narrow canal network during the 19th century, and remains unique as the only complete example of a canal and tramway terminus in Britain. **'Bugsworth Basin'** was granted the status of a Scheduled Ancient Monument in 1977.

Buxworth used to have several public houses. Nowadays there is one inn, the Navigation, and a war memorial club known as 'Buggy Club'.

WHALEY BRIDGE

7 miles N of Buxton off the A5004

Known locally as the *'Gateway to the Goyt Valley'*, this Area of Outstanding Natural Beauty is a magnet for walkers, tourists and those seeking adventure. The village grew up around the coal-mining and textile industries. Both have now gone, but many feel the real glory of Whaley Bridge is the **Peak Forest Canal**, flowing through the town. Many visitors come by water, and there is a thriving barge-restaurant base at the canal head; boats can also be hired to those who want to explore the delights of the waterways in the area.

The **Toddbrook Reservoir**, often seen in summer with small yachts, is in an exceptionally beautiful setting. It was built in 1831 to be a feeder for the Peak Forest Canal, and is situated to the west of the town. The wharf here is dotted with picturesque narrowboats.

The whole area round the canal basin is very historic, with a large conservation area. Every year, usually in June, the basin provides the setting for one of the biggest local events, the **Whaley Water Weekend**. It is their starting point for the annual **Rose Queen Carnival**, which usually follows a week later.

To the east of the town lies a weird natural feature on the hillside. The curiously named **Roosdyche** is a strange flat-bottomed valley, 3/4 mile long, 40 yards wide and with sides sloping up to 30 feet high. Local legend decrees that The Roosdyche was a Roman racecourse as nobody could explain its creation, but it is now believed the great

Toddbrook Reservoir, Whaley Bridge

scoop taken out of the hillside was the result of glacier erosion dating from the last ice age.

A map detailing many of the walks in and around Whaley Bridge is available from many outlets in the town.

LYME PARK

8 miles NW of Buxton off the A6

Lyme Park is an estate and park in the county of Cheshire, although the estate lies wholly within the Peak District National Park. It is an ancient estate that was given to Sir Thomas Danyers in 1346 by a grateful King Edward III after a battle at Caen. Danyers then passed the estate to his son-in-law, Sir Piers Legh, in 1388. It remained in the family until 1946, when it was given to the National Trust. The principal feature of the park is **Lyme Hall**, which offers a memorable glimpse of a genteel and extravagant age and has now become even better known since its use as the location for "Pemberley", the home of Mr. Darcy, the BBC's 1995 production of Jane Austen's novel *Pride and Prejudice*. The grounds now form a country park owned and managed by the National Trust and supported by Stockport Metropolitan Borough Council. A leaflet has been produced to help you get the best out of the grounds and gardens.

Not much remains of the original Elizabethan manor house; in the 18th century the house was redesigned to resemble an Italian palazzo, the work of Venetian architect Giacomo Leoni. Undaunted by the bleak landscape and climate of the surrounding Peak District, Leoni built a corner of Italy here in this much harsher countryside. Inside the mansion there is a mixture of styles: the elegant Leoni-designed rooms with rich rococo ceilings, the panelled Tudor drawing room, and two surviving Elizabethan rooms. Much of the three-dimensional internal carving is attributed to Grinling Gibbons, though a lot of the work was also undertaken by local craftsmen. Another glory of the house is the collection of early 17th-century Mortlake tapestries, produced in what was then the village of Mortlake outside London.

As well as the fantastic splendour of the manor house, the estate includes a 17-acre Victorian garden, laid out with impressive bedding schemes, a sunken parterre, an Edwardian rose garden, Jekyll-style herbaceous borders, a reflection lake, a ravine garden and Wyatt conservatory. The garden is surrounded by 1,400 acres of medieval moorland, woodland and parkland, and is home for many Red Deer and Fallow Deer. Also within the garden is an unusual landmark, **The Cage**: built as a hunting lodge, it served as a watchtower from which to follow the stag hunts but was later used as a lockup for poachers. After years of disuse it has now been restored.

NEW MILLS

9 miles N of Buxton off the A6015

Situated by the River Sett, New Mills takes its name from Tudor corn mills that once stood on the riverbanks, though an earlier mill, known as the "Berde Mill", built in 1391, gave it the name New Mill before that. Later, in the 18th and 19th centuries, water power was used to drive several cotton-spinning mills in the town and, as New Mills grew, the textile industry was joined by engineering industries and the confectionery trade. There is still a rich legacy of this industrial heritage to be found in the town. The Torr Mill is featured on the millennium series of postage stamps issued by the Post Office. The elevated **New Mills Millennium Walkway**, built on stilts rising from the River Goyt, sits directly opposite the Torrs Mill. The walkway answered public demand for a route through

New Mills Millennium Walkway

the impassable gritstone **Torrs Gorge**, reached by the **Torrs Riverside Park**. The gorge is an area of exceptional natural beauty and unique industrial archaeological heritage. The 175-yard-long steel walkway is fixed to the rock face and adjoining railway retaining wall at a height of about 20 feet from the base of the 100-feet deep gorge. The **New Mills Heritage and Information Centre**, near the walkway, contains a fine model of how the town looked in the 1840s.

The **Little Mill** at Rowarth still retains a working water wheel, although the mill building is now a well-known public house. Opposite the library is the Police Station, where the ringleaders of the 'Kinder Trespassers' were kept in the cells, following their arrest in 1932 after the mass public trespass on Kinder Scout. Although it is now a private house, the site is identified by a plaque on the wall. The trespass was a significant factor in the creation of National Parks, to allow public access to the countryside (see also the introduction to this chapter).

The serious walker or stroller can use New Mills as a starting point for various way-marked walks. The **Goyt Valley Way** leads south to Buxton via Whaley Bridge and the Goyt Valley north to Marple. There are local signposted walks below the Heritage Centre, and the **Sett Valley Trail** follows the line of the old branch railway to Hayfield and then on to Kinder Scout. Opened in 1868, the single track line carried passengers and freight for over 100 years. However, by the late 1960s much of the trade had ceased and the line closed soon afterwards. In 1973 the line was reopened as a trail and is still used by walkers, cyclists and horse riders and it takes in the remains of buildings that were once part of the prosperous textile industry.

HAYFIELD

9 miles N of Buxton off the A624

Beneath the western slopes of **Kinder Scout**, Hayfield sits peacefully in the narrow valley of the River Sett surrounded by some of the wildest hills in the Dark Peak. The first written record of the place is to be found in the *Domesday Book* when it was called 'Hedfeld' and was a natural clearing in the vast forest that once covered the whole of North Derbyshire. It was once a staging post on the packhorse route across the Pennines. The old packhorse route went up the Sett valley and by Edale Cross, where the remains of an old cross can still be seen, down to Edale by Jacob's Ladder. Some ancient cottages still survive around the centre of the old village, and some local farmhouses date from the 17th century.

Things were much different in its industrial past, when cotton and paper mills, calico printing and a dye works made it a busy and anything but a peaceful place. As the 18th century progressed Hayfield began to share in the great expansion of textiles, which was taking place in its neighbour town, New Mills. Three-storey weavers' houses replaced many of the thatched cottages; three woollen mills were built by the river and later in 1810, a dye works. However, the prosperity did not last and handloom weaving began to decline, although Hayfield still had woollen mills until the mid 19th century.

A curious building can be found in Market Street, on the left of a small square known as

Pennine Way, nr Kinder Scout, Hayfield

Dungeon Brow. Built in 1799, this was the town's lock-up and was referred to as the new prison. However, the stocks in front of the building appear to be somewhat newer than the prison itself.

The elegant parish **Church of St Matthew** was completed in 1818, and is a reminder of this Pennine town's former prosperity. It stands on the site of a medieval church built in 1386 at the command of Richard II. The freemen of the parish had the right to appoint their own vicar, recommending him to the local bishop. This right was given to the freeholders when the church was built.

Tourists now come to walk on Kinder Scout, which at 2,088 feet is the highest point in the Peak District National Park, or to explore the much gentler valley of the River Sett. Hayfield is a popular centre for exploring the area and offers many amenities for hill walkers. The old station site has been turned into a picnic area and information centre. For many years Kinder Scout was barred to walkers, being preserved as a grouse moor until the peace was interrupted on 24th April 1932 by the famous 'Mass Trespass', when four hundred ramblers set off walking across the moors. Five ramblers were

10 THE SPORTSMAN	
Hayfield	
Lying at the foot of Kinder Scout, this inn is a great place to start your walks and well known for its delicious home cooked food, real ale and great accommodation.	
See entry on page 145	

11 THE PACK HORSE	
Hayfield	
This pub and restaurant offers a unique, stylish and sassy take on the traditional country inn with decor, facilities and cuisine a cut above the rest.	
See entry on page 146	

later arrested and imprisoned for their part in the demonstration. But it was not made in vain: as a result of the trespass access restrictions were gradually reduced. The walk started from **Bowden Bridge Quarry**, just to the west of the village centre, which is now a car park with public toilets and a Peak Park campsite opposite.

Three miles northeast of the town is **Kinder Downfall**, a spectacular waterfall and at over 90 feet is the highest waterfall in the county. It lies on the River Kinder, where it flows over the edge of **Kinder Scout**. The waterfall was formerly known as '*Kinder Scut*', and it is from this that the plateau derives its name. In winter when the fall freezes solid it forms an imposing and fascinating sight – one not to be missed! In such conditions, climbers use it for ice-climbing training. It is also renowned for its blow-back effect, hence the phrase 'Kinder blow-back': where the prevailing wind forces the fall's water back against the rock so the water appears to run uphill! Not far from the bottom of the fall is a small lake known as **Mermaid's Pool**. Legend has it that those who go to the pool at midnight on the night before Easter Sunday will see a mermaid, or water sprite, swimming in the dark waters. The legend is said to date back to the times when pools and lakes were places of worship.

CHARLESWORTH
12 miles N of Buxton on the A626

Located on the western edge of the Pennines, Charlesworth has many old and typically Pennine cottages. The cotton mills established in the 19th century have long since ceased to operate but the village has two rows of small cottages where the

occupants used to weave cotton.

As well as the neat mock-Gothic **St John the Baptist Parish Church** (1849), there is also a Catholic church (1985), which was built primarily for the many Irish immigrants who came over to this country after the potato famine to work in the nearby mills.

The site of a Roman fort, Melandra Castle is situated nearby and can be reached by a path from the Glossop to Stalybridge road.

GLOSSOP
13 miles N of Buxton off the A624

Glossop stands at the foot of an exhilarating stretch of road with hairpin bends, known as the **Snake Pass**, and the town is an interesting mix of styles: the industrial town of the 19th century with its towering Victorian mills and the 17th century village with its charming old cottages and cobble streets. The name Glossop is thought to be of Saxon origin, derived from "Glott's Hop" - where 'hop' is a small valley and 'Glott' was probably a chieftain's name.

Further back in time, when the Romans arrived here the area was under the control of the Brigantes, who were in the midst of a civil war. This led to Roman intervention and

Snake Pass, nr Glossop

---

12 **DUKE OF YORK**

Romiley

Just two minutes from the Peak Forest Canal this traditional pub offers a warm welcome to all with seven award winning ales and a Mediterranean menu on offer.

See entry on page 147

---

13 **STAR INN**

Glossop

A real pub with a wide range of real ales, close to the town centre and with accommodation too.

See entry on page 147

the establishment of a fort, now known as **Melandra Castle**, though it is thought that the Roman name for the fort was 'Ardotalia'. The early, wooden fort probably dates from the seventies of the first century AD in the course of the 'pacification' of Brigantia. The timber fort has disappeared completely under the present stone fort and very little survives today but the stone foundations. The settlement developed further as part of the monastic estates of Basingwerk Abbey in north Wales and the village received its market charter in 1290. Subsequently there was a decline in its importance, and little now remains of Old Glossop except the medieval parish **Church of All Saints.**

Planned as a new town in the 19th century by the Duke of Norfolk, the original village stood on the banks of the Glossop Brook at the crossing point of three turnpike roads. The brook had already been harnessed to provide power for the cotton mills, as this was one of the most easterly towns of the booming Lancashire cotton industry. Many still refer to the older Glossop as Old Glossop and the Victorian settlement as Howard Town, named after the Duke, Bernard Edward Howard.

Latest news suggests that Glossop is set to become one of the country's most attractive areas for birdlife with the creation of a huge nature reserve bordering the National Park. The Royal Society for the Protection of Birds (RSPB) is believed to be in the final stages of negotiations and it hopes to turn a huge swathe of land into a conservation area where normal activities such as farming can continue but always with the birdlife in mind. The proposed site will stretch from Saddleworth in the north to Glossop in the south, taking in the Arnfield and Dovestones reservoirs and the Chew Valley. These areas are rich in wildlife, especially moorland birds such as the curlew, ring ouzel and the golden plover. There are also peregrine falcons, short-eared owls and many wetland birds. And in addition to the many species of birds there is also an abundance of roe deer, which were first spotted in the area by locals twenty years ago.

You can keep yourself up-to-date with daily newsworthy stories about what's going in the area at www.glossopadvertiser.co.uk.

DINTING

13 miles N of Buxton off the A624

The village is well served by the Dinting Railway Station, which is notable for the impressive **Dinting Arches**: a 120 feet viaduct built to carry the main Sheffield to Manchester railway line, which crosses the narrowest point of the valley, to the west of Glossop. Its graceful yet sturdy and even structure lends its name to a pale medium strength beer that is hugely popular in the county. The village church of the **Holy Trinity** was built in 1875 in Victorian gothic style and has a tall and elegant spire.

HADFIELD

14 miles N of Buxton off the A624

Once upon a time this was a small, inconspicuous town at the dead end of a branch railway line.

The main attraction of Hadfield is that it marks the start of the **Longdendale Trail**, which follows the line of the former Manchester to Sheffield railway line and forms part of the longer Trans-Pennine Trail that runs from coast to coast (Liverpool to Hull). It is now a safe, traffic-free trail for biking and walking. Its level sandy surface makes it suitable for wheelchair users and less agile people, as well as for families with small children and pushchairs. You can get onto the Longdendale Trail at Platt Street, Hadfield.

Longdendale itself is the valley of the River Etherow, and is a favourite place for day-trippers. Along the footpath through this

---

14 **REVIVE COFFEE LOUNGE**

Glossop

A charming mother and daughter team open this relaxing coffee lounge seven days a week serving delicious homemade food and sweets from the Glossop area.

See entry on page 148

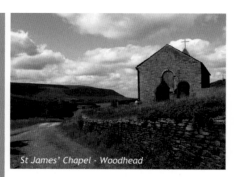
St James' Chapel - Woodhead

Shrewsbury, Talbot used the road with great frequency as he travelled from Glossop to his father's castle at Sheffield.

EDALE

8 miles NE of Buxton off the A625

Edale is a justly popular destination for people who want to walk, climb, mountain-bike, hang-glide or just sit and admire the magnificent scenery. Though the valley has changed over the centuries, it remains unspoilt, and there are many places where even in the bustle of today it is possible to escape from the crowds. Many travellers have spoken of Derbyshire as a county of contrasts, and nowhere is this more apparent than at Edale. Not only does the landscape change dramatically within a short distance from the heart of the village, but the weather - as all serious walkers will know - can alter from brilliant sunshine to snowstorms in the space of a couple of hours.

Edale is famous for being the start of the **Pennine Way National Trail**. Opened in 1965, this long-distance footpath winds up the watershed of England to Kirk Yetholm, across the Scottish border. The 300-year-old Nag's Head Inn is the traditional start of the 270-mile (435-km) Pennine Way. Though the footpath begins in the lush meadows of this secluded valley, it is not long before walkers find themselves crossing the wild and bleak moorland of Featherbed Moss before heading further north to Bleaklow.

The village, nestling at the foot of Kinder Scout, is in the heart of dairy-farming and stock-rearing country and began as a series of scattered settlements. The five hamlets, which punctuate its length, are all called 'booths', an old word meaning a temporary shelter for herdsmen. The true name of the village is actually Grindsbrook Booth, but it is commonly known by the name of the valley. Tourism first came to Edale with the completion of the Manchester to Sheffield railway in 1894, though at that time there was little in the way of facilities for visitors. Today there are several hotels, camping sites, a large youth hostel and adventure and walking centres. **The Moorland Centre** is a

wild and desolate valley there are many reminders of the past, including **St James' Chapel**, the graveyard of which has numerous memorials to the navvies, and their families, who died in an outbreak of cholera in 1849 while working on the two tunnels on the Sheffield to Manchester railway line. The chapel was originally built in 1487, though it has been rebuilt several times since.

NORTH EAST OF BUXTON

From Glossop the A57 east is known as **Snake Pass**, an exhilarating stretch of road with hair-pin bends. The road is frequently made impassable by landslides, heavy mist and massive snowfalls in winter but, weather permitting, it is an experience not to be missed. For much of the length of the turnpike road that Thomas Telford built across Snake Pass in 1821, the route follows the line of an ancient Roman road, known as Doctor's Gate, which ran between Glossop and a fort at Brough. The route was so named after it was rediscovered, in the 16th century, by Dr Talbot, a vicar from Glossop. The illegitimate son of the Earl of

---

15 THE FLEECE INN

Holme

This homely inn is known for its great hospitality, entertainment and quality cuisine, just a stone's throw from some of the area's best reservoir walks.

See entry on page 149

visitor and learning centre at Fieldhead, with interactive exhibits, a living roof of sedum turf which acts as eco-friendly insulation, and much helpful information about the area and especially the Pennine Way. The Duke of Devonshire, speaking at the opening ceremony in September 2006, said: "In order to love these uplands properly we need to learn about them and educational facilities and functions are high on the list of priorities here and rightly so".

Not far from the village is the famous **Jacob's Ladder**. Nearby is the tumbledown remains of a hill farmer's cottage; this was the home of Jacob Marshall, who some 200 years ago cut the steps into the hillside leading up to **Edale Cross**, an ancient boundary marker erected by the monks of Holywell abbey, Flintshire, who owned lands here in medieval times.

CASTLETON

8 miles NE of Buxton off the A62

Situated at the head of the lovely Vale of Hope, Castleton is sheltered by the Norman ruin of **Peveril Castle** (English Heritage). The castle, originally called *'Castle of the Peak'* was built as a wooden stockade in 1080 by William Peveril (illegitimate son of William the Conqueror). In 1155 Henry II, thinking that the Peverils had become too powerful, seized the castle and its lands. Later rebuilt in stone, the keep was added by Henry in 1176. It was originally about 60 feet high and faced with gritstone blocks, which still remain on the east and south sides and still dominates the view across Castleton. In Tudor

Peveril Castle and Cavedale

times the building fell into disrepair, and the keep was used as a courthouse. Soon after, the castle was abandoned completely, with the stone being used for building cottages. In 1832 Sir Walter Scott published *Peveril of the Peak*, set in and around the castle. The foundations of the Great Hall and kitchens can be seen inside the courtyard. It remains the only surviving example of a Norman castle in Derbyshire, and is among the best preserved and most complete ruins in Britain.

Approaching Castleton from the west along the A625, the road runs through the **Winnats Pass**, a narrow limestone gorge hemmed in on both sides by steep limestone hills. It is thought to have been created when huge caverns, carved out by swift-flowing underground rivers, collapsed. The gorge, over a mile in length, has been used as a road for centuries and is still the only direct route to the village from the west.

Aside from the castle, some of the older buildings in the village are the Castle Hotel, which dates back to the 17th century and is one of several pubs here, and Castleton Hall, a fine 13th-century house, now a YHA Youth Hostel. Two and a half miles west of the village at Rushup Edge is **Lord's Seat**, a Bronze Age burial mound. **St Edmund Parish Church** was heavily restored in 1837, but retains its box pews and a fine Norman arch,

16 YE OLDE CHESHIRE CHEESE INN
Castleton

A true English country inn offering traditional décor, log fires, wholesome food and cask ales with four poster accommodation available.

See entry on page 150

17 THE PEAKS INN
Castleton

This traditional country inn provides an ideal base from which to explore the Peak District.

See entry on page 151

Winnats Pass, Castleton

the throne in 1660 after the rule by the parliamentarians.

The Garland is a wooden frame, with bunches of wild flowers attached and a small wreath of garden flowers on top called the 'Queen'. The 'King', dressed in Stuart costume, with the garland on his shoulders, tours the village on horseback followed by a procession and a band. At the end of the ceremony the garland is left on the top of the tower of St Edmund's Church to wither and the Queen's wreath is placed on the war memorial.

The hills to the west of Castleton are famous for their caves, which have been in the hands of the Ollerenshaw family for many years and are probably one of Derbyshire's most popular attractions. Amazing trips down into the caves themselves can be made. During these trips, as well as seeing the incredible natural beauty of the caverns and the unique rock formations, there are collections of original 19th-century mining tools. Above ground, in the gift shops, various items can be bought made with the distinctive "Blue John" fluorspar with its attractive purplish veining, which is only found in the Castleton area.

The **Blue John Mine** is a natural cavern system with some old workings. The name "Blue John" was given to the fluorspar in the

as well as a Breeches Bible.

Castleton has a lot to offer visitors in terms of interest and history. **Castleton Visitor Centre** is situated at the very heart of the village. The centre houses a fascinating museum as well as a full range of tourist information services including accommodation bookings, local theatre bookings, brochures, and up-to-date information on events, attractions and the Peak District National Park. In addition, there are constant changing displays in the exhibition room, which show off the talents of local artists, photographers and crafts people.

If you visit Castleton you can learn about the numerous traditions, customs and annual events for which Castleton has become famed. Where else will you find a Garland Ceremony held on **Oak Apple Day** or the ancient practice of ringing a curfew bell?

On Oak Apple Day, 29th May, the ancient ceremony of garlanding takes place in the village, and after the three feet high Garland has been paraded though the streets, it is hoisted to the top of Saint Edmund's Church tower. The ceremony celebrates the ending of winter, and the restoration of Charles II to

18 DENEWOOD

Castleton

Four star luxury en-suite B & B in the Heart of the Peak District. Offering unique Chocolate Heaven breaks. Four Star Holiday Cottage also available.

See entry on page 152

19 CAUSEWAY HOUSE

Castleton

Modern comforts in a 15-century cottage, and an award-winning breakfast all greet guests at the Causeway in Castleton.

See entry on page 153

18th century by two miners, John Kirk and Joseph Hall. The best caverns within the system are the Crystallised Cavern and the Variegated Cavern.

At the bottom of Winnats Pass, only 1,000 metres (0.6 miles) from the centre of the village, lies **Speedwell Cavern**. It is a very gentle walk along the road to this former lead mine, which used boats on an underground canal to ferry the miners and lead ore to and from the rock face. Half way along is a small chamber known as Halfway House, which allows boats to pass as they go in and out. The mine had a short life: it opened in 1771 and, following an investment of £14,000, closed in 1790 after only £3,000 worth of iron ore had been extracted. This underground canal is about 800 metres long, finally reaching a glorious cavern with a huge subterranean lake known as the Bottomless Pit.

Treak Cliff Cavern is on the Mam Tor Road and contains superb stalagmites and stalactites. The cavern is not a natural formation, as it was dug by miners for the Blue John fluorspar. However, while digging in 1926, the miners broke through into some natural caverns, which have some features now known as the Frozen Waterfall and Aladdin's Cave.

Only **Peak Cavern** is a true cave. Directly beneath the castle, it has an awe-inspiring entrance and is said to have the widest opening of any cave in the British Isles. More recently the cave has been promoted using its older, more vulgar name the "Devil's Arse" (so-called because of the flatulent-sounding noises from inside the cave). Up until the 17th century, little cottages used to stand within the entrance. The rope-makers who lived in these tiny dwellings used the cave

entrance for making rope, the damp atmosphere being a favourable environment for rope-making. Bert Marrison, the last rope-maker in Castleton, worked here and his ashes, along with some of his tools, are buried here. The ropewalk, which dates back some 400 years, can still be seen and guides re-enact the process of making rope. One rope-maker's cottage still exists.

HOPE

9 miles NE of Buxton off the A625

Tradition says that a great battle took place here in the 7th century between the troops of Mercia, under King Penda, and Northumbrian troops under King Edwin. The tradition further states that two hills to the north of the village, **Win Hill** and **Lose Hill**, were so named because of the battle. However, the village gets its first recorded mention in a charter dated AD 926, where it mentions a great battle won by King Athelstan. By the time of the *Domesday Book* of 1086, the parish of Hope had extended to embrace much of the High Peak area and included places such as Buxton, Chapel-en-le-Frith and Tideswell, and was one of the largest parishes in England. It remained so until the 19th century, though a market charter was not granted it until 1715.

21 THE OLD HALL HOTEL

Hope

This traditional inn offers rustic Derbyshire dishes, real ales and luxury four poster accommodation with separate tea rooms adjacent.

See entry on page 154

20 TREAK CLIFF CAVERN

Castleton

This spectacular underground cavern contains a wealth of rock formations, minerals and fossils. A fascinating day out for all the family.

See entry on page 153

22 THE COURTYARD CAFÉ

Hope

This secluded café is nestled within a hidden garden, serving delicious homemade soups, sandwiches and fair trade teas and coffees.

See entry on page 154

The parish **Church of St Peter** was built at the beginning of the 13th century. The only part remaining from that original church is the Norman font. Its tower is 14th-century with a squat spire on top and, though the chancel was rebuilt in 1881, 14th-century piscina and sedilia are incorporated into the walls. The Latin inscription on a chair in the north aisle reads (in translation), 'You cannot make a scholar out of a block of wood', and is said to have been carved for Thomas Bocking, the vicar and schoolmaster here during the 17th century. His name also appears on the fine pulpit, and his Breeches Bible is displayed nearby. From the outside, the squat 14th-century spire gives the church a rather curious shape. In the churchyard can be found the shaft of a Saxon cross.

The **Hope Agricultural Show** is held every year on August Bank Holiday Monday, and offers something for all the family.

BROUGH

9 miles NE of Buxton off the A6187

Brough is the site of the Roman fort of **Navio**, meaning 'place by the river'. Excavations of the site in the early 20th century revealed an enclosure with walls six feet thick, though little can be seen today. This rectangular fort was built in AD 158 to control the Romans' lead mining interests in the area. You can visit the riverside fort and wonder what the garrison thought of the surrounding hills as they kept lookout.

BRADWELL

9 miles NE of Buxton off the B6049

'Bradder' as this Hope Valley village is known locally, has a long and chequered history. People have taken baths in Bradwell ever since the Romans built the fort of *Narvio* at nearby Brough (also see Brough). Near the New Bath Hotel, where there is a thermal spring, the remains of a Roman Bath were found. Legend has it that Bradwell was also once a Roman slave camp, with the slaves working in the lead mines.

Later, when the Roman Empire fell just after AD400, Bradwell became a tribal border

and the mysterious earthwork known as the **Grey Ditch** was constructed north of the village. The boundary is a massive embankment that runs from Bradwell Edge to Mick Low to protect the limestone plateau from the north. We still don't know who built it or when.

During the Middle Ages and later Bradwell was an important centre for lead mining, and is famous as the place where miners' hardhats - hard, black, brimmed hats in which candles were stuck to light the way underground - were made; thus these hardhats came to be known as 'Bradder Beavers'.

The centre of the village is a maze of narrow lanes with tiny cottages. A narrow street called Smalldale follows the line of the Roman road between Brough and Buxton.

Most buildings in Bradwell date from the 19th century. Built in 1549, Hazelbadge Hall is one of the oldest houses in the area.

Bradwell is also the birthplace of **Samuel Fox**, the 19th-century inventor of the modern umbrella. His house is marked with a plaque and lies just off the main street.

A key attraction here is the massive **Bagshawe Cavern**, a cave reached by descending a flight of 98 steps through an old lead mine. It was named after Sir William Bagshawe, who owned the land when it was discovered in 1806 by lead miners. For the

---

23   **YE OLDE BOWLING GREEN INN**

Hope Valley

Traditional country pub in a great location in the Peak District National Park, appealing to food and drink lovers alike. Accommodation is available too.

See entry on page 155

---

24   **STONEY RIDGE**

Bradwell

This long serving bed and breakfast is run by a friendly local couple offering delicious breakfasts, en suite accommodation and their own indoor heated swimming pool.

See entry on page 156

more adventurous, caving trips are available.

On the Saturday before the first Monday in August, four wells are dressed in the village. Although wells were dressed even at the turn of the 20th century, the present custom dates back only to 1949, when the Bowling Green Well was dressed during Small Dale Wakes. The village has its own particular method for making the colourful screens, section by section, so that the clay does not dry out.

BAMFORD

11 miles NE of Buxton off the A6187

Bamford is a hillside village beneath the **Bamford Edge** and on the road to the **Ladybower** and **Upper Derwent** dam. When the Derwent and Howden dams were built in the early years of the 20th century, the valley of the Upper Derwent was flooded, submerging many farms under the rising waters. The 1,000 or so navvies and their families were housed at Birchinlee, a temporary village which came to be known locally as 'Tin Town', for its plethora of corrugated iron shacks. During the Second World War the third and largest reservoir, the **Ladybower**, was built. This involved the inundating of two villages — Derwent and Ashopton. Many buildings were lost including ancient farms and Derwent Hall, dating from 1672 and which had been made into a youth hostel in 1931. The spire of the parish church was still visible at first, but was demolished in 1947.

Ladybower Reservoir

St John the Baptist Parish Church in Bamford was built between 1856 and 1860,

and is unlike any other in Derbyshire. It was designed by the famous church architect William Butterfield, with a slender tower and an extra-sharp spire. It was here, within the churchyard, that the dead from Derwent's church were re-interred. The survivors were re-housed in Yorkshire Bridge, a purpose-built hamlet located below the embankment of the Ladybower Dam. The **Visitor Centre at Fairholmes** (in the Upper Derwent Valley) tells the story of these 'drowned villages'. Here you can also learn all about **The Derwent Dam**, which was built in 1935 and was the practice site for the Dambusters, who tested their bouncing bombs here.

Also worthy of note, particularly to lovers of industrial architecture, is **Bamford Mill**, just across the road by the river. This cotton mill, built in 1780 and rebuilt in 1791-1792 after a fire, retains its huge waterwheel and also has a 1907 tandem-compound steam engine. It ceased to operate as a cotton mill in 1965 and was used by an electric furnace manufacturer until a few years ago. It has now been converted for luxury housing.

Along the A57 towards Sheffield, the road dips and crosses the gory-sounding **Cutthroat Bridge**. The present bridge dates back to 1830, but takes its gruesome name from a 16th-century murder, when the body of a man with his throat cut was discovered under the then bridge.

Bamford Sheepdog Trials, held on Spring Bank Holiday Monday, are among the best-attended and most famous in the Peak.

HATHERSAGE

12 miles NE of Buxton off the A625

This is the fictional home of **Little John**, loyal friend of Robin Hood. According to legend Little John, after he had buried his comrade Robin Hood at Kirklees Priory, made his way sadly back to Hathersage where he spent his last remaining days. Whether or not the legend is to be believed, it is worth mentioning that when the grave in the churchyard was opened in the 1780s, a 32-inch thighbone was discovered. This would certainly indicate that the owner was well over seven feet tall. The whole area

Highlow Hall, Hathersage

surrounding Hathersage has features with such names as Robin Hood's Cave, Hood Valley, Hood Brook and Robin Hood's Moss.

As well as its historical association to Robin Hood it also has interesting literary connections. **Charlotte Brontë** stayed at Hathersage vicarage in 1845, and the village itself appears as 'Norton' in her novel *Jane Eyre*. The name Eyre was probably gleaned from the monuments to the prominent local landowners with this surname, which can be seen in the village churchyard.

The Eyre family has been associated with this area for over 800 years. Legend has it that the family was given their name by William the Conqueror. During the Battle of Hastings, so it is said, William was knocked from his horse and, wearing his now battered helmet, found it difficult to breathe. A Norman, Truelove, saw the King's distress and helped him take the helmet off and get back on his horse. In gratitude the King said that from thenceforth Truelove would be known as 'Air' for helping the King to breathe.

Later the King learned that Air had lost most of a leg in the battle, and made arrangements for Air and his family to be cared for and granted land in this part of Derbyshire. The name became corrupted to Eyre over the years, and the family's coat of

arms shows a shield on top of which is a single armoured leg. The 15th century head of the family, Robert Eyre, lived at Highlow Hall. Within sight of this Hall he built seven houses, one for each of his seven sons. **North Lees** was one, which Charlotte Brontë took as a model for Rochester's house, Thornfield Hall. It is one of the finest Elizabethan buildings in the region - a tall square tower with a long wing adjoining and the grounds are open to the public. Another was **Moorseats**, where Charlotte Brontë stayed on holiday and used as the inspiration for Moor House in *Jane Eyre*.

St Michael's Parish Church is said to date from 1381, though it has been much altered and extended over the years. There are brasses of the Eyre family, and an Eyre family chapel once stood on the north side of the chancel, on the other side of the tomb to Robert Eyre, dating from 1459.

Highlow Hall is a fine, battlemented manor built in the 1500s by the Eyre family. It is said to be haunted by a ghost known as The White Lady, thought to be the older sister of the wife of Nicholas Eyre, founder of the Eyre family. Nicholas had promised to marry her, but instead jilted her in favour of her younger sister. She was so humiliated she killed herself.

Until the late 18th century Hathersage was a small agricultural village with cottage industries making brass buttons and wire, until in 1750 a Henry Cocker started the **Atlas Works**, a mill for making wire. By the early 19th century it had become a centre for the manufacture of needles and pins. Though water power was used initially for the mills, by the mid-19th century smoke from the industrial steam engines enveloped the village. The fragments of dust and steel

---

25 **ELLIOTTS COFFEE SHOP & BISTRO**

Hathersage

This contemporary Coffee Shop & Bistro offers speciality drinks, and a daily changing menu of homemade food served in a pretty and relaxed setting.

See entry on page 157

---

26 **THE LITTLE JOHN INN**

Hathersage

This inn has been run for twenty years by the same charming couple who offer bed and breakfast or self catering accommodation, fine real ales and food in a friendly atmosphere.

See entry on page 158

dispersed in the process of sharpening the needles destroyed the lungs of the workers, reducing their life expectancy to 30 years. There was also a paper mill, with the paper being used to wrap the needles and pins. The last mill here closed in 1902, as needle making moved to Sheffield, but several of the mills still stand, including the Atlas Works.

EAST EDGES OF THE DARK PEAK

FROGGATT

5 miles N of Bakewell off the B6054

This neat village sits below the gritstone escarpment known as **Froggatt Edge** - a favourite place for climbers. The village's position has lead to its name - there are 17 fresh water springs in the village of which three can still be seen. The river Derwent is close by together with its attractive 17th-century bridge, which is rather unusual in that it has two different shaped and sized arches.

The Froggatt Show is held on August Bank Holiday and is an offshoot of the former village 'cow club'. There are very few pubs or

Froggatt Edge

shops but the quaintness still attracts many tourists on hot summer weekends.

Nearby **Stoke Hall**, situated high above the Derwent Valley, was built in 1757 for Reverend John Simpson. The Hall remains home to a ghost, said to have been haunting the building for well over 100 years. The ghost is claimed to be that of a maid at the Hall who, while pining for a soldier fighting overseas, was brutally murdered. Her employers at the Hall were so shocked by this that they built a memorial to her in the front garden. However, the memorial was seen to move not long after it had been erected, and so it was rebuilt in a quiet corner of the estate, where it remains undisturbed.

CURBAR

5 miles NE of Bakewell off the A623

Although it is Eyam that is famous as the 'Plague Village', Curbar suffered much the same way, though about 30 years earlier. During the height of the infection bodies were taken away from the centre of the village, and usually as quickly as possible, to prevent the spread of the disease. Many of the graves were left unmarked, but at Curbar the **Cundy Graves** (dating from 1632) can be seen on the moors above the village. They are named after the Cundy family, who farmed nearby. Below the Wesleyan Reform Church there are other graves.

Missionaries have trained at **Cliffe College**, since 1883. It is now a theological college and conference centre sponsored by the Methodist Church. Interesting older features of the village include a circular pinfold or stock compound on top of Pinfold Hill, where stray animals were kept until claimed by their owners. There is also a covered well and circular trough, and an unusual village lock-up with a conical roof.

The coarse gritstone ridge of **Curbar Edge**, which shelters the village, is popular with rock climbers and walkers alike.

CALVER

4 miles NE of Bakewell off the A623

In 1870 James Croston, in his book *On Foot*

Calver Bridge

BASLOW

4 miles NE of Bakewell off the A619

Standing at the northern gates to Chatsworth, Baslow is inextricably linked with the fortunes of the Cavendish family. The village has three distinct parts – Bridge End, the oldest part around the church, Over End, a residential area to the north of the village, and Nether End, next to the Chatsworth Estate. At Nether End, near one of Baslow's two fine bridges over the Derwent River, you can see one of the few remaining thatched cottages in the National Park.

The **Old Bridge** was built in 1603. It is the only bridge across the Derwent that has never been destroyed by floods. It replaced a wooden bridge, and one of the tasks of able-bodied men in the village at one time was to guard this bridge to ensure its weight limit was not exceeded. The watch house still exists, and it has an entrance that is only three-and-a-half feet high. The **Devonshire Bridge** was built just after the First World War, and carries most of the traffic across the river nowadays.

The parish **Church of St Anne's** dates partly from the 15th century, and has an unusual clockface decorated with the legend 'Victoria' and '1897' in place of numerals - the idea of a local man, Lieutenant-Colonel E. M. Wrench. These were added to commemorate Queen Victoria's Diamond Jubilee. It is beautifully situated by the River Derwent, and has a squat broach spire that dominates the village. The fragment of an ancient Saxon cross shaft can also be found in the porch. Inside the church

Through The Peak noted that the air at Calver was 'full of pale blue smoke that wreathed itself into a variety of fantastic looking clouds' - a reference to the lime-burning and lead-smelting which still took place in late Victorian times. Sixty years later just before the Second World War, travel writer Thomas Tudor remarked, 'Calver is not pretty for it has mills and lime works and ugly houses, and gives little suggestion of the rural charm which agriculture and its attendant interests can throw over these Derbyshire dales'.

These days the polluting smoke of industry is consigned to Calver's past and despite heavy traffic over the **Calver Bridge**, built in 1974, the village still wears a cloak interwoven with threads of rural charm.

Calver is also home to one of the most sinister buildings known to television viewers with long memories. The handsome, though austere, **Georgian Cotton Mill**, which is now converted into luxury flats, was the infamous Colditz Castle of the television series of that name. It was built between 1803 and 1804 by Arkwright to replace a mill built in the 1780s.

---

27 **THE EATING HOUSE**

Calver Bridge

The home-cooking draws visitors to the Eating House over and over again, in the delightful setting of the Derbyshire Craft Centre.

See entry on page 159

Baslow Village

another unusual feature is preserved: a whip that was used to drive stray dogs out of the church during services in the 17th and 18th centuries. Some people claim it was also used to waken people who fell asleep during a service and snored.

Baslow sits beneath its own Peakland 'edge', which provides fine views across the Derwent Valley towards Chatsworth House. From the **Eagle Stone**, a 6 metre high block of gritstone on Baslow Edge, to the north of the village, there are wonderful views. Climbing to the top of this isolated rock was a test for every young Baslow man before he married. It is here that the same Lieutenant-Colonel Wrench who had the unusual clock face installed, erected the **Wellington Monument** in 1866 to celebrate the Duke's victory at Waterloo and to counterbalance the monument to Nelson on Birchen Edge not far away. It is in the form of a ten-feet-high cross.

THE CHESHIRE PEAK DISTRICT

MACCLESFIELD

The earliest written reference to Macclesfield is found in the *Domesday Book* of 1086. Macclesfield is a medieval town, as evidenced by its street patterns and their names. Look to the end of Macclesfield's historic streets and you'll see the dramatic Peak District hills. Macclesfield is the major market town for East Cheshire and was once an important silk manufacturing town.

Charles Roe built the first silk mill here, beside the River Bollin, in 1743 and for more than a century-and-a-half, Macclesfield was known as *the* silk town, renowned for the skill of its designers and for its richly patterned woven fabrics. Whilst Macclesfield established its reputation many years ago as the greatest silk weaving centre in England, this industry has now declined in international attention. Some of the early mill buildings survive and a number of them

Old Mill, Macclesfield

are of great architectural interest. It's appropriate then, that Macclesfield can boast the country's only **Silk Museum** where visitors are given a lively introduction to all aspects of the silk industry, from cocoon to catwalk! Originally the Macclesfield School of Art, built in 1877 to train designers for the silk industry, the museum has an award-winning audio-visual presentation, fascinating exhibitions on the Silk Road across Asia, silk cultivation, fashion and other uses of silk. A shop dedicated to silk offers a range of attractive and unusual gifts – scarves, ties, silk cards and woven pictures along with inexpensive gifts for children.

The silk theme continues at nearby **Paradise Mill**. Built in the 1820s, it is now a working museum demonstrating silk weaving on 26 restored jacquard hand looms. Exhibitions and restored workshops and living rooms capture the working conditions and lives of mill workers in the 1930s. It is also possible to buy locally-made silk products here. Within the town's **Silk Heritage Centre** is another silk museum, which has some interesting displays on Macclesfield's rich and exciting past, (the town was occupied for five days by Scottish troops during the Jacobite Rebellion of 1745, for example). The Heritage Centre is housed within a former Sunday School which was built in 1813 and finally closed in 1970.

The Heritage Centre is situated in the centre of Macclesfield. The Silk Museum, Paradise Mill and West Park Museum (see below) are situated within easy walking distance of the Heritage Centre.

One of the Macclesfield area's most famous sons is **Charles Frederick Tunnicliffe**, the celebrated bird and wildlife artist, who was born at the nearby village of Langley in 1901. He studied at the Macclesfield School of Art and first came to public attention with his illustrations for Henry Williamson's *Tarka the Otter* in 1927. A collection of Tunnicliffe's striking paintings can be seen at the **West Park Museum** on the northwest edge of the town. This purpose-built museum, founded in 1898 by the Brocklehurst family, also includes exhibits of ancient Egyptian artefacts, as well as fine and decorative arts.

Much less well-known is **William Buckley**, (the 'Wild White Man') who was born in Macclesfield around 1780. As a young man he joined the army and became a respected soldier. However, his military career came to an abrupt end in 1802, when he took part in a mutiny at Gibraltar against the Rock's commanding officer, the Duke of York, father-to-be of Queen Victoria. The mutiny failed and Buckley was transported to the convict colony of Australia. There he escaped into the outback and became the leader of an aboriginal tribe (the Wathaurung people) who took this giant of a man, some 6 feet 6 inches tall, as the reincarnation of a dead chief. For 32 years Buckley never saw a white man or heard a word of English. When the explorer John Bateman, on his way to found what is now Melbourne, discovered him, Buckley had virtually forgotten his mother tongue. He was pardoned, given a pension and was killed in an accident at Hobart at the age of 76. His survival against the odds, his determination to be free, and his life with the Wathaurong make his story remarkable.

28 THE RYLES ARMS

Higher Sutton

The food here is a real winner and its reputation is growing daily. Definitely worth a look.

See entry on page 160

AROUND MACCLESFIELD

PRESTBURY

3 miles N of Macclesfield off the A538

Prestbury, several times voted one of Cheshire's best-kept villages, has riverside walks along the Bollin Valley towards Wilmslow and includes a great deal of dairy-farming country. It is widely known as one of the most attractive villages in the northwest, with its atmospheric and historic landscape,

Priest's House, Prestbury

13th-century church and ancient buildings including the timber-framed **Priest's House**.

Dominating the centre, however, is the **Parish Church of St Peter**, a building largely of the 13th century but restored in 1879 by Sir George Gilbert Scott. In the churchyard is the church's Norman predecessor, a chapel largely rebuilt in 1747. Even today it still maintains a tradition that began in 1577, as every autumn and winter evening at 8pm a curfew bell is rung, with the number of chimes corresponding to the date of the month. Close by is a building known as the **Norman Chapel** with a striking frontage carved with the characteristic Norman zigzags and beaked heads. Even older are the carved fragments of an 8th-century Saxon cross, preserved under glass in the graveyard.

Opposite the church is the Priest's House, a remarkable building dating back to about 1448 and now a bank. Also of interest is the

Reading Room, a building erected in 1720, which is now housing a branch library, a bank, an estate agent's and the Parish Council Chamber.

Prestbury Hall is in a commanding position facing down the village street. Ford House is at the other end of the street, near Prestbury Bridge, which crosses the River Bollin. Although not a listed building, it has a pleasing appearance and is an important component of the Conservation Area.

Charles Edward Stuart's Jacobite army passed through the village in late November 1745 on its way south to London. Four or five regiments marched through, followed by the prince and his bodyguard. An eyewitness described him as being a 'very handsome person of a man', in Highland dress, with a blue waistcoat trimmed in silver and wearing a blue Highland bonnet.

The village has several excellent restaurants and is a favourite destination for sightseers.

ADLINGTON

4 miles N of Macclesfield off the A523

Adlington Hall is one of the country's most popular attractions, with a history that can be traced back to 1040 when the Legh family of Adlington chose the site for a hunting lodge in the Forest of Macclesfield. The present structure, quadrangular in shape, dates back to 1315 and incorporates both Medieval and Tudor architecture, further wings and rooms having been added down the centuries. There is much to see as you tour the hall, with beautifully-polished wooden floors and lovely antique furnishings enhancing the air of elegance and grandeur. The Great Hall is a breathtaking sight, a vast room of lofty proportions that sets off perfectly the exquisitely painted walls. One of Adlington Hall's most interesting and historic possessions is the organ in the Great Hall, standing in the balcony supported at each end by the two original oak trees, their roots still in the ground. It is one of the finest examples of a large 17th century organ in Britain as well as being one of the oldest. Being virtually unaltered since it was built, it now re-creates the authentic sounds of its day and has responded to the touch of many maestros, none more famous than George Frederick Handel who visited the hall in the 1740s.

Equally impressive are the Hall's gardens. Landscaped in the style of Capability Brown in the 18th century, these are truly a delight to behold, with a Lime Avenue planted in 1688, and the splendid folly 'Temple to Diana' with its painted ceiling. More recent additions to the gardens include a maze, rose garden and the beautiful Father Tiber Water Garden.

It wasn't long after Handel's visit to Cheshire that the county was gripped by a mania for building canals, a passion that has left Cheshire with a uniquely complex network of these environmentally-friendly waterways.

BOLLINGTON

4 miles NE of Macclesfield on the B5091

Known to its residents as the Happy Valley, this town, as the name suggests, lies on the River Bollin, which flows from here down across the Cheshire plain. It's difficult to determine if this is a town or a village, because its 7,300 population is strung out over a distance of about two miles, giving the

---

29 **ADLINGTON HALL**

Adlington

A superb historic house with interesting original features and a delightful garden.

See entry on page 161

---

30 **THE HOLLY BUSH**

Bollington

With its focus on good beer and keeping the customer satisfied, the Holly Bush is a fine example of a traditional British pub.

See entry on page 160

---

feeling of one long village. Present-day Bollington is really based around three villages that became merged together – Bollington, West Bollington and Bollington Cross.

Like Macclesfield, in its 19th-century heyday there were 13 cotton mills working away at Bollington but producing cotton rather than silk. Two of the largest mills, the Clarence and the Adelphi, still stand, although now adapted to other purposes. The Victorian shops and cottages around Water Street and the High Street recall those busy days.

A striking feature of the town is the splendid 20-arched viaduct which once carried the railway over the River Dean. It is now part of the **Middlewood Way**, a ten-mile, traffic-free country trail that follows a scenic route from Macclesfield to Marple. The Way is open to walkers, cyclists and horse riders and during the season cycles are available for hire, complete with child seats if required.

Just as remarkable as the viaduct, although in a different way, is **White Nancy**. This curious dome-shaped, whitewashed monument stands on Kerridge Hill, more than

900 feet above sea level. It was erected in 1817 and has been the subject of considerable discussion though it is generally believed to have been built to commemorate the Battle of Waterloo, and was named Nancy after a member of the Gaskell Family.

Today, Bollington enjoys a strong sense of community spirit and this is no more apparent than at the **Discovery Centre** in Clarence Mill. It was opened by cousins John & Terry Waite, in 2005 and provides an insight into Bollington's heritage.

Visit the Happy Valley site (www.happy-valley.org.uk) for maps, pubs and restaurants, local history, organisations, businesses and artisans, and to learn about local heritage initiatives.

SUTTON

2 miles S of Macclesfield off the A523

Sutton Hall is honoured by scholars as the birthplace of **Raphael Holinshed**, whose famous *Chronicles of England, Scotland & Ireland* (1577) provided the source material for no fewer than 14 of Shakespeare's plays including the plot of *Macbeth*, and for portions of *King Lear* and *Cymbeline*. As well as drawing heavily on the facts in the Chronicles, the playwright wasn't above plagiarising some of Holinshed's happier turns of phrase.

This semi-rural village includes the hamlets of Gurnett and Jarman and it was in Gurnett that the notable engineer James Brindley did his apprenticeship in about 1733. A plaque commemorating this fact can still be seen on Plough Cottage.

White Nancy, Bollington

 THE CHURCH HOUSE INN

Bollington

This traditional stone-built inn combines real ales with really fine food, and a warm northern welcome.

See entry on page 162

Macclesfield Canal, Gurnett

BOSLEY

6 miles S of Macclesfield on the A523

Bosley takes its name from the wild boar that used to be prevalent in the area; in the *Domesday Book* of 1086 it was described as 'Boslegh'. Whilst Bosley is technically part of Macclesfield, it is on the Leek Road, and is a stone's throw from Congleton via the Bosley Crossroads.

To the east of Bosley town centre is the **Macclesfield Canal**, one of the highest waterways in England, running for much of its length at more than 500 feet above sea level. It was one of the last canals to be built and was designed by Thomas Telford. Between Macclesfield and Congleton, the canal descends over 100 feet in a spectacular series of 12 locks at Bosley, before crossing the River Dane via Telford's handsome iron viaduct. Also to the east of the village is the reservoir created to feed the canal. It is used by anglers and is visited by ornithologists.

Macclesfield Canal, Bosley

Other unusual features of this superbly-engineered canal are the two 'roving bridges' south of Congleton. These swing from one bank to the other where the towpath changes sides and so enabled horses to cross over without having to unhitch the tow-rope.

LOCATION MAP

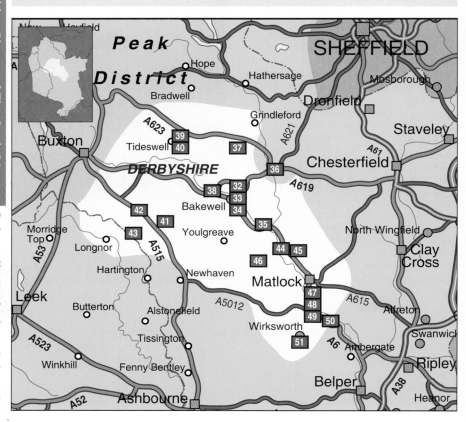

BAKEWELL, MATLOCK AND THE WHITE PEAK

These regions of the Derbyshire Dales occupy the central area of the Peak District National Park between the two major towns of Ashbourne and Buxton. It is altogether a more gentle, feminine kind of landscape than the Dark Peak. Its rich lands are more intensely farmed, and sheep and cattle dot the fields, which are separated by dry-stone walls. The estimated 26,000 miles of dry-stone walls in the White Peak are believed to make the most lasting impression on first-time visitors to the Peak District.

Considered to be part of the White Peak, Bakewell and Matlock are built on sedimentary rock deposited 350 million years ago, when the land lay under a warm tropical sea. Today Bakewell is nearly 400 feet above sea level, but it is by no means among the highest place in the Peak District – parts of which rise to over 2,000 feet. The landscape is a geologist's dream, displaying the effects of millions of years of change.

The two main rivers, the Wye and the Derwent, which both have their source farther north, are, in this region, at a more gentle stage of their course. Over the centuries, the fast-flowing waters were

Countryside near Bakewell

harnessed to provide power to drive the mills situated on the riverbanks; any walk taken along these riverbanks will not only give the opportunity to discover a wide range of plant and animal life, but also provide the opportunity to see the remains of buildings that once played an important part in the economy of north Derbyshire.

Most of the White Peak is now used for dairy farming (for which calcium soil is essential). In the past it supported a number of creameries and the famous Hartington Cheese Factory, which sadly recently closed its doors.

Food & Drink

Places of Interest

BAKEWELL

World famous puddings, annual shows, steeped in history and packed with attractions - Bakewell is a 'must see' town at the geographical (and spiritual) heart of the Peak District National Park. The Park Authority has its headquarters here at **Aldern House** on Baslow Road, but these modern planners are following in the footsteps of an administrative history that goes back to Saxon times.

During Saxon times, Bakewell was in the Anglican kingdom of Mercia, and by Norman times had gained a great level of importance, with the town itself, and its church, being mentioned in the *Domesday Book*. An entry refers to the town as 'Badequella', meaning 'Bath-well', which is said to derive from a cluster of thermal springs in the area.

The **All Saints Parish Church** dates from the 10th century (although most of the building is medieval, it was restored in 1841). The site, on which the church stands contains the largest and most varied group of medieval monuments in Britain. Inside the church, there are many references to the 'Manners' and 'Vernon' families, the story of the elopement of John Manners and Dorothy Vernon being one of the Peak District's most romantic tales.

The Romans had a station here and the town became established as a meeting and crossing point on the River Wye. The three original fords were eventually superseded by bridges and two of these remain: the distinctive **Five-Arched Bridge**, at around 800 years old one of the oldest in the country, and the **Old Packhorse Bridge** further upstream.

There has been a market in Bakewell since 'time immemorial', but King Edward III granted its market charter in 1330. Held every Monday, the farming community flocks from miles around for the weekly sale of livestock, domestic goods and provisions. In 1826 the market was moved to a site in Granby Road to clear the streets and relieve congestion. In recent years the livestock market has moved across the river to the new award-winning **Agricultural Business Centre**, and is currently enjoying something of a resurgence with the recent revival of monthly farmers' markets.

River Wye, Bakewell

Today, Bakewell attracts a multitude of visitors and tourists, and has gained fame as being the unofficial 'Capital of the Peak'. It contains many interesting historic buildings and monuments. A couple of miles east of Bakewell is one of Britain's most celebrated and best loved historic houses and estates, **Chatsworth**. It offers something for everyone to enjoy, from world-famous works of art and spectacular fountains to miles of free walks.

The Rutland Arms was built in 1804. It is claimed that Jane Austen stayed there in 1811 and she based *Lambton* in *Pride and*

---

32 FARMERS FEAST CAFE & BAR

Bakewell

It would be hard to find a cafe serving better quality meat and vegetables. It is well worth a visit.

See entry on page 163

---

33 BAKEWELL TART SHOP & COFFEE HOUSE

Bakewell

This popular shop has a little something for everyone with an impressive range of gifts and treats to suit every budget, appetite and taste.

See entry on page 164

Chatsworth House, Bakewell

Prejudice on the town. However the Rutland Arms' (known then as the White Horse Inn) chief claim to fame is as the place where the **Bakewell Pudding** was stumbled upon. Legend has it that the dish was an accidental invention during the 1860s. The story goes that a nobleman visited the Inn and ordered a strawberry tart. The cook, instead of stirring the egg mixture into the cake as would normally happen, spread it over the jam, and the Bakewell Pudding was born. However similar puddings were made in the area as early as the 16th century and this 'accident' story is now seen as doubtful.

This popular dessert is traditionally served with hot custard, but smaller versions (usually known as Bakewell tarts or Bakewell slices) can be bought in bakeries and supermarkets throughout the country. Two shops within the town each claim to have the oldest recipe: **The Old Original Bakewell Pudding Shop** on Bridge Street, and **Bloomers Original Bakewell Pudding Shop** on Water Street.

Those who enjoy old buildings should take time to look at the town's historic **Almshouses** (King Street) – a classic sandstone terrace built by charity 300 years

ago to give shelter to destitute townsfolk.

Other places of historical interest include **Bagshawe Hall**, a fine 17th-century house built by a rich lawyer, and the **Old House** in Cunningham Place, behind the parish church. The latter building is one of the few genuinely medieval buildings of the area and serves as the local history museum and is in the care of the Bakewell Historical Society. **Old House Museum** (as it's known today) houses a fascinating collection of rural bygones.

Also worth a visit is the **Market Hall**, which adjoins the Market Square, originally built as an open-sided market hall. Since those early days it has been used as a washhouse, dance hall and library before taking on its latest lease of life as the **Bakewell Information Centre**.

Not all of Bakewell's attractions are immediately obvious. Take the 'pink building', tucked away behind the walls of a picturesque medieval courtyard. With its lopsided walls and latticed windows, the house (now a florist's shop) has all the charm of a gingerbread cottage – and Kings Court is just one of many secluded squares to be discovered in the higgledy-piggledy backstreets of Bakewell.

There is little evidence of industry in the town, which is not very surprising considering Bakewell is surrounded by farming country, but the remnants of **Lumford Mill** can still be seen. Originally built in 1778 by Sir Richard Arkwright as a cotton-spinning mill, over 300 people, mainly women and children, were employed here. Badly damaged by fire in 1868, the Mill has been rebuilt and it is used

34 THE MANNERS HOTEL

Bakewell

This lovely little hotel serves mouth-watering traditional pub grub and has two comfortable en-suite guest bedrooms.

See entry on page 165

Lumford Mill, Bakewell

as offices today. Here can also be found a very fine example of a low-parapeted packhorse bridge across the Wye, dating from 1664. **Holme Hall** to the north of town dates from 1626. This Jacobean hall faces the water meadows of the Wye.

Just down the A6 toward Matlock is the romantic pile of medieval **Haddon Hall**, home of the Duke of Rutland. Haddon Hall is the star of many films. *Jane Eyre, Elizabeth* and *Pride and Prejudice* have all been shot in the lavish surrounds.

Bakewell has an annual well dressing and carnival, held in late June.

NORTH OF BAKEWELL

EDENSOR

2 miles E of Bakewell off the B6012

Pronounced 'Ensor', this pretty village was demolished then re-built in a different location by the 6th Duke of Devonshire between 1838 and 1842, after he deemed the original village was too close to **Chatsworth House** and spoiled the view. Only Park Cottage remains in its original location.

Unable to decide on a specific design for the buildings, an eccentric, though somehow pleasing, mixture of architectural styles characterises the village, with the graceful spire of Sir George Gilbert Scott's **St Peter's Church** dominating the scene.

PILSLEY

2 miles NE of Bakewell off the A619

There are two Pilsleys in Derbyshire, one being in northeast Derbyshire near

Chesterfield and this one, the Chatsworth Estate Village. This Pilsley is a pretty, unspoilt village with magnificent views over the Derwent Valley. It lies about one mile east of Chatsworth House, and along with Edensor and Beeley makes up the three Chatsworth Estate villages. The village is in a sheltered position and the limestone cottages are enriched by gardens full of colour. The Shire Horse Stud Farm, built by the 9th Duke of Devonshire in 1910, has been converted into a variety of craft workshops and the Chatsworth Estate Farm Shop.

HASSOP

3 miles N of Bakewell off the B6001

This little village is dominated by its fine Roman Catholic **Church of All Saints** (1818) and **Hassop Hall**, which is now a luxurious country house hotel. The church was built by the Eyre family who, as well as being devout Catholics, also owned some 20 manors in the area. Dating from the 17th century, Hassop Hall was garrisoned for the King by Thomas Eyre during the Civil War and it remained in the family until the mid-19th century when there were a series of contested wills.

GREAT LONGSTONE

3 miles NW of Bakewell off the B6465

This one-street village has attractive 18th- and 19th-century houses, notably **Longstone Hall** built in 1747 of red brick and which was the home of the Wright family. Nearby, Longstone Edge is being quarried for fluorspar, the mineral that lead miners threw away as waste, although the National Park Authority is campaigning to stop further mining from taking place in the area, which

---

35 HADDON HALL

nr Bakewell

Haddon Hall is thought by many to have been the first fortified house in the country, although the turrets and battlements were actually put on purely for show.

See entry on page 165

---

36 AVANT GARDE OF BASLOW

Baslow

Wonderful Aladdin's Cave of a shop filled with all your home and gift needs, with inspirational ideas at every turn.

See entry on page 166

is one of the most attractive within the National Park.

STONEY MIDDLETON

4 miles N of Bakewell off the A623

This village, known simply as "Stoney" locally, is certainly well named as, particularly in this part of **Middleton Dale**, great walls of limestone rise up from the valley floor. Further up the Dale there are also many disused limestone quarries as well as the remains of some lead mines. Not all industry has vanished from the area, as this is the home of nearly three-quarters of the country's fluorspar industry. Another relic from the past also survives - a shoe- and boot-making company operates from the village and is housed in a former corn mill.

An ancient village, the Romans built a bath here, and it is mentioned in the *Domesday Book* as Midletune. It is thought that the place originated when a motte and bailey castle was built on **Castle Hill**, but was abandoned in the 14th century due to the Black Death. Nearby is the odd octagonally-shaped **St Martin's Parish Church**. Joan Eyre built it in thanksgiving for the safe return of her husband from the field of the Battle of Agincourt in the 15th century. It is said that she actually built the church at a place where she and her husband-to-be met and courted in secret, as her family did not approve of him.

Middleton Hall dates originally from about 1600, but was much altered by the Denman family in the 19th century. The most famous Denman was a lawyer who became Lord Chief Justice of England in 1832.

During the Great Plague of 1665-1666, the 17th-century villagers of Stoney Middleton left food and clothing out for those quarantined in nearby Eyam.

In January 2007 some of the houses in the village were ruined when a wall of mud pounded the village after a dam near the top of the dale burst following heavy rainfall. Despite this, Stoney Middleton has preserved its village identity and character and also partakes in the custom of well-dressing, when two wells around The Nook are dressed in late July/early August.

EYAM

5 miles N of Bakewell off the B6521

Eyam, pronounced 'Eem', cannot escape its infamous label as **'the Plague Village'**. In 1665, a local tailor, George Vicars, received a bundle of plague-infected clothing from London. Within a short time the infection had spread and the terrified inhabitants prepared to flee the village. However, the local rector, William Mompesson, and his predecessor Thomas Stanley persuaded the villagers to stay put and, thanks to his intervention, most neighbouring villages escaped the disease. Eyam was quarantined for over a year, relying on outside help for supplies of food which were left on the village boundary (see Stoney Middleton).

Plague Cottage, Eyam

Out of a total of 350 inhabitants, only 83 survived. Whole families were wiped out, and there were no formal funerals. People were buried close to where they died without ceremony. At Riley Farm, the farmer's wife buried her husband and six children within eight days. The **Riley Graves**, as they are called nowadays, are still there.

An open-air service is held each August at Cucklet Delf to commemorate the villagers' brave self-sacrifice, and the well-dressings are also a thanksgiving for the pureness of the water. Taking place on the last Sunday in

37 EYAM MUSEUM

Eyam

Learn the full story behind this village, once devasted by plague.

See entry on page 167

August, known as Plague Sunday, this also commemorates the climax of the plague and the death of the rector's wife, Catherine Mompesson.

The village itself is quite large and self-contained, and typical of a mining and quarrying settlement. For all its plague associations, it is said that it was the first village in England to have a public water system. In the 16th century a series of troughs were placed throughout the village, with water being brought to them by pipes. An interesting place to stroll around, there are many information plaques documenting events where they took place. **Eyam Museum** tells the story of the heroic sacrifice and the **Parish Church of St Lawrence**, which dates partly from the 12th century and was restored in the 19th century, houses an excellent exhibition of Eyam's history, including Mompesson's own chair and the plague register. Also inside the church are two ancient coffin lids; the top of one of the lids is known as St Helen's Cross. Born in what is now Turkey, St Helen is said to have found a fragment of the cross on which Jesus was crucified. In the churchyard is the best-preserved Saxon cross to be found in the Peak District, along with an unusual sundial which dates from 1775. There is also a memorial to Catherine Mompesson and Thomas Stanley.

The home of the Wright family for over 300 years, **Eyam Hall** is a wonderful, unspoilt 17th-century manor house that is open to the public. As well as touring the house and seeing the impressive stone-flagged hall, the tapestry room and the magnificent tester bed, there is also a café and gift shop. The Eyam Hall Crafts Centre, housed in the farm building, contains several individual units which specialise in a variety of unusual and skilfully-fashioned crafts.

A mile or two north of the village is **Eyam Moor**, where there are cairns and stone circles.

GRINDLEFORD

6 miles N of Bakewell off the A625

Strung out for 2 miles along the River

Derwent, Grindleford gets its name from the grindstones that were quarried from nearby Froggatt and Curbar Edges for many years.

Across from Padley Chapel is **Brunt's Barn**, a conservation centre founded in 1981 in memory of Harry Brunt, a local man who helped found the Peak District National Park.

ASHFORD IN THE WATER

1 mile NW of Bakewell off the A6

Not exactly in the water, but certainly on the River Wye, Ashford is another candidate for Derbyshire's prettiest village. It developed around a ford that spanned the river and was once an important crossing place on the ancient Portway. Originally a medieval packhorse bridge, **Sheep Wash Bridge** crosses the Wye, with overhanging willows framing its low arches. It is one of three bridges in the village, and a favourite with artists. There is a small enclosure to one side that provides a clue to its name, as this is still occasionally used for its original purpose - crowds gather to witness sheep being washed in the river to clean their fleece before they are shorn. The lambs would be penned within the enclosure and the ewes would be thrown in the water at the other side. Seeing their offspring, they would swim across, their wool getting a good wash as they went.

So-called Black Marble, or Ashford Marble, actually a highly polished grey limestone from quarries near the village, was quarried nearby for some considerable time, and particularly during the Victorian era when it was fashionable to have decorative items and fire surrounds made from the stone. It was also exported all over the world. Within the village there was once a thriving cottage industry inlaying Black Marble with coloured

38 **AISSEFORD TEA ROOM**

Ashford-in-the-Water

Home-cooked food that's full of flavour in a lovely tea room in beautiful Ashford-in-the-Water.

See entry on page 167

Churchdale Hall, Ashford in the Water

marbles, shells and glass. Another industry was candle making, and the house that now stands on the site of the factory is called The Candle House. It stands in Greaves Lane, "greaves" being the unusable dregs of melted tallow.

The great limestone **Parish Church of the Holy Trinity** was largely rebuilt in 1871 but retained the base of a 13th-century tower and a 14th-century north arcade. A fine Ashford Marble table is on show as well as a tablet to the memory of Henry Watson, the founder of the marble works who was also an authority on the geology of the area. Several of the pillars within the church are made of the rare Duke's Red marble, which is only found in the mine at Lathkill Dale owned by the Duke of Devonshire. The church also boasts a Norman tympanum, complete with Tree of Life, lion and hog, over the south door. Hanging from the roof of Ashford's church are the remains of four 'virgin's crantses' - paper garlands carried at the funerals of unmarried village girls. One of them dates from 1747.

Near the village is **Churchdale Hall**, which dates from the 18th century and was once part of the vast Chatsworth estate. It was also the home, until his death in 1950, of the 10th Duke of Devonshire, who never resided at Chatsworth. Churchdale Farm is now a working sheep farm tucked down a private drive and is a haven of rural peace. The Monsal Trail is at the end of the drive and it offers gentle walks to Monsal Head and Bakewell, wild flowers in profusion and safe cycle-riding for the children. To the south of Ashford is another manor House, **Ashford**

Hall, overlooking a picturesque lake formed by the River Wye. Built by the Dukes of Devonshire in 1785 to a design by Joseph Pickford of Derby, it was occupied by them for a time, but then sold in the early 1950s. It now belongs to the Olivier family. **Thornbridge Hall** dates from 1781, but was extensively refurbished in Victorian times. It has been a teacher training college and a conference centre but is now a private residence once more, though it is open for weddings, private events and occasional open days.

The village also has a pleasant range of mainly 18th-century cottages, and a former tithe barn.

MONSAL HEAD

3 miles NW of Bakewell off the B6465

Monsal Head, standing high above the dale, affords the best viewpoint for admiring **Monsal Dale**, through which the River Wye flows. The view is spectacular, with the river far below, winding through a steep-sided valley with many rocky outcrops. It forms part of the **Monsal Trail**, a popular route with walkers at weekends. The viaduct here is now an accepted feature of the landscape, but when the railway was built in the 1870s, John Ruskin campaigned against the damage done to this unique environment, simply "so that any fool from Bakewell can be in Buxton by lunchtime".

WARDLOW

6 miles NW of Bakewell off the B6465

At a crossroads near Wardlow, the body of Anthony Lingard (who had earlier been hanged at Derby) was publicly gibbeted in 1815 for the murder of a local widow. The body was placed in a cage and hung from the gibbet, a sight that drew an enormous crowd - so large that the local lay-preacher at Tideswell found himself preaching to virtually empty pews. Determined not to waste this opportunity to speak to so large a congregation, he made his way to the gibbet and gave his sermon there.

A wonderful track leads from Wardlow to

the edge of Cressbrook Dale, known as **The Pingle**. In spring the sides of this wonderful dale are covered with orchids and cowslips.

LITTON

6 miles NW of Bakewell off the A623

Although this is only a small village there is a real sense of spaciousness about Litton; a wide grass verge runs down the side of the street of this attractive village, situated almost 1,000 feet above sea level. An old world village pub, The Red Lion, and an attractive triangular green complete with its ancient cross and village stocks make up Litton's idyllic picture.

Equally attractive are the stone built cottages. Although the oldest house dates from 1639 - many of the buildings have date stones - most date from the mid-18th century, a time of prosperity for the area when the local lead mining industry was booming.

A macabre historical reference is that of **Litton Mill**. The mill still stands beside the Wye Mill stream about 2 miles from Litton village (also see Millers Dale). It used a workforce made up largely of orphaned and pauper children, who were treated so badly by the mill owners that many of them died (see Miller's Dale below).

Litton was the also birthplace, in 1628, of **William Bagshawe**, who earned the title the "Apostle of the Peak" (see also Chapel-en-le-Frith).

CRESSBROOK

5 miles NW of Bakewell off the B6465

Clinging to the slopes of the Wye Valley, the village cottages of Cressbrook are found in terraces amongst the ash woodland. The handsome **Cressbrook Mill**, built in 1815, was closed down in 1965, and has now been converted into flats. The apprentice house, used to house the pauper children from London and elsewhere who worked long hours in the mill, also exists. The owner of the Mill, William Newton, known as the "Minstrel of the Peak" because he wrote poetry, saw that the apprentices were treated well (see

Cressbrook Mill

also Tideswell), unlike those at the nearby Litton Mill. The stretch of the River Wye between Cressbrook and Litton mills is known as Water-Cum-Jolly Dale.

TIDESWELL

8 miles NW of Bakewell off the B6049

Dubbed 'the Cathedral of the Peak', the magnificent 14th century **Parish Church of St John the Baptist** has a wealth of splendid features, and is one of the grandest parish churches in Derbyshire. The tower is impressive, the windows are beautiful and there is a fine collection of brasses inside. The 'Minstrel of the Peak', William Newton, is buried in the churchyard (see also Cressbrook).

In other parts of Derbyshire, natives of Tideswell are said to come from 'Tidsa', which takes its name from a Saxon chieftain called Tidi. Over 900 feet above sea level, the surrounding countryside offers many opportunities to wander, stroll, or take a leisurely (or energetic) hike through some varied and impressive scenery.

The village is one of the most ancient in the Peak District, and was granted its market charter in 1251. This was where the Great Courts of the Royal Forest of Peak met during the reign of Edward I, and some of buildings in the village may have foundations going back to that time.

Eccles Hall, overlooking the Market Place, was built in 1724 and became the home of the headmaster of the Grammar School in 1878.

By the 14th century the village was a flourishing centre for the local wool trade.

Today it is home to a number of craftspeople working in buildings converted from other uses. The excellence of their work is apparent, not only in the items they make, but also in the splendid well-dressing they help to arrange annually on the Saturday nearest St John the Baptist's Day, 24th June.

PEAK FOREST

11 miles NW of Bakewell off the A623

Despite its name, Peak Forest doesn't boast any trees. Instead, it takes its name from the medieval Royal Forest of the Peak, which was an open area used as a Royal hunting park rather than a forested area. At Chamber Farm, rebuilt in the 18th century, the Forest courts were held, attended by some 20 foresters whose job it was to maintain the special laws of the area.

The village grew from an earlier settlement called Dam, a hamlet that still exists. The **Parish Church of King Charles the Martyr** speaks of the fierce independence of the village inhabitants, and is one of the few in England dedicated to someone who was never a saint, but who was, nevertheless, revered by many. It was built in 1657 by the wife of the 2nd Earl of

Eldon Hole, Peak Forest

Devonshire, during a time when there was a ban on building churches. It became known as the 'the Gretna Green of the Peak', because of a quirk of ecclesiastical law - it was not subject to the laws regarding posting the banns before marriage. The church that stands today was built in 1878 on the site of the former chapel.

Within walking distance of Peak Forest is one of the original 'Seven Wonders of the Peak' as described by the poet Charles Cotton in 1682. **Eldon Hole** is the largest open pothole in Derbyshire, it was once thought to be bottomless and home to evil spirits. In the 1500s the Earl of Leicester had a man lowered on a rope to find the true depth. He went crazy and died speechless shortly afterwards. A traveller was fatally thrown in here after being robbed by two villains in the 18th century. Local legend also tells how a goose was thrown down Eldon Hole and reappeared inside Peak Cavern (also called the Devil's Arse) 2 miles (3 km) away. It had been singed down to its pimples by some infernal flames. Potholers, who view the hole as no more than a practice run, maintain that it is, in fact, 'only' 245 feet deep (75 metres).

TADDINGTON

5 miles E of Buxton off the A6

Now lying just off the main Bakewell to Buxton road, Taddington was one of the first places to be bypassed, and it has made a great improvement to village life. An ancient village and one of the highest in England at 1,100 feet, the cottages here are simple but the **Parish Church of St Michael and All Angels** is well worth looking at. Like many in the Peak District, it was rebuilt in the 14th century with money gained from the then-booming woollen and lead industries in the area. In 1891 it was considerably restored. The churchyard entrance is through a magnificent lych-gate, a gift to the church from Samuel Bramwell in 1910, and the churchyard is one of the best kept in the county.

Taddington Hall, one of the smaller of the Peak District manor houses, dates back to the 16th century though much of the building seen today was constructed in the 18th century. As with all good halls, Taddington has its share of ghost stories. One in particular concerns two brothers. The pair ran a hessian factory from the Hall and one day they quarrelled. The next day one of the brothers, named Isaac, was found dead in the cellar. The other brother was found guilty of the act. It is said that Isaac has been heard wandering around the passages of the Hall from time to time. The other ghost is of a drunken farmer who fell from his horse on his way home from Bakewell Market. Intriguingly, it was the farmer's ghost that revealed to his wife that he was dead before she knew about it.

MILLER'S DALE

7 miles NE of Buxton off the B6049

Miller's Dale is very near to the infamous **Litton Mill**. The original 19th century mill became notorious during the Industrial Revolution for its unsavoury employment practices. It was at Litton Mill where Robert Blincoe arrived as a child from a London poorhouse. He later wrote a harrowing tale

Litton Mill, Miller's Dale

of the cruelty and inhumane treatment meted out to the mill workers, many of the children died as a result of the harsh treatment they received at the hands of Ellis Needham and his sons. They were buried away from the mill to try and hide the truth about what went on, though in reality in those days, few people cared as long as these children were not a burden on local parishes. The mill, now luxury apartments, is said to be haunted by the ghosts of the orphans who were exploited as cheap labour.

The hamlet takes its name from one of several charming and compact dales that lie along the River Wye and provide excellent walking. The nearby nature reserve occupies land that was originally a limestone quarry, which was last used in 1971. This tiny settlement, situated in the narrow valley of the River Wye, began life as late as the 1860s when it was built to provide housing for the workers building the London to Manchester railway. All this has now gone but the dramatic **Monsal Dale Viaduct** (built in the 1860s to carry the railway line) remains and is now used by walkers taking the Monsal Trail. It has stone piers and a wrought iron superstructure. There is another viaduct to the north, built in 1905, to cope with increased traffic on the line.

The disused railway has been converted to a track for walkers, cyclists, horse riders and less active people, including wheelchair users. Between Blackwell and Monsal Head the trail follows the deep limestone valley of the River Wye for eight-and-a-half miles. It is unsuitable for cycling and wheelchairs at its western half, with rocky diversions around tunnels. Level access is available from Miller's Dale Station, for half-a-mile west or two miles east.

---

39 **HORSE AND JOCKEY**

Tideswell

Full of character, this inn is run by a locally born and bred family who offer delicious homemade food, ale and bed and breakfast accommodation.

See entry on page 168

---

40 **GEORGE HOTEL**

Tideswell

This historical 18th century hotel has a tradition for excellence serving innovative and delicious English food.

See entry on page 169

Monsale Dale Viaduct, Miller's Dale

The **Parish Church of St Anne's** is on a hillside, and is comparatively modern, dating from 1879.

WORMHILL

4 miles E of Buxton off the A6

Wormhill, originally named 'Wolfhill', is a sleepy village with an attractive village green, old church and majestic hall. Its original name is thought to have been taken from the numerous wolves which roamed the nearby woods – rest assured, there are no wolves here today!

The village is surrounded by varied scenery of rocks known as **Chee Tor** and the beautiful dale through which runs the River Wye. The Bagshawes have been chief land owners in this village for several generations. They built **Wormhill Hall** in 1679, a stone mansion (privately owned) that can be seen on the approach to the village.

Within the village is a drinking fountain erected in 1875 to the memory of James Bridley (also see Tunstead). This fountain is the scene of the village well-dressing each year, normally in late August or early September.

TUNSTEAD

3 miles E of Buxton off the A6

High in the hills above the valley of the River Wye, Tunstead is a small hamlet with a very famous son, James Brindley, born here in 1716. He became a civil engineer and the greatest canal-builder of his time, and is known as the father of the canal system.

Although Brindley never learned to read or write, his skills in engineering brought him to the attention of the Duke of Bridgewater, who commissioned Brindley to build the Bridgwater Canal to carry coal between Manchester and Worsley.

KING STERNDALE

2 miles SE of Buxton off the A6

The regally named King Sterndale is a tiny hamlet, with a population of barely 30 souls, high above Ashwood Dale. Hundreds of wonderful beech trees were planted around King Sterndale by the Pickford family to transform the bleak and desolate moorland landscape into a more cultured and sheltered parkland.

SOUTH AND WEST OF BAKEWELL

SHELDON

3 miles W of Bakewell off the A6

Situated 1,000 feet up on the limestone plateau, Sheldon was mentioned in the *Domesday Book* as Scheldhaun. However, its heyday was in the 18th and 19th centuries when black marble was mined here, as it was at nearby Ashford in the Water. However, due to a lack of water to power the many manufacturing processes, it was not as successful as its neighbour.

The village itself is chiefly a single row of mainly 18th century cottages lining the main street. The 19th century **Parish Church of St Michael and All Angels**, with some notable features, is well worth a visit. Prehistoric monuments litter the limestone plateau above the village and, from Sheldon numerous footpaths lead through the surrounding countryside to Monyash, Flagg and Monsal Dale.

FLAGG

5 miles W of Bakewell off the A515

Each year on Easter Tuesday, thousands of

enthusiastic spectators enjoy **Flagg Races**, the thrilling spectacle of thoroughbreds racing across spectacular open countryside. Flagg Races is a unique event that reflects the early days of horse racing when riders rode from one point to another with no defined course. It's a great day out!

The Elizabethan manor house, **Flagg Hall**, now known as Flagg Hall Farm, is visible from the main road, and is well worth seeing, although it is not open to the public.

CHELMORTON

7 miles W of Bakewell off the A5270

This 'mountain village' is the second highest village in the county, with the **Parish Church of St John the Baptist** standing at 1,209 feet above sea level. The layout of the village is unchanged since Saxon times. It is linear, with farms built on either side of the gently sloping main street, which runs downhill in a south westerly direction from the parish church to the Flagg Lane crossroads. The remains of the narrow strips of land that were allotted to each cottage in medieval times can still be seen.

MONYASH

5 miles W of Bakewell off the B5055

Monyash, which is situated at the head of **Lathkill Dale**, can really only be experienced by walking along the path by the banks of the quiet river, is noted for its solitude and, consequently, there is an abundance of wildlife in and around the riverbank meadows. The upper valley is a National Nature Reserve; those who are lucky enough may even spot a kingfisher or two. One of the country's purest rivers, the Lathkill is

River Lathkill, Monyash

famed for the range of aquatic life that it supports as well as being a popular trout river. Renowned for many centuries, it was Izaak Walton who said of the Lathkill, back in 1676, 'the purest and most transparent stream that I ever yet saw, either at home or abroad; and breeds, 'tis said, the reddest and best Trouts in England.' The **River Lathkill**, like others in the limestone area of the Peak District, disappears underground for parts of its course. In this case the river rises, in winter, from a large cave above Monyash, known as Lathkill Head Cave. In summer, the river emerges further downstream at Over Haddon.

Farming and tourism are its main industries now but it was once at the centre of the Peak District's lead mining industry (from medieval times to the end of the 19th century) and had its own Barmote Court (one of the oldest industrial courts in the country). Its market charter was granted in 1340 and the old market cross still stands on the village green. Due to its isolated position, Monyash had, for many years, to support itself and this led to a great many industries within the village. As far back as prehistoric times there was a flint-tool 'factory' here and, as well as mining, candle-making and rope-making, mere-building was a village speciality.

The **Parish Church of St Leonard** was founded in 1178, though it has been much altered and added to over the years. Its parish chest is still preserved as one of its

---

41 **OLD SMITHY TEAROOMS**

Monyash

Food hearty enough to satisfy a smithy's appetite, in the picturesque Peak District village of Monyash.

See entry on page 170

greatest treasures. It is 10-feet long and thought to date from the 13th century, when it was used to store the silver vessels and the robes worn during mass. Monyash was once a centre for the Quaker movement, and John Gratton, a prominent preacher, lived at One Ash Grange.

POMEROY

7 miles W of Bakewell on the A515

Pomeroy is a charming hamlet with lovely buildings, some dating back to medieval times. The alehouse, the Duke of York, was first opened in 1618 as part of the farmstead owned by John and Maria White. The chestnut tree in the car park was planted in the 1900s by the then Prince of Wales, later King Edward VIII, on an occasion when he was visiting the area with Sir Thomas Pomeroy.

EARL STERNDALE

7 miles W of Bakewell off the A515

At the less well-known northern end of Dove Valley, Earl Sterndale is close to the limestone peaks of Hitter Hill and High Wheeldon, where there is Fox Hole Cave, which has been a shelter for people since Stone Age times. Over 1,100 feet above sea level, it is surrounded by lovely farmland. A number of the farmsteads are called 'granges', a relic of the Middle Ages when the granges were where monks of the local Abbey lived. The **Parish Church of St Michael**, built in the early 19th century, was the only church in Derbyshire to suffer a direct hit from a Second World War bomb. It was refurbished and restored in 1952, and retains a Saxon font.

The village inn, the Quiet Woman, has a sign showing a headless woman, with the words 'Soft words turneth away wrath'. It is supposedly of a previous landlord's nagging wife, known as 'Chattering Charteris', whose husband cut off her head.

CROWDECOTE

8 miles W of Bakewell off the B5053

Viewed from the tiny hamlet of Crowdecote are the sharply pointed summits and knife-edge ridges of **Chrome Hill** and **Parkhouse Hill**. They dominate the dale with a fair impression of real Alpine giants, especially after a snowfall. Over 350 million years ago, these knolls were actually coral reefs within a shallow, warm sea - hard to believe, but perhaps not so puzzling when one remembers that much of this landscape has been formed by the action of water. Unlike the softer limestone, they retained their original structure and are richer in marine fossils than limestone, containing trilobites and corals.

The original Crowdy Coat Bridge over the river Dove was a wooden footbridge. In 1709 this was replaced by a stone packhorse bridge, which was constructed to enable the heavily laden packhorse ponies to cross. The nearby Packhorse Inn dating back to 1723 was used by traders when this was the main road to Leek and Buxton.

LONGNOR

8 miles W of Bakewell off the B5053

On a ridge between the River Manifold and the River Dove, Longnor, has one of the oldest cobbled **Market Squares** in Britain, dating back to medieval times. Its **Market Hall** was built in 1873 and now houses the **Longnor Craft Centre**; at present there are

---

42 THE DUKE OF YORK

Pomeroy

This fine establishment has a fascinating history and today attracts plenty of customers who enjoy real ales, good food and top hospitality.

See entry on page 171

---

43 THE PACK HORSE INN

Crowdecote

This picturesque hostelry is a popular stop off point for walkers and cyclists and definitely worth a visit.

See entry on page 170

over seventy exhibitors, and an outlet for craftspeople, artists and publishers. The village also has some fascinating narrow flagged passages, which seem to go nowhere but suddenly emerge among some beautiful scenery.

Though the late 18th-century **Church of St Bartholomew** is grim and plain, it sits on foundations at least 800 years old, and contains a Norman font. The churchyard has an interesting gravestone. The epitaph tells the tale of the life of William Billinge, who was born in 1679, and died in 1791. This means that he died at a grand old age of 112 years. As a soldier Billinge served under Rooke at Gibraltar and Marlborough at Ramilles. After being sent home wounded, he recovered to take part in defending the King in the Jacobite Uprisings of 1715 and 1745.

On the first Thursday after the first Sunday in September, the annual 'Wakes Races', or 'Longnor Sports', takes place in the village. They go back to 1904, and are held at Waterhouse Farm.

OVER HADDON

1½ miles SW of Bakewell off the B5055

Sitting at the top of a steep valley there are beautiful views south over the Lathkill Dale and river. Over Haddon is now visited by walkers as it lies on the **Lathkill Dale Trail** which follows the River Lathkill up the valley to beyond Monyash. For several centuries the valley was alive with the lead mining industry that was a mainstay of the economy of much of northern Derbyshire, and any walk along the riverbanks will reveal remains from those workings as well as from limestone quarries.

There is an old engine house at **Mandale Mine** that was built in 1847 and further upstream from the mine are the stone pillars of an aqueduct, built in 1840, which carried water down to the engine house. Downstream from the village is the first National Nature Reserve established in the Peak District in 1972. Set mainly in an ash and elm wood, the reserve is home to many varieties of shrubs.

Over Haddon enjoys several claims to fame: the Gold Rush of 1854, when iron pyrites ('fool's gold') was found, and Martha

Mandale Mine, Over Haddon

Taylor, the 'Fasting damsel', who didn't eat for almost two years! Maurice Oldfield, head of the MI6 from 1973 – 1978, lived in the village and is buried in the churchyard.

BEELEY

3 miles SE of Bakewell off the B6012

Anyone compiling a list of the most picturesque villages in Derbyshire would have to include Beeley. It is a pretty, unspoilt village sheltered by Beeley Moor with wonderful views in all directions. What makes the village so beautiful is that almost all the farm and domestic buildings are built from the same honey-coloured sandstone, quarried locally close to Fallinge Edge. The ancient **Parish Church of St Anne**, close to the gabled vicarage (now a private house), is one of the oldest in Derbyshire. Its considerably mutilated round-headed doorway dates back to the middle of the 12th century. However, the star attraction, at least as far as age is concerned, is a gnarled old yew - once a massive tree - said to be older than the church. There is a tradition that, when marriages take place, the bride and groom must not enter the churchyard by the west gate, and must pay a token sum, after the ceremony, to leave by the east gate.

To the west of Beeley a small road climbs up onto Beeley Moor and here, along a concessionary path from Hell Bank, can be found **Hob Hurst's House**. Local folklore tells that this was the home of a goblin but it is just one of 30 or so Bronze Age barrows to be found on the moor.

ROWSLEY

4 miles SE of Bakewell off the A6

The River Derwent and the River Wye merge at this village, giving the impression of two separate settlements. Not surprisingly they are called Great Rowsley and Little Rowsley, but perhaps more unexpectedly it is the latter that has the larger population. The older part of this small village, Great Rowsley, lies between the two rivers, while to the east is the 'railway village' around the former Midland railway station. The two areas are quite distinct. The old part has gritstone cottages and farmhouses, while the newer part is clearly Victorian.

The oldest surviving structure in the village is the bridge over the Derwent which was originally a 15th-century packhorse bridge, widened to carry increasingly motorised traffic in 1925. However, there are some architectural gems and the most prominent of these is undoubtedly the magnificent **Peacock Hotel** whose visitors' book includes the names of many famous guests, including royalty, who have enjoyed a brief sojourn in the luxuriant surroundings since it became a hotel in 1828. The house was built in 1652 by John Stevenson of Elton, founder in 1636 of the Lady Manners School in Bakewell. It is aptly named as a carved Peacock stands over the porch and is actually part of the family crest of the Manners family, whose descendents live at nearby Haddon Hall. The hotel was recently bought by Lord Edward Manners, from Haddon Hall. It lies to the west of the village, and is reckoned to be the most perfect house to survive from the Middle Ages in England.

The **Parish Church of St Katherine** dates

from 1855, and contains the fine chest tomb of Lady Catherine Manners, first wife of the 7th Duke of Rutland, who died in 1859.

On the banks of the River Wye lies **Caudwell's Mill**, a unique Grade II listed historic roller flour mill. A mill has stood on this site for at least 400 years. The present mill was built in 1874, powered by water from the River Wye, and was run as a family business for over a century up until 1978. Since then the Mill has undergone extensive restoration by a group of dedicated volunteers and, using machinery that was installed at the beginning of this century, the mill is once again producing wholemeal flour. Other mill buildings on the site have been converted to house a variety of craft workshops, shops and a restaurant.

On Chatsworth Road, **Peak Village** is an extensive shopping centre but aside from shops, it boasts a coffee house, restaurant and is home to the fascinating **Toys of Yesteryear** exhibition. The impressive displays feature over 6,000 toys dating from the early 1900s right up until the 1970s, including a model of the 'Herbie' and 'Chitty Chitty Bang Bang' cars. It is also the home of the award-winning Wind in the Willows Attraction, an enchanting re-creation of Kenneth Grahame's magical tale that brings Toad's adventures to life and delights young and old alike.

MATLOCK

Matlock and its surrounding townships are built on the banks of the River Derwent. There are actually eight Matlocks that make up the town, but most have simply been engulfed and have lost their identity as the town grew. Just downriver of the main town **Matlock Bath**, the site of the spa, still maintains some individuality and contains the main tourist attractions of the locality. The Matlocks are just outside the boundaries of the National Park, but for many visitors marks the southern entrance to the Peak District. The towns, villages and much of the surrounding countryside have plenty of the typical Peak District characteristics. There are also some fine views over the Lower Derwent Valley from its well planned vantage points.

Matlock lies right on the divide between the gritstone of the Dark Peak and the limestone of the White Peak. The whole area is dominated by the imposing cliffs of High Tor and the Heights of Abraham, which tower 120 metres above the gorge. Though the hilltops are often windswept and bleak, the numerous dales, cut deep into the limestone, provide a lush and green haven for all manner of wildlife and plant life. Several of the rivers are famous for their trout, particularly the Lathkill, which was greatly favoured by the keen angler and writer Sir Izaak Walton. The attractive four-arched bridge across the Derwent was built in the 1400s. It was made famous by Joseph Turner's painting - 'The Bridge at Matlock'.

In many respects Matlock seems quite a new town, certainly when compared with Buxton or Bakewell for instance. This is because until relatively recently Matlock was a collection of insignificant hamlets, but then the thermal springs were discovered and harnessed to make Matlock's name as a fashionable Victorian retreat. In the early Matlock village, known as Old Matlock you will find most of the buildings that predate the town's spa heyday.

The **Parish Church of St Giles** is an attractive building with fragments of masonry dating from its foundation in the 13th century, and its tower, in the perpendicular style, dates from the 16th century. However, most of the medieval church was destroyed in the 18th century during alterations, and in 1859 the chancel was completely rebuilt. Inside the church can be seen a preserved funeral garland or 'virgin crantse', though the church has others in storage. These were once common all over Derbyshire, and were bell-shaped, decorated with rosettes and ribbons and usually containing a personal item. They were made in memory of a deceased young girl of the parish. At her funeral the garland was carried by the dead girl's friends and, after the service, it would be suspended from the church rafters above the pew she had normally occupied.

Matlock is famed as, at one time, having

the steepest gradient (a 1-in-5½) tramway in the world. It ran between the railway station and the hydro of John Smedley, and it was so steep that a cable beneath the road connected the two trams - one going uphill and one going downhill. It was also the only tram system in the Peak District. Opened in 1893, the tramcars ran until 1927 and the depot can still be seen at the top of Bank Road. The old ticket office and waiting room at Matlock station have been taken over by the **Peak Rail Society** and here can be found not only their shop, but also exhibitions explaining the history and aims of the society.

For train enthusiasts, the **Peak Rail** run regular steam and diesel hauled heritage passenger trains between Matlock Riverside station, through the charming rural station of Darley Dale to the terminus at Rowsley South. Run entirely by volunteers, this lovely old line operates on different days throughout the year. The full journey (one way) takes just 20 minutes, and passengers can alight to enjoy the picnic area at the entrance to Rowsley South Station, or the exhibition coach at Darley Dale platform to learn about the history of the reopening of the line. Special events are held throughout the year, and engine-driving courses can be taken.

Peak Rail, Matlock

High up on the hill behind the town is the brooding ruin of **Riber Castle**, which sits 850 feet above sea level. The castle was built between 1862 and 1868 by John Smedley, as his residence. He was a local hosiery manufacturer who became interested in the hydropathic qualities of Matlock, and drew up

NORTH OF MATLOCK

DARLEY DALE

2 miles NW of Matlock off the A6

Riber Castle, Matlock

the designs for the building himself. It was lavishly decorated inside, and Smedley constructed his own gas-producing plant to provide lighting for the castle and it even had its own well. The castle has been the former site of a boys' school, a food store during the Second World War, and later a nature reserve before it was left to become a ruined shell. It is currently privately owned, and not open to the public, with planning permission to convert it into luxury flats.

A popular attraction in the area is **Matlock Farm Park**, set in 600 acres of working farm and providing a great day out for all the family. The Park is home to a wide variety of animals including llamas, red deer, donkeys and peacocks, which children can feed. The Two Dales Riding School and Trekking Centre is part of the farm park. This offers riding lessons as well as pony trekking in the nearby forests (booking is essential).

To the west of Matlock, down a no-through road, can be found one of Derbyshire's few Grade I listed buildings, the secluded and well-hidden **Snitterton Hall**. The hall, built in the 1630s, is a rare surviving example of an Elizabethan manor house in a substantially original state. It was bought in 1996 for use as a private home and underwent a seven-year restoration project relying on authentic materials and traditional craftsmanship. The gardens were also restored in the late Elizabethan-Jacobean style with extensive terraces and lawns and formal box hedging. The main architect was quoted having said: "Snitterton was saved just in time. Another two or three years and it might have been too late".

This straggling village along the main road north from Matlock dates only from the 19th century, and was created out of several smaller settlements, three of them being Darley Bridge, Darley Hillside and South Darley. Indeed, Darley is mentioned in the *Domesday Book* as 'Derelie', showing that the name at least is ancient. The all-encompassing 'Darley Dale' was either devised by the commercially-minded railway company at work in the area or by the romantically-inclined vicar of the parish. Darley Dale makes up one of three stops on the Matlock-to-Rowsley South Peak line.

One of the most unassuming heroines of this part of Derbyshire must be Lady Louisa Whitworth. She was the second wife of Sir Joseph Whitworth, the famous Victorian engineer whose name is associated with the Great Exhibition of 1851 and who invented the screw thread. Sir Joseph made a fortune manufacturing, amongst other items, machine tools, munitions and nuts and bolts. Following his death in 1887, Lady Louisa brought sweeping changes to the lifestyle of the local poor and needy. She allowed the grounds of her home, Stancliffe Hall, to be used for school outings and events. In 1889, the Whitworth Cottage Hospital was opened under her auspices.

The **Whitworth Institute** was opened in 1890, bringing to the community a wide range of facilities including a swimming pool (the first heated pool in Britain), an assembly

---

44   **THE WHITWORTH PARK HOTEL**

Darley Dale

This is one of the most popular places to dine. If you fancy a drink you can always stay the night, with five en-suite rooms available.

See entry on page 172

hall, a natural history museum and a library. At a time when a woman was required to take a secondary role in society, Lady Louisa was determined to credit her late husband with these changes, which so benefited Darley Dale. Lady Whitworth died in France in 1896, and is buried next to her husband at the **Parish Church of St Helen**, in the hamlet of Churchtown. The church as we see it today dates from at least the 12th century, and has the tomb of Sir John de Darley dating from 1322. It also contains two fine examples of Burne-Jones stained glass windows.

A tree that can be seen at the top of **Oker Hill** is a lobe sycamore, and an unusual tale is attached to it. It seems that two brothers planted sycamore trees at the same time. One tree flourished, just as the brother who planted it did, while the other one died, just like the other brother, who died soon after. A different tale claims that a local man named Shore planted the twin trees to provide in due course of time, the wood for his coffin! William Wordsworth, passing through Darley in 1838 on his way to Dovedale was sufficiently inspired by the legend that he composed a sonnet about it called 'The Keepsake'.

Much of the stone used for local buildings came from nearby Stancliffe Quarry, which also supplied stone for the Thames Embankment and Hyde Park Corner in London, and the Walker Art Gallery in Liverpool. To the north of the 15th century **Darley Bridge**, which carries the road to Winster over the River Derwent, are the remains of **Mill Close Mine**. This was the largest and most productive lead mine in Derbyshire until 1938, when flooding caused it to be abandoned.

Darley Dale has an extensive park that is

very pretty in all seasons. Another of this small village's attractions is the **Red House Stables Working Carriage Museum**, featuring some fine examples of traditional horse-drawn vehicles and equipment. One of the finest collections in the country, it consists of nearly 40 carriages, including one of the very few surviving Hansom cabs, a stage coach, Royal Mail coach, Park Drag and many other private and commercial vehicles. Carriage rides are available, making regular trips through the countryside to places such as Chatsworth and Haddon Hall, and the carriages and horses can be hired for special occasions.

STANTON IN PEAK

5 miles NW of Matlock off the B5056

Stanton is a hillside village which climbs up the western flank of **Stanton Moor**, rising to some 1,096 feet, one of the richest prehistoric sites in the Peak. The moor contains at least 70 barrows as well as stone circles, ancient enclosures and standing stones and is of such interest to archaeologists that the whole area is now protected. However, don't go expecting anything on the scale of Stonehenge, or even Arbor Low - most of the monuments and remains are very small-scale and overgrown with heather. There are interesting features on the moorland, such as the folly, **Earl Grey's Tower**, which was built in 1832 to commemorate the reform of Parliament.

This is a typical Peak District village, with numerous alleyways and courtyards off its main street. A quick glance at the village cottages and the visitor will soon notice the initials WPT that appear above most of the doorways. The initials are those of William Pole Thornhill, the owner of Stanton Hall, which stands near the church and is still home to his descendents. There are some fine 17th and 18th century cottages, one of which, Holly House, has some of its windows still blocked since the window tax of 1697.

The village pub, The Flying Childers, is named after one of the 4th Duke of Devonshire's most successful racehorses.

---

45 **TALL TREES COFFEE SHOP & RESTAURANT**

Two Dales, nr Matlock

Home cooking of the finest kind in the heart of the Derbyshire Dales.

See entry on page 173

ALPORT

*5½ miles NW of Matlock on a
minor road off the B5056*

Derbyshire has three similarly-named places, the others being Alport Heights between Wirksworth and Ambergate, and Alport Moor in the High Peak. Better known is this charming village of Alport which stands at the confluence of the Bradford and Lathkill rivers, near Youlgreave. What connects the three Alports and, indeed, is responsible for the place name, is the ancient track known as the Portway. This ancient way pre-dates the Roman occupation and runs roughly south-east to north-west through the county.

The cottages here mainly date from the 17th and 18th centuries, but the village itself is much older than these dwellings would suggest. Much its wealth was found, like so many other White Peak villages, on lead mining.

River Bradford, Alport

The surrounding countryside (its lead mining area) was owned by the Duke of Rutland and, by the end of the 18th century, the industry was struggling due to flooding. In order to prevent the mines filling up with water, the Duke had a 4-mile sough (underground drainage canal) built to run the water off into the River Derwent. Begun in 1766, this project took 21 years to complete and, in an attempt to recover some of the construction costs, a levy was put on any ore being taken from below a certain level.

Sometime after completion of the project, in 1881, the **River Bradford** disappeared underground for several years. As with other rivers in this limestone landscape, it had channelled a route out underground, only this time it was taking the route of the sough to the River Derwent. After sealing the chasm through which the river had joined up with Hillcar Sough, it was restored to the above-ground landscape.

Among Alport's many fine houses, **Monk's Hall** (private) is one of the best, dating from the late 16th or early 17th century and probably, at one time, connected to a monastic grange. Another is **Harthill Hall Farm**, a gabled 17th century yeoman's farmhouse with stone mullioned and transomed windows.

YOULGREAVE

*6 miles NW of Matlock on a
minor road off the B5056*

This straggling village can also be spelled Youlgrave, and to confuse matters further, it is known locally as Pommy. There have been over sixty variations on the name of this busy, one-street village. The name is thought to mean 'the yellow grove' or 'Geola's grove' – an old name for a lead mine – and Youlgreave was certainly once at the centre of the Derbyshire lead mining industry. In fact, fluorspar and calcite are still extracted from some of the old mines.

The **Parish Church of All Saints**, one of the most beautiful churches in Derbyshire, contains some parts of the original Saxon building though its ancient font is, unfortunately, upturned and used as a sundial. Inside, the working font is Norman and still retains its stoup for holding the Holy Water. It is well worth taking the time to have a look at, as it is the only such font in England. The Church also contains a small tomb with an equally small alabaster effigy; dated 1488. It is a memorial to Thomas Cockayne, who was killed in a brawl when only in his teens. A fine alabaster panel in the north aisle, dated 1492, depicts the Virgin with Robert Gylbert, his wife and seventeen children. There is a glorious Burne-Jones stained-glass window, which was added in 1870, when Norman Shaw very sensitively restored the church.

Conduit Head, Youlgreave

Further up the village's main street is **Thimble Hall**, the smallest market hall in the Peak District. It dates from 1656 and there are also some rather grand Georgian houses to be found in the village. Nearby, the old shop built in 1887 for the local Co-operative Society is now a youth hostel. It featured in the film of DH Lawrence's *The Virgin and the Gypsy*, much of which was filmed in the village. Standing opposite is the **Conduit Head**, a gritstone water tank that has the unofficial name of The Fountain. Built by the village's own water company in 1829, it supplied fresh soft water to all those who paid an annual fee of sixpence. In celebration of their new, clean water supply, the villagers held their first well-dressing in 1829. Today, Youlgreave dresses its wells for the Saturday nearest to St John the Baptist's Day (24th June). Such is the standard of the work that the villagers, all amateurs, are in great demand for advice and help.

Two or three miles to the west of the village is the Bronze Age **Arbor Low**, sometimes referred to as the 'Stonehenge of the Peak District'. About 250 feet in diameter, the central plateau is encircled by a ditch, which lies within a high circular bank. On the plateau is a stone circle of limestone blocks, with a group of four stones in the centre cove. There are a total of 47 stones each weighing no less than eight tonnes, and a further three stones in the centre. Probably used as an observatory and also a religious site, it is not known whether the stones, which have been placed in pairs, ever stood upright. There is no archaeological evidence to suggest that they did. Gaps in

the outer bank, to the northwest and southeast, could have been entrances and exits for religious ceremonies.

Arbor Low dates to the Early Bronze Age period, and there is much evidence in the dales along the River Lathkill that they were inhabited at that time. Nearby there is a large barrow known as **Gib Hill**, which stands at around 16 feet. When it was excavated a stone cist was discovered, containing a clay urn and burned human bones. This circular mound to the south of the stone circle, offers some protection against the weather and it is from this that Arbor Low got its name – 'sheltered heap'.

MIDDLETON BY YOULGREAVE

7 miles NW of Matlock on a minor road east of the A515

Thomas Bateman, the local squire, rebuilt the entire village in the 1820s, though more famous is his grandson. Thomas Bateman Jnr., a pioneer archaeologist who, in the 19th century, excavated some 500 barrows in the Peak District, revealing many valuable Bronze Age artefacts, many of which can be seen at Weston Park Museum in Sheffield. His book *Ten Years Digging* was published just two weeks before he died. Before his grandfather's death, he built **Lomberdale Hall** in 1844, which he enlarged in 1856 to house his growing collection of archaeological artefacts. In the village is a small building with a signpost pointing to Thomas Batemans Jnr's grave. His tomb is surmounted with a replica of a Bronze Age urn.

WENSLEY

2½ miles W of Matlock off the B5057

Derbyshire, like Yorkshire, has a Wensley and a Wensleydale – yet there's not a cheese factory in sight! Its name derives from Woden, the Norse God of War, however the following rhyme suggests the village now has more romantic connotations.

'At Winster Wakes there's ale and cakes
At Elton Wakes there's quenchers
At Bircher Wakes there's knives and forks
At Wensley Wakes there's wenches'.

This is a modest village that often goes unnoticed as you drive through, but as a result provides a peaceful and pleasant alternative to many other villages.

BIRCHOVER

4 miles W of Matlock off the B5056

Birchover's name means 'the ridge where the birch trees grow'. Its main street meanders gently up from the unusual outcrops of **Rowtor Rocks** at the foot of the village, heading up towards neighbouring Stanton Moor. The village was once home to father-and-son amateur antiquarians J.C. and J.P. Heathcote, who excavated over seventy Bronze Age burial mounds. They kept a detailed and fascinating private museum in the old village post office in the main street and it is now in Sheffield's Weston Park Museum.

The strange Rocks of Rowtor, behind The Druid Inn, are said to have been used for Druidical rites. The Reverend Thomas Eyre, who died in 1717, was fascinated by these rocks and built the strange collection of steps, rooms and seats which have been carved out of the gritstone rocks on the summit of the outcrop. It is said that the reverend would take his friends there to admire the view across the valley below - a view which, nowadays, is obscured by trees. Prehistoric cup-and-ring marks have been discovered on the rocks and several rocking stones can be moved by the application of a shoulder. One of these, weighing about 50 tons, could once be rocked easily by hand, but in 1799 fourteen young men decided to remove it for a bit of a lark. However when they put it back, they couldn't get the balance right.

---

46 RED LION INN

Birchover

This historic public house is one of Derbyshire's most popular destination pubs for lovers of fine food and excellent ales.

See entry on page 173

Thomas Eyre lived at the Old Vicarage in the village below Rowtor Rocks, and also restored the lovely tiny church known as the Jesus Chapel or **Rowtor Chapel**. The chapel later became the village cheese shop, and it now features, among fragments of Norman work, unusual carvings and some wonderful decorative features, including modern stained glass by the artist Brian Clarke, who lived at the vicarage for a time during the 1970s.

Nearby across the fields are two equally strange outcrops **Robin Hood's Stride** (also known as 'Mock Beggar's Hall') and **Cratcliff Tor**. A medieval hermit's cave, complete with crucifix, can be seen at the foot of Cratcliff Tor, hidden behind an ancient yew tree.

WINSTER

4 miles W of Matlock off the B5056

This attractive gritstone village was once a lead mining centre and market town, the last mine at Mill Close, two miles to the northeast, closing down in 1938. Today it is a conservation village, with a pleasant high street and some fine late 18th century houses. Less splendid than the surrounding houses, but no less interesting, are the ginnels - little alleyways - which run off the main street. The name 'Winster' is a corruption of 'Wysterne', the name under which it appears in the Domesday Book. It is thought to mean 'Wyn's thorn tree', though who Wyn is no one knows. The most impressive building here, however, must be the **Market House**, owned by the National Trust and found at the top of the main street. This was the Trust's first purchase in Derbyshire, back in 1906. The lower portion, with its built-up arches, is over 500 years old, while the upper portion was added on in the 18th century, and rebuilt in 1905 using old materials. The house is open to the public and acts as an information centre and shop for the Trust.

Within the Burton Institute, Winster's village hall, is a more modern attraction, the **Winster Millennium Tapestry**. It took six years to make, and involved the whole village. For a payment of 25p, villagers could get their name woven into it.

Winster Hall

Winster Hall was built in 1628 by Francis Moore, a local businessman, and like all good manor houses has its own ghost, which haunts the grounds. The ghost, in the form of a 'white lady', is said to be that of a daughter from the Hall, who fell in love with one of the coachmen. Her parents were horrified at her choice of husband and vowed to find a more suitable partner. However, before such a match could be made the girl and her lover climbed to the top of the Hall and jumped, together, to their deaths.

The **Bank House** is another building with a gruesome tale attached to it. It was built around 1580, and was occupied in the early 19th century by the local doctor, William Cuddie. The owner of nearby Oddo House, William Brittlebank, was visiting in 1821 and murdered Cuddie. He then fled and a reward of £100 (a vast sum in those days) was offered for his capture, but he was never heard of again.

The **Parish Church of St John** stands on the site of an ancient chapel built by the Ferrers family, who were given the manor soon after the Conquest. The nave was built in 1833, tacked on to a tower of 1721, which itself was added to the original Norman building. It has a curfew bell which still rings at 8pm every evening.

Finally, although Morris Dancing is traditionally associated with the Cotswolds area, two of the best known and most often played tunes, The Winster Gallop and Blue-eyed Stranger, originate from the village. Collected many years ago by Cecil Sharpe, a legend in the world of Morris Dancing, they were rediscovered in the 1960s. The Winster

Morris Men traditionally dance through the village at the beginning of Wakes Week in June, finishing, as all good Morris Dances do, at one of the local pubs.

ELTON

5 miles W of Matlock off the B5056

Elton is one of the coldest places in Derbyshire. This isn't surprising, given that it sits at an altitude of 900 feet, with no shelter from the cold north and east winds. This must raise the inevitable question as to why the village was built in such an exposed position. The facts that lead was in plentiful supply, as was water, were probably the major factors behind the location of the village.

Interestingly the village is set on a division in the underlying rocks: to the north is limestone and to the south is gritstone. This produces an unusual effect with gritstone vegetation on one side (e.g. oak trees) and limestone on the other (e.g. ash trees). The houses too reflect the division, some of limestone, some of gritstone, or a mixture of both. This is nowhere more apparent than along the main street, where The Old Hall, which for many years acted as a Youth Hostel before being turned into a private residence, is built of girtstone. In contrast, Greenacres Farm, which is just across the road, is built of pure limestone.

The surrounding area contains traces of barrows, Bronze or Iron Age enclosures and hut circles, but the most visible monument is the stone circle called the **Nine Stones** (though in fact only four are left standing) or **'Grey Ladies'**. It is another Bronze Age monument connected with the Portway, and is probably the most impressive in the area.

SOUTH OF MATLOCK

MATLOCK BATH

1 mile S of Matlock off the A6

Known as "Little Switzerland" to generations of tourists, Matlock Bath began its life as a craggy limestone gorge cut by the River

Derwent. Developed as one of the country's first tourist destinations, it retains much of the character and interest that impressed early visitors. Matlock Bath was formed as a Spa Town, famous for its healing waters.

A turnpike road built in 1818, and the coming of the railways in 1849, brought Matlock Bath within cheap and easy reach to many more people and it became a popular destination for day excursions. Many famous people have visited the town, including the young Victoria before she succeeded to the throne. Lord Byron confirmed its romantic character, comparing it with alpine Switzerland, hence its nickname "Little Switzerland".

Today, it is still essentially a holiday resort and manages to possess an air of Victorian charm left over from the days when many Victorians descended on the town looking for a 'cure'. Attractions in and around the village include High Tor, the Heights of Abraham including the cable cars, Gulliver's Kingdom, an Aquarium and the Peak District Mining Museum to name but a few. The town is also known as a meeting point for motorcyclists.

High Tor is a spectacular 390 feet high limestone cliff that towers above Matlock Bath, giving wonderful views of the town and its environs. Nothing beats a walk on High Tor Grounds, where there are 60 acres of nature trails to wander around, while, far below, the River Derwent appears like a silver thread through the gorge. A popular viewing point for Victorian visitors to the town, today rock climbers practice their skills on the precipitous crags. For those a little less energetic, a relatively steady walk to the top provides magnificent views over the town and surrounding area.

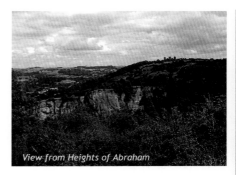
View from Heights of Abraham

On the opposite side of the valley are the beautiful wooded slopes of Masson Hill, the southern face of which has become known as the **Heights of Abraham**. This particular name was chosen after the inhabitants of Matlock had shown great enthusiasm for General Wolfe's victory in Quebec in 1759. This part of the Derwent Valley was seen to resemble the gorge of the St Lawrence River and the original Heights of Abraham lying a mile north of Quebec. Today it is a well-known viewing point, reached on foot or, more easily, by cable car.

For a family fun day out there is **Gulliver's Kingdom Theme Park**, nestled within breathtaking woodlands. All the rides are centred on family fun with just enough thrills to make your visit an unforgettable one!

One of the great attractions of the town is **The Matlock Bath Aquarium**, which occupies what was once the old Matlock Bath Hydro that was established in 1833. The original splendour of the Bath Hydro can still be seen, in the fine stone staircase and also in the thermal pool. The pool, maintained at a constant temperature of 68 degrees Fahrenheit, was where the rheumatic

---

47 **RIVERSIDE TEA ROOM & OLD BANK CAFE BAR**

Matlock Bath

These popular establishments have an ambience all of their own - a sanctuary from the bustling weekend days of the summer, and warm and friendly on quieter days.

See entry on page 174

---

48 **HEIGHTS OF ABRAHAM**

Matlock Bath

Overlooking the spa town, this country park with its spectacular views, makes an ideal day out .

See entry on page 173

patients would come to immerse themselves in the waters to ease their symptoms. Today the pool is home to a large collection of Common and Koi carp, while the upstairs consulting rooms now house tanks full of native, tropical and marine fish. Visitors are welcome to feed the fish with food obtainable from the Aquarium.

Down by the riverbank and housed in the old Pavilion can be found the **Peak District Mining Museum**. Opened in 1978, the Museum offers an enthralling insight into the many facets of mining from as far back as Roman times through to the modern day.

Life in a Lens is a museum of popular photography set in a beautiful renovated Victorian house. Displays include cameras of all ages, toy and novelty cameras, postcards and much more. also a Victorian Teashop and a live webcam on their website.

Being a relatively new town, Matlock Bath has no ancient place of worship, but the **Parish Church of the Holy Trinity** is a fine early Victorian edifice which was built in 1842 and enlarged in 1873/74 to accommodate the growing congregation. Of greater architectural merit is, however, the **Chapel of St John the Baptist**, found on the road between Matlock and Matlock Bath and built into a cliff. Built in 1897, it was designed by architect Guy Dawber to be a chapel-of-ease for those finding it difficult to attend St Giles in Matlock, but it also became a place of worship for those who preferred a High Church service.

Matlock Bath is of course famous for its Illuminations and Venetian nights. In 1898 a Venetian Fete was conceived when a number of tradesmen in Matlock Bath decided to purchase 2,500 coloured-glass bucket lanterns to illuminate the gardens on the promenade

and on Lover's Walk. They are now firmly part of the tourism year, and are held annually from the end of August to the end of October.

LEA

4 miles SE of Matlock off the A615

Lea is mentioned briefly in the *Domesday Book* when it was spelt 'Lede' and was owned by Ralph fitzHerbert. But it is better known now for its association with John Marsden-Smedley (1867-1959) who spent much of his life in the village. As well as being the local squire, he was the owner of John Smedley Ltd, a manufacturer of quality woollen garments.

Lea Gardens offer a rare collection of rhododendrons, azaleas, alpines and conifers in a superb woodland setting. This unique collection including kalmias and other plants of interest has been introduced from all over the world to this area in the heart of Derbyshire. The gardens provide a stunning visual display to enthral the whole family. Covering an area of some four acres, the site is set on the remains of a mediaeval millstone quarry and includes a lovely rock garden with dwarf conifers, alpines, heathers and spring bulbs. A mile of walks takes visitors through a blaze of spring colour. The house at Lea Gardens was a later addition, built in 1967.

Lea Gardens

HOLLOWAY

4½ miles SE of Matlock off the A6

Not far from Lea, this attractive village has one famous daughter, Florence Nightingale, who lived here at **Lea Hurst**, a 17th-century

49	THE PEAK DISTRICT MINING MUSEUM

Matlock Bath

An exciting insight into the world of the Derbyshire Mines.

See entry on page 175

gabled farmhouse. Although she was named after the city of her birth, Florence spent much of her childhood in the Derbyshire mansion. Florence was the second daughter of William Edward Shore, who had to adopt the name of a distant relative, in order to benefit from his inheritance, including the family seat of Lea Hurst.

Florence Nightingale is most remembered as a pioneer of nursing and a reformer of hospital sanitation methods. But perhaps the most interesting member of the early Nightingale family was Peter, born in 1736. His nickname was 'Mad Peter' on account of his lifestyle, which consisted of heavy drinking, gambling and horse riding. However, he was an astute businessman and established a lead smelting business and extended an arm of the Cromford Canal.

Florence's father left Lea Hurst to her in his will and, after her courageous work in the dreadful conditions of the Crimean War, she retired to the house and spent the next 50 years writing, specifically on the subject of hospital organisation. Florence died in London in 1910 and the house remained in the family until 1940. Still in private hands, Lea Hurst is occasionally opened to the public.

TANSLEY

1 mile SE of Matlock on the A615

Around the village a network of footpaths lead through beautiful and varied countryside to Matlock, a lane to the left of The Gate Inn leads down to Oaksedge Lane which continues northward up a steep hill to a track below a magnificent pinewood. There are outstanding views towards Matlock and Masson Hill to be had from here and soon the track arrives at the head of the Lumsdale Valley.

This tiny and picturesque village has an 18th-century mill, **Tansley Wood Mill**, and some good 18th-century houses including Knoll House with an impressive carved doorway. Today there are no more working mills and quarries but there are six garden centres within half a mile of the village, making it well worth a visit by keen gardeners.

CROMFORD

2 miles S of Matlock off the A5012

Although at first sight not a 'pretty' village, Cromford does have a charm of its own, with plenty to surprise and please the visitor. It was here in 1771 that Sir Richard Arkwright started to build **Cromford Mill**, the world's first successful water-powered spinning mill. Though some of the buildings predate Arkwright, he also built a new town round the mill, providing decent housing and other amenities for his workers, such as an inn, shops, a school and a village lock-up for miscreants. In this respect, Cromford became possibly the first purpose-built industrial town in the world.

The area Arkwright had chosen for his mill was perfect. The River Derwent described by Daniel Defoe as 'a fury of a river', provided an ample power supply; there was an unorganised but very willing workforce, as the lead mining industry was experiencing a decline, and probably most importantly, Cromford was away from the prying eyes of Arkwright's competitors. In 1792 he commissioned the building of the village church, where he now lies. The mill proved

Cromford Mill

to be a great success and became the model for others both in Britain and abroad, earning Arkwright the accolade 'Father of the Factory System'. His pioneering work and contributions to the great Industrial Age resulted in a knighthood in 1786, and one year later he became High Sheriff of Derbyshire. Cromford Mill was last in use as a Colour Works, but is now a Visitor Centre owned and run by the Arkwright Society, with a variety of shops and businesses occupying the old buildings. Tours of the mill and Cromford village are available throughout the year.

For lovers of waterways there is an opportunity, at **Cromford Canal**, to wander along the five-mile stretch of towpath to Ambergate. At **Cromford Wharf** there is a warehouse dating back to 1794, a counting house from the same year and a couple of canal cottages. The old **Leawood Pumping Station**, which transferred water from the River Derwent to the Cromford Canal, has been fully restored. Inside, the engine house is a preserved Cornish-type beam engine and is occasionally steamed up. Close by the Pump House is the **Wigwell Aqueduct**, (also known as the Derwent Aqueduct) dating from 1793, which carries the canal high over the River Derwent. It had to be rebuilt when it partially collapsed during construction.

The **High Peak Trail**, which stretches some 17-and-a-half miles up to Dowlow near Buxton, starts at Cromford and follows the track bed of the Cromford and High Peak Railway. First opened in 1880, the railway was built to connect the Cromford Canal with the Peak Forest Canal. It is somewhat reminiscent of a canal as it has long level sections interspersed with sharp inclines (instead of locks) and many of the stations

are known as wharfs. After walking the trail it is not surprising to learn that its chief engineer was really a canal builder! The railway was finally closed in 1967; the old stations are now car parks and picnic areas and there is an information office in the former Hartington station signal box. Surfaced with clinker rather than limestone, the trail is suitable for walkers, cyclists and horses.

The **Cromford Venture Centre** is an ideal base for study visits, holidays, training and self-development courses. It offers self-catering accommodation for parties of up to 24 young people and four staff. It is run by the Arkwright Society in association with the Prince's Trust, and is housed in a listed building.

"Celebrating Cromford", is a weekend festival celebrating the village and the talents of the people who live there; it began in June 2005 and has become an annual event.

BONSALL

2 miles SW of Matlock off the A5012

In a steep-sided dale beneath Masson Hill, Bonsall has a long history of lead mining, possibly going back to Roman times, and is mentioned in the *Domesday Book*. Many of the fields and meadows around are still littered with the remains of the miners' work. Bonsall inhabitants have also been involved in the textile industry, pre- and post-Arkwright. The village was also at one time a centre of framework knitting, and east of the village cross is an old knitting workshop, with its large windows and outside staircase.

Bonsall owes its size and relative prosperity almost exclusively to the numerous industries which once flourished beside the **Bonsall Brook**. Indeed, the Bonsall Brook is responsible for the shape of the village which follows every twist of the stream from its rising at the highest point above Uppertown to its cascading plunge down the Clatterway.

It is also one of the Derbyshire villages which continues the tradition of well-dressing, usually on the last Saturday in July.

| **50** | **THE BOAT INN** |

Cromford

A village inn full of charm, character, history – and good food and drink.

See entry on page 175

Bonsall Village Cross

Beside the market square cross stands The King's Head inn, dating from the late 17th century and said to be haunted. Another pub in the village reflects the traditional occupations of its residents, as it is called the Barley Mow. Another was called the Pig of Lead but is now a private residence. Above the village centre stands the battlemented **Parish Church of St James**, with its pinnacled tower and spire. Dating originally from the 1200s, it has a wonderful clerestory lighting the nave, though the outer walls were substantially rebuilt in 1862-63. From one end of the main street the road climbs up some 400 feet to the Uppertown, which lies just below the rim of the limestone plateau. In order to cope with the steep hill, the village church is split-level.

MIDDLETON BY WIRKSWORTH

4 miles SW of Matlock off the A5012

From Middleton-by-Wirksworth there are lovely far-reaching views, despite the scars of the quarrying industry. Just north of the village, which is also known as Middleton, lies the **Good Luck Mine**, which is now a lead mining museum. Usually open the first Sunday in the month, this old mine, found on

the Via Gellia, is typically narrow and, in places, the roof is low. Not a place for the claustrophobic, it does, however, give an excellent impression of a lead mine. The village also has another mine, where a particularly rare form of limestone is quarried. Hopton Wood marble from here has been used in Westminster Abbey, York Minster and the Houses of Parliament.

The Cromford and High Peak Railway had many inclines, and no less than nine steam-powered winding engines to haul the wagons and engines up them. **Middleton Top Winding Engine**, to the west of the village, was built in 1829, and is the only survivor. On certain days of the year between April and October it can still be seen in action. At **Middleton Top** is a visitor centre that explains the Cromford and High Peak Railway.

A lead mining disaster occurred in 1797 close to Middleton-by-Wirksworth and involved two miners named Job Boden and Anthony Pearson. There was a huge fall of earth and a rush of water while these men were working 50 yards underground. It was thought that Job and Anthony had surely perished. Other miners rushed to clear the debris, and after three days they came across the body of Anthony Pearson who was found in an upright position. Eight days after the disaster Job was found and still alive. Although badly emaciated, he recovered from his ordeal, and lived for many years to tell the story of his rescue.

In Balleye Quarry between Matlock Bath and Middleton-by-Wirksworth there was an amazing discovery recorded in 1663. George Mower found the bones and molar teeth of an elephant! He also found a huge natural cavern large enough to contain a great church, and there was also the skeleton of a man said to be of monster proportions.

WIRKSWORTH

4 miles S of Matlock off the B5023

Standing as it does virtually at the centre of Derbyshire, where north meets south, Wirksworth was once the leading lead-mining town in the Peak District when the industry was at its height.

Babington House Garden, Wirksworth

Babington House dates back to Jacobean Wirksworth. Another former lead merchant's house, **Hopkinsons House**, was restored in 1980 as part of a number of restoration schemes initiated by the Civic Trust's 'Wirksworth Project'. The ancient **Parish Church of St Mary's** is a fine building dating originally from the 13th century and standing on a site previously occupied by a Saxon and then a Norman church. It sits in a tranquil close bounded by the former (Georgian) grammar school and the Elizabethan **Gell's Almshouses**, named after Sir Philip Gell who founded them in 1584. The church holds one of the oldest stone carvings in the country. Known as the Wirksworth Stone, it is a coffin lid dating from the 8th century, and was found beneath the chancel floor in the 1820s. There are also tombs of the Gell family, local lords of the manor in Tudor times and lead mine owners. The ancient ceremony of 'clypping the church' takes place here on the first Sunday after 8th September each year. It is thought to date from pre-Christian times, and consists of the people of the village circling the church and linking hands. Another ceremony is that of well-dressing,

which takes place during the last few days of May/first week of June.

The **National Stone Centre** in Porter Lane tells 'the story of stone', with a wealth of exhibits, activities such as gem-panning and fossil-casting, and outdoor trails tailored to introduce topics such as the geology, ecology and history of the dramatic Peak District landscape.

At **North End Mills**, visitors are able to witness hosiery being made as it has been for over half a century; a special viewing area offers an insight into some of the items on sale in the factory shop.

The town has connections with Mary Ann Evans, the author who wrote under the pen name of George Eliot. At the southern end of the town is a cottage known as **Adam Bede Cottage**. This is where Samuel Evans and his wife Elizabeth lived, in real life Mary Ann's aunt and uncle. In the book *Adam Bede*, Wirksworth is called Snowfield, and Samuel and Elizabeth are portrayed as Adam Bede and Dinah Morris. Another literary connection is to be found at the Crown Inn, which Baroness Orczy featured in her novel *Beau Brocade*. Wirksworth was also where D.H. Lawrence's mother came from, and indeed Lawrence lived close to the town at Mountain Cottage for a year with his German-born wife.

An impressive exhibit in the courtyard is the Kugel Stone, a massive ball of granite weighing over one tonne, which revolves on a thin film of water under pressure and can be moved with a touch of the hand. Some half a million trees and shrubs have been planted and are managed here, to attract wildlife and to enhance the landscape. There are two bird hides and a wildlife centre to help visitors understand the variety of wildlife and observe the birdlife that visits the reservoir. The reservoir is stocked for fishing either from the bank or from boats available for hire. There is a large adventure playground and numerous open spaces for families to relax.

For those wanting to know more about Wirksworth a visit to the highly acclaimed **Wirksworth Heritage Centre** is essential. Situated just off the market place in Crown Yard, the Heritage Centre is housed in a

---

51 RED LION HOTEL

Wirksworth

Open all-day every day, the Red Lion has been offering traditional Derbyshire hospitality for well over 200 years.

See entry on page 176

former Silk and Velvet Mill and takes visitors through time from when the bones of a Woolly Rhino were found, to the Romans in Wirksworth through to the present day, with all this being explained over three floors. Excellent views over the town are obtained from the windows. One of the town's most interesting sights is the jumble of cottages linked by a maze of tiny lanes on the hillside between The Dale and Greenhill, in particular the area known locally as 'The Puzzle Gardens'.

Wirksworth wells are dressed on spring bank holiday and there is also an annual arts and crafts festival in September.

Heritage Centre, Wirksworth

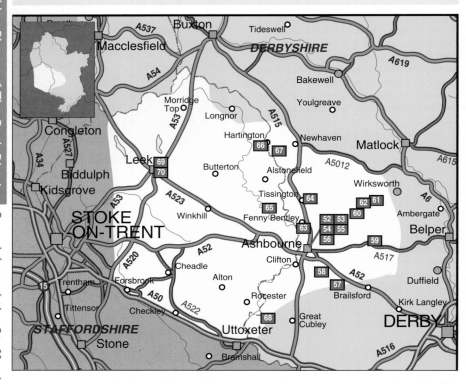

Accommodation

53	White Hart Hotel, Ashbourne	*pg 63, 178*
54	Ye Olde Vaults, Ashbourne	*pg 63, 178*
59	The Black Horse Inn, Hulland Ward, Ashbourne	*pg 66, 182*
60	The Red Lion Inn, Hognaston	*pg 67, 182*
63	Bentley Brook Inn, Fenny Bentley, Ashbourne	*pg 70, 184*
67	Biggin Hall Country House Hotel, Biggin-by-Hartington, Buxton	*pg 77, 187*
69	The Swan, Leek	*pg 79, 188*

Food & Drink

52	The Coach & Horses, Ashbourne	*pg 63, 177*
53	White Hart Hotel, Ashbourne	*pg 63, 178*
54	Ye Olde Vaults, Ashbourne	*pg 63, 178*

Food & Drink

55	The Flower Cafe, Ashbourne	*pg 63, 179*
56	Chimes Cafe, Ashbourne	*pg 64, 179*
57	Saracen's Head, Shirley, Ashbourne	*pg 65, 180*
58	Shoulder of Mutton, Osmaston, Ashbourne	*pg 65, 181*
59	The Black Horse Inn, Hulland Ward, Ashbourne	*pg 66, 182*
60	The Red Lion Inn, Hognaston	*pg 67, 182*
61	Mainsail Restaurant, Carsington Water, Ashbourne	*pg 67, 183*
62	Brackendale Restaurant & Function Room, Carsington Water, Ashbourne	*pg 68, 184*
63	Bentley Brook Inn, Fenny Bentley, Ashbourne	*pg 70, 184*
66	Beresford Tea Rooms, Hartington, Buxton	*pg 77, 186*

DOVEDALE AND THE STAFFORDSHIRE MOORLANDS

This area of Derbyshire, which includes a southern section of the Peak District, is probably best known for the beautiful Dovedale. For the walker, the area holds mile after mile of paths, both alongside the River Dove and over the surrounding countryside, linking villages and hamlets. A walk in Dovedale – perhaps the most famous dale of all thanks to its connections with Izaak Walton, who published his famous book, *The Compleat Angler*, in 1653 – passes a whole collection of fancifully-named rock features and a dozen fascinating and beautiful villages.

River Dove

Standing either side of the entrance to Dovedale are the shapely twin southern sentinels of Bunster Hill and Thorpe Cloud. They are followed in swift succession by features like the Twelve Apostles, Lover's Leap, Tissington Spires, Ilam Rock and Pickering Tor. All can be reached by car, but to discover the best of the dales or the hilltops it is advised to walk. Watch out for a wide variety of birdlife from kingfishers to dippers and the odd heron, grey wagtails and moorhens. Wild flora abounds with mosses, lichens and flowers such as Herb Robert

Food & Drink

Places of Interest

everywhere. An aura of peaceful seclusion hangs over the valley, making a walk in Dovedale one of the highlights of a visit to the Peak District.

The Stepping Stones at the entrance to Dovedale appear on thousands of post cards and have delighted visitors for years. The footing in the river is uncertain to say the least, so be careful, and wear good footwear. For those who don't want to cross the river at this point there is a foot bridge closer to the car park, below Thorpe Cloud.

The River Dove meanders slowly through Dovedale and takes its name from the British Gaelic word 'dutho', meaning dark. It is 45 miles long from its source at Axe Edge to the River Derwent, and for much of its length it forms the boundary between Derbyshire and Staffordshire. It is a favourite place for fishermen, and is forever associated with the aforementioned Izaak Walton.

Izaak Walton was born in Stafford and later moved to London, where he was an ironmonger. He afterwards lived in Farnham, Surrey, but spent a lot of time with his poet friend Charles Cotton at the latter's fishing cottage on the Dove. An old farmhouse at the head of the Dale was converted, many years ago, into the well-known and much-loved Izaak Walton Hotel.

The spectacular scenery was perfect for the television and camera crews that were on location late in 2006 filming scenes for a BBC documentary which celebrated the Centenary of the work of the National Trust in Derbyshire, and heralded the dawning of Dovedale as a National Nature Reserve.

Dovedale, however, is not the only dale worth exploring. The River Manifold offers some equally wonderful scenery, as does Ilam. A beautifully preserved estate village, with a well-established youth hostel, Ilam is also a popular starting point from which to explore the Manifold Valley. But look out for the phantom Cromwell Coach riding along the lane from Ilam to Throwley. During the day it is heard though not seen, but its lights can be seen at night.

On the southern edge of the Peak District, the Staffordshire Moorlands certainly rival those of Derbyshire in terms of scenery and tranquil atmosphere. There are attractions for everyone from Britain's favourite theme park, Alton Towers, to steam railways, animal parks and gardens to stir the imagination. Then there are the undulating pastures of the moorlands, along with the fresh air and ancient weatherworn crags, all making this the ideal place to walk, cycle or trek.

It is also an area full of character, with charming scattered villages, historic market towns and a wealth of history. Many of the farms and buildings date back hundreds of years, and the Industrial Revolution also left its mark. This region is also blessed with the two great reservoirs of Rudyard and Tittesworth, which make for pleasant and easy-to-navigate walks and cycle routes while offering peaceful havens for a wide variety of plants, animals and birds. There is a visitor centre, café and large car park, as well as recreational facilities such as fishing and boating at each site.

Most of this area is now used for dairy farming (for which calcium soil is essential). In the past it supported a number of creameries and the famous Hartington cheese factory, which sadly recently closed (see also Hartington).

Let us leave the last words with Lord Byron, who wrote with Dovedale in mind, to his friend, 'I can assure you there are things in Derbyshire as noble as Greece or Switzerland'.

ASHBOURNE

There can be no doubt left in the mind of the visitor who leaves the limestone plateau of the White Peak and travels south to the cobbled Market Place at Ashbourne that they have well and truly left the highlands behind.

Although just outside the National Park boundary, Ashbourne proclaims itself as 'the Gateway to Dovedale'. But there is much more to this charming Georgian town than that, including its famous gingerbread and unique Shrovetide football match. It is one of Derbyshire's finest old towns having celebrated the 750th anniversary of its market charter in 2007. It is a pleasure to visit and the cobbled market place is still used twice weekly (Thursday and Saturday) – a popular haunt for bargain-hunters, whether locals or visitors. It has an enviable reputation for its abundance of antique shops, other shopping facilities and its modern leisure centre.

Mentioned in the *Domesday Book* as 'Essiburn', - derived from the local stream with its many ash trees - it was originally a small settlement lying on the northern bank of Henmore Brook, which already had a church. It was a 13th-century lord of the manor who laid out the new town to the east, around its unusual shaped market place. Many of the town's traders, in order to continue to enjoy the benefits without paying the town's tolls, built themselves houses on the south side of the Brook. The area became known as Compton (or 'Campdene') and it was slowly absorbed into the town.

The triangular, sloping **Market Square**, in the heart of Ashbourne, was part of the new development begun in the 13th century that shifted the town to the east, away from the church. It was from this market place during the height of the Jacobite Rebellion in 1745, that Bonnie Prince Charlie proclaimed his father to be King James III.

Though the old bull ring no longer exists, the town boasts many fine examples of 18th-

Ashbourne Gingerbread Shop

52 THE COACH AND HORSES

Ashbourne

The aroma of home cooked food attracts plenty of diners to this fine public house, which dates in parts to the 18th century.

See entry on page 177

53 WHITE HART HOTEL

Ashbourne

This traditional and picturesque British pub offers the same hospitality to travellers today as it always has.

See entry on page 178

54 YE OLDE VAULTS

Ashbourne

It has been a pub for over 200 years, and Ye Olde Vaults is as popular as ever, with locals and visitors alike.

See entry on page 178

55 THE FLOWER CAFÉ

Ashbourne

The kind of café you hope to find in every town, serving the best local food, lovingly prepared and cooked.

See entry on page 179

century architecture as well as some older buildings. On the **Gingerbread Shop** can be seen the original wattle and daub and probably dates from the 15th century but for many years was covered by a mock Elizabethan front. Ashbourne Gingerbread has a fascinating history, and the recipe is said to have been acquired from French prisoners during the Napoleonic Wars. The personal chef of a captured French general reputedly made it in 1805, and his recipe was copied and used locally. You can buy it today at Spencers bakery in the town centre.

Also worthy of a second glance is the unique double inn sign for the **Green Man and Black's Head Royal Hotel**. The inn sign stretches over St John's Street and was put up when the Blackamoor Inn joined with the Green Man in 1825. Though the Blackamoor is no more, the sign remains and it claims to be the longest hotel name in the country. If you look carefully, you will see that the blackamoor's head is smiling on one side and scowling on the other. Of Georgian origin, the amalgamated hotel has played host to James Boswell, Dr Johnson and the young Princess Victoria. Ashbourne was, in fact, one of Dr Johnson's favourite places; he came to the town on several occasions between 1737 and 1784 to visit Dr John Taylor, an old friend. He also visited the hotel so often that he had his own chair with his name on it! The chair can still be seen at the Green Man. Today one of the two bars in named after him.

A stroll down Church Street, described by Pevsner as one of the finest streets in Derbyshire, takes the walker past many interesting Georgian houses - including the Grey House, which stands next to the **Grammar School**. Founded by Sir Thomas

Cockayne on behalf of Elizabeth I in 1585, the school was visited on its 400th anniversary by the present Queen. Almost opposite the Grey House is **The Mansion**, the late 17th-century home of the Reverend Dr John Taylor, oldest friend of Dr Johnson. In 1764 a domed, octagonal drawing room was added to the house, and a new brick façade built facing the street. Next to The Mansion are the **Owfield's Almshouses**, dating from the early 17th-century. Next to them, at right angles to the street, are **Pegg's Almshouses**, founded in 1669. Ashbourne also retains many of its narrow alleyways and, in particular, there is Lovatt's Yard, where the town lock-up can be seen.

St Oswald's Church

The **Parish Church of St Oswald**, with its elegant 212 feet spire, was described by Victorian novelist George Eliot as 'the finest mere parish church in England'. The town was a regular haunt of George Eliot, who used it as a model for the fictional town of 'Oakbourne' in the novel *Adam Bede*. James Boswell said that the church was 'one of the largest and most luminous that I have seen in any town of the same size'. St Oswald's stands on the site of a Minster church mentioned in the *Domesday Book*, though most of what we see today dates from rebuilding work in the 13th century. There is a dedication brass in the south transept dated 1241. The south doorway, with its dog-toothed decoration and ribbed moulding, reflects the church's classic early-English style. St Oswald's has chapels to its transepts, adding to the spacious feeling that

---

56 CHIMES CAFÉ

Ashbourne

Chimes Café is a one-of-a-kind place where you can buy an antique clock, have a glass of wine or eat a rump steak – all under the same roof.

See entry on page 179

is more reminiscent of a small cathedral than a parish church. To the southeast of the church are the **Spalden Almshouses**, built between 1723 and 1724.

Don't miss the monuments to the Bradbourne and Cockayne families in the north transept chapel or that of Penelope Boothby, who died in 1791 at the tender age of five. It is perhaps sculptor Thomas Banks's most famous work, and is in white Carrara marble. The figure of the child is so life-like that it appears that she is only sleeping. Queen Charlotte, wife of George II, is supposed to have burst into tears when she saw the sculpture at the Royal Academy exhibition. The moving epitaph reads:

'She was in form and intellect most exquisite. The unfortunate parents ventured their all on this frail bark, and the wreck was total.'

It is said that Penelope's parents separated at the child's grave and never spoke to each other again.

More recently Ashbourne was the birthplace in 1829 of Catherine Mumford, who later married William Booth and helped him found the Salvation Army. Catherine became known as the 'Mother of the Army'. She was responsible for many of the changes in the new organization, designing the flag and bonnets for the ladies, and contributed to the Army's ideas on many important issues and matters of belief. There is a bust of her in the War Memorial Gardens.

Ashbourne is home, too, to the famous Royal Shrovetide football match, played on Shrove Tuesday and Ash Wednesday – an annual game of 'traditional' football, played with a leather ball stuffed with sawdust. Apart from the pubs the whole of the town closes for this event. The two teams, the 'Up'ards' (those born north of the Henmore Brook) and the 'Down'ards' (those born south of it) begin their match at 2pm behind the Green Man Hotel. The game continues until 10pm unless a goal is scored after 5pm. The two goals are situated three miles apart, along the Brook, on the site of the old mills at Clifton and Sturston. Despite there being hundreds of participants, it is rare for more than one goal to be scored in this slow-moving game. To describe it as boisterous would be an understatement. The violence involved has led to intermittent attempts to ban it, but the game has been played here for hundreds of years and fortunately it still continues.

AROUND ASHBOURNE

YELDERSLEY

3 miles SE of Ashbourne off the A52

Yeldersley has long been the home of gentlemen farmers and those who love the countryside. This picturesque village offers many scenic delights. **Yeldersley Hall** is a spacious country mansion, dating back to the 18th century and with a fascinating history. It also has a royal connection - the Duchess of York's grandfather was born here. Today the mansion is made up of luxury self-catering holiday apartments.

OSMASTON

2½ miles SE of Ashbourne off the A52

Five minutes drive from Ashbourne, the visitor must think they are in another world when they arrive at Osmaston. Formerly

57 SARACEN'S HEAD

Shirley

This award-winning gastro-pub mixes historic surroundings with the absolute best of modern English cuisine.

See entry on page 180

58 SHOULDER OF MUTTON

Osmaston

On the edge of the Peak District is one of the best pubs in Derbyshire, serving quality food and drink in a picturesque village setting.

See entry on page 181

Osmaston-in-the-Wood, this sleepy, beautiful village, neither crowded nor bustling, offers the visitor a real haven of tranquillity. It is the archetypal English village, with thatched cottages, village green, duck pond, pub and church. Thatched cottages are rare in Derbyshire, but at Osmaston even the village hall has a thatched roof.

However - not everything is as it seems - it was built in the 19th century as an estate village to house the workers at the Butterley Iron Works. The manor house, Osmaston Manor, was built in 1849 for Francis Wright (his memorial stands in the market place at Ashbourne), the owner of the ironworks, and was demolished in 1964; the main staircase is now in Wooton Lodge, Staffordshire. The park, formerly the manor grounds, is open to the public and has an abundance of wildlife; it is also the location for the internationally recognised annual Osmaston Horse Trials and the more local annual Ashbourne Shire Horse Show.

The Gothic **Parish Church of St Martin** dates from 1845 and replaced an earlier church whose register dates back to 1606.

BRADLEY

3 miles E of Ashbourne just off the A517

A regular visitor to the Georgian **Bradley Hall** (private) was Dr Johnson, who would visit the Meynell family here when he was staying in Ashbourne with his friend, Dr John Taylor. The Meynells had come to Bradley in 1655 and bought the hall from Sir Andrew Kniveton, who had been ruined by the Civil War.

Opposite the hall stands the rather squat **Parish Church of All Saints**, which is interesting in having a bell turret but no

tower on its 14th-century nave and chancel. The original wooden bell tower was struck by lightning. There are several memorials to the Meynell family in the church. The base and part of the shaft of a Saxon cross stand in the churchyard. The archway, crossing the formerly-gated road between cottages at Moorend, is known locally as 'The Hole in the Wall'. The former village pub had the distinction, common in Derbyshire, of two official names, The Jinglers and the Fox and Hounds. Nearby **Bradley Wood** was given to the people of Ashbourne in 1935 by Captain Fitzherbert Wright.

KNIVETON

3 miles NE of Ashbourne on the B5035

This tiny village of grey stone houses lies close to Carsington Reservoir, sheltered in a dip in the hills. Its beautiful little **Parish Church of St Michael** has a 13th-century tower and font, a Norman doorway, small lancet windows, battlements and a short spire. The medieval glass in the chancel depicts the arms of the family of Kniveton. Sir Andrew Kniveton became so impoverished through his loyalty to Charles I that he had to sell most of the family estates. A huge sycamore tree and an ancient yew stand in the churchyard. The yew has grooves in its bark, said to have been made by archers sharpening their arrows.

Close by is the Bronze Age burial mound of **Wigber Low**, which has revealed some important remains from the village's past.

KIRK IRETON

6 miles NE of Ashbourne off the B5023

Nestled in the hills near **Carsington Reservoir**, Kirk Ireton sits at 700 feet above sea level. Its name means 'church of the Irish enclosure', and at one time a Celtic monastery is supposed to have stood here. Much of the village is 17th century and one of the oldest buildings is the 15th-century Barley Mow Inn. Tradition here was so strong that when decimal coinage was introduced in 1971, the 87-year-old landlady refused to accept the new currency. This caused

---

59 THE BLACK HORSE INN

Hulland Ward

Picturesque and historic country inn with a fine reputation for good food and drink.

See entry on page 182

regulars a great deal of amusement to watch the faces of visitors when asked for 'five shillings and eleven pence'. Customers had to pay in 'old money' up to the time of the owner's death in 1977. The Barley Mow was one of the last places in the country to go decimal.

The **Parish Church of the Holy Trinity** is partly Norman, with 14th-century additions. There is an interesting custom observed here at weddings known as 'roping for weddings', when children would stretch a rope across the road as the bride and broom leave the church. They can only pass if they pay a toll.

According to village records, on the 12th May 1811 the village and neighbourhood were visited by an awful tornado, accompanied by lightning and loud claps of thunder; large trees were twisted from their roots, most of the houses were unroofed, and the church was stripped of its lead, which was blown into the adjoining fields.

HOGNASTON

4 miles NE of Ashbourne off the B5035

In 1675, John Ogilby compiled the first practical road map of England. On his map, the only road in Derbyshire is shown going through Hognaston, when it would have been little more than a cart track. People have lived on the site of the village for at least 1,000 years and it was entered in the *Domesday Book* as 'Ochenaueston': King's land. It used to be a busy place in coaching days when the London to Manchester coaches passed through, also the famous stagecoach 'The Devonshire' used to call here en route from Wirksworth to Ashbourne.

According to some of the old village records, Hognaston was not always as

picturesque as it is today. One court order read, 'Every person who has a Dunghill Town Street to remove it out of town'. While another order required a villager to remove his 'Necessary House', to stop the fouling of a neighbour's water.

The **Parish Church of St Bartholomew**, dating back to the late 12th century, has some extraordinary Norman carvings over the doorway in the tympanum, and an early Norman font. Two of the bells date back to the 13th century. The clock was a gift from John Smith and Sons, the famous Derby clock-makers as a memorial to John Smith who lived in the village. John Smith and Sons maintain the clock each year.

CARSINGTON WATER

7 miles NE of Ashbourne off the B5023

Carsington Water, just outside Wirksworth, is one of Britain's newest reservoirs. This 741-acre expanse of water is a beauty spot that has attracted well over a million visitors a year since it was opened by Queen Elizabeth in 1992. It can be reached on foot from Wirksworth along a series of footpaths, and aims to be disabled-friendly with wheelchairs

Carsington Reservoir, Wirksworth

---

60 THE RED LION INN

Hognaston

This family run public house, which has a strong focus on serving local produce, boasts a stunning location on the edge of the Peak District National Park.

See entry on page 182

---

61 MAINSAIL RESTAURANT

Carsington Water, nr Ashbourne

With fabulous views and a wonderful menu, the Mainsail shows off what's best about Derbyshire.

See entry on page 183

available and access to as many attractions as possible. Sailing, windsurfing, fishing and canoeing can be enjoyed here, as well as quiet strolls or bike rides. The Visitor Centre on the west bank offers visitors the opportunity to learn about all aspects of Severn Trent Water, who own it, and water supplies in general. The reservoir is unusual in that it is not fed by streams and rivers, but by water pumped into it from the River Derwent when the water is high. It can hold up to 7.8 billion gallons of water at any one time.

HOPTON

8 miles NE of Ashbourne off the B5035

Hopton is the ancestral home of the famous Derbyshire family of the Gells. They are recorded as holding an estate at Hopton since at least the 14th century, until it was sold in 1989. Their influence is apparent throughout both Hopton and neighbouring Carsington. The **Sir Philip Gell Almshouses** were built between 1719 and 1722 for two men and two women. The Gell family made their fortune in the nearby limestone quarries and they were also responsible for the construction of the **Via Gellia**, a road which runs along a

Hopton Incline

---

62 **BRACKENDALE RESTAURANT & FUNCTION ROOM**

Nr Carsington Water

With a farm location, this restaurant is renowned for its delicious homemade cuisine and is talked about all over the county.

See entry on page 184

---

valley to the west of Cromford.

This village, now by-passed by the main road, is dominated by the Carsington Water reservoir. The land rises to the north of Hopton and here can be found the **Hopton Incline**, once the steepest railway incline in the British Isles. Lying on the **High Peak Railway**, carriages were hauled up using fixed engines on their journey from Cromford to Whaley Bridge. It is now part of the High Peak Trail.

BRADBOURNE

4 miles NE of Ashbourne off the A5056

"I have travelled in many lands, but never seen a more beautiful place"; so wrote author Nat Gould of Bradbourne, which is indeed a 'beautiful place' set in sylvan surroundings just beyond the south-eastern boundary of the Peak District National Park. Gould was born in 1857, and was a journalist who emigrated to Australia. There he worked on the Brisbane Telegraph, where his first fiction appeared. Eventually he returned to England and by the time of his death in 1919 had written 130 horse racing novels. That Nat Gould chose this as his final resting place speaks volumes: his grave is in the **Parish Church of All Saints** churchyard.

The pastoral beauty of Bradbourne is enhanced by its elevated position on a ridge between the valleys of Bradbourne Brook and Havenhill Dale, and this hill-top village of just over 100 inhabitants enjoys some fine views over the surrounding countryside.

Bradbourne may be a small village but it has a large and straggling parish. The church is essentially Norman, but with some fragments of Saxon work , especially on the north side of the nave where typical long-and-short work is visible. The church's large, unbuttressed west tower is Norman and has an elegantly decorated south door. Most of the rest of this appealing little church dates from the 14th century, but there are some fine modern furnishings which owe much to William Morris' Arts and Crafts movement. Some of the wall paintings date from the 17th and 18th centuries. The church is surrounded by its hilltop churchyard which contains not only the remains of a Saxon cross, dated approx AD 800, but also a scene of the crucifixion. The **Bradbourne Stone**, dating from ancient times, stands well north of the church.

While in the village it is also worth taking a look at the fine grey-stone Elizabethan manor house, **Bradbourne Hall** (private), with its three gables and beautiful terraced gardens. **The Old Parsonage**, which has a rather peculiar appearance as it was built in three completely different styles and materials, is also worthy of note.

BRASSINGTON

7 miles NE of Ashbourne off the B5056

According to the *Oxford Dictionary of English Place-Names*, Brassington derives from Old English and is said to mean 'the farm by the steep path'. At the time of the *Domesday Book*, the Manor of 'Branzincton' belonged to Henry de Ferrers and had a population of around 100, who were mostly farm workers. The men of `Brass'on', as it is still known locally, have earned their daily bread for centuries by working either on the land or under it: in the limestone quarries or the lead mines. The hollows and bumps in the green meadows tell of 200 years of underground industry in pursuit of lead, and now lead-tolerant flowers such as mountain pansy, sandwort and orchids flourish here.

Protected from the wind by the limestone plateau that soars some 1,000 feet above sea level, the village sits by strange-shaped rocks, the result of weather erosion, with names like **Rainster Rocks** and **Harborough Rocks**. At Rainster Rocks there is evidence of a Roman British settlement, and at Harborough there are the remains of a chambered cairn. Stone Age man found snug dwellings amongst these dolomite limestone formations and there is evidence that animals like the sabre-toothed tiger, brown bear, wolf and hyena also found comfort here in the caves. As late as the 18th century, families were still living in the caves.

Nearby is the Wesleyan Reform Chapel, one of the so-called 'Smedley Chapels' built by local mill owner, Mr Smedley, in 1852.

Brassington

Smedley was a keen Revivalist and his two other chapels in the village are now the village hall and a private house.

Episodes of the TV series *Peak Practice* have been filmed in the village, as was a sequence in the film version of DH Lawrence's *The Virgin and the Gypsy*, which starred the Derbyshire-born actor Alan Bates.

BALLIDON

5 miles N of Ashbourne off the B5056

You can see a well-preserved deserted medieval village and open fields at Ballidon. According to the 2001 census it had a population of just 79 souls, but in medieval times this was a thriving community. It dates originally from the Norman period, but it was so heavily restored in 1882 that most Norman details have been obliterated. There are four rather grand 17th-century farms, and the **Chapel of All Saints** stands isolated in a field.

Overshadowed by its gigantic limestone quarry, the legacy of this tiny hamlet's days as a robust medieval village remain in the numerous earthworks, lynchets and evidence of ridge-and-furrow cultivation in its fields. One-and-a-half miles north is **Minning Low**, one of the most impressive Bronze Age chambered tombs. It was the best discovery of its kind in Derbyshire at the time.

ALDWARK

9 miles NE of Ashbourne off the B5056

Close to the High Peak Trail, just inside the Peak Park boundary, Aldwark is one of the most unspoilt villages in Derbyshire. A quiet and tranquil backwater, its name comes from the Saxon for 'Old Fort', meaning that even then it was considered an ancient settlement. The highest recorded population was 97 in 1831, though at this time it was one of the staging posts on the coaching route between Derby and Buxton. A chambered tomb dating from 2000 BC was discovered at **Green Low**, just to the north of the village, which contained pottery, flints and animal bones.

FENNY BENTLEY

2 miles N of Ashbourne off the A515

Fenny Bentley is the first village of the Peak for visitors coming from the south, with a steep hill up into the Peak District and the old railway bridge where the Tissington Trail passes through the village (see also Tissington).

The **Parish Church of St Edmund's** has a dominant position in the village and dates back to the 13th century, although it has been heavily restored in later years. You can find some wonderful examples of the Arts and Crafts movement art works in many of the surrounding churches. At Fenny Bentley you can see angels lined up behind the altar and a stunningly painted aluminium ceiling in the northeast aisle. Also, inside the church can be found the tomb of Thomas Beresford, the local lord of the manor who fought, alongside eight of his 16 sons, at Agincourt. The effigies of Beresford and his wife are surrounded by those of their 21 children - each covered by a shroud as, by the time the tombs were built, nobody could remember what they had looked like! It is said that everyone with the surname of Beresford is

descended from Thomas and his wife, and the annual meeting of the Beresford Family Society takes place in the village each year.

The 15th-century square tower of the Beresford's fortified manor house is now incorporated into **Cherry Orchard Farm**. It was also the home of poet Charles Cotton at one time, and is a local landmark that can be seen from the Buxton road.

TISSINGTON

4 miles N of Ashbourne off the A515

The 'modern' tradition of well-dressing is said to have been started at Tissington in 1350. But it is almost certain that the tradition goes back much further than that, to pagan times when the life-giving gift of water was so important to communities like this. Today the ceremony takes place on Ascension Day, the 40th day after Easter (usually the middle of May), and draws many crowds who come to see the spectacular folk art created by the local people. The significance of the event in Tissington may have been to give thanks for their pure springs that had saved them from the ravages of the Black Death of 1348-49. During this time some 77 of the 100 clergy in Derbyshire died; the surviving villagers simply returned to the pagan custom of well-dressing. Another plausible theory dates back only as far as the great drought of 1615, when the Tissington wells kept flowing though water everywhere was in very short supply. Whichever theory is true, one thing is certain: in the last 50 years or so many villages that had not dressed a well for centuries, if ever, began to take part in this colourful tradition.

A total of six wells are dressed at

---

63 BENTLEY BROOK INN

Fenny Bentley

For lovers of history and gardens as well as fine food and drink, the Bentley Brook is a Derbyshire landmark.

See entry on page 184

---

64 TISSINGTON HALL

Tissington

Home to the FitzHerbert family, the hall and gardens are open to the public on selected dates during the year.

See entry on page 185

Tissington - the Hall, the Town, the Yew Tree, the Hands, the Coffin and the Children's Wells. Each depicts a separate scene, usually from the Bible. Visitors should follow the signs in the village or ask at the Old Coach House.

Very much on the tourist route, particularly in the early summer, Tissington has plenty of tea rooms and ice cream shops to satisfy the hot and thirsty visitor, as well as that essential of any picturesque English village - a duck pond. The village itself, though often overlooked in favour of the colourful well-dressings, has some interesting buildings. The **Parish Church of St Mary**, situated on a rise overlooking Tissington, dates originally from Norman times, and is still essentially Norman, even though it was restored in 1854, with many mock Norman features being added. It has an unusual tub-shaped font, which dates back to the original Norman Church. The pulpit too is unusual. Converted from a double-decker type, it once had a set of steps leading out from the priest's stall below.

Home of the FitzHerbert family for 500 years, **Tissington Hall** is a distinguished and impressive stately home which was built by Francis FitzHerbert in 1609, though there may be fragments of an earlier building incorporated. During the Civil War, the Fitzherberts were for the king, and the then Fitzherbert was a colonel with the Royalist forces. He used the hall as a garrison for his troops.

The estate consists of 2,405 acres, and the Hall boasts a wealth of original pieces, artwork, furnishings and architectural features tracing the times and tastes of the FitzHerbert family over the centuries. The oak-panelled main hall has the original stone-flagged floor and is dominated by a stunning Gothic fireplace installed in 1757. Here visitors will also find a pair of late-18th-century Chippendale bookcases, a rosewood piano and other fine pieces. The Dining Room, originally the old kitchen, is also panelled in oak and has an original Waring & Gillow table with a matching set of 13 chairs. The frieze work was added in the early 1900s. Paintings of country scenes and family

Tissington Hall Well

portraits adorn the walls. The Library is a repository of over 3,000 books, and is adorned with a frieze depicting a woodland scene. Other fine pieces include a bracket clock made by Jasper Taylor of Holborn in about 1907. The East and West Drawing Rooms can also be visited.

Tissington Hall and Gardens are open to the public on certain afternoons throughout the summer. Please call the Estate Office for details. In addition, the gardens are open on several days for charity including the National Gardens Scheme. Private groups and societies are welcome by written appointment throughout the year.

Following the old Ashbourne to Parsley Hay railway line, the **Tissington Trail** is a popular walk which can be combined with other old railway trails in the area, or country lanes, to make an enjoyable circular country walk. The trail passes through some lovely countryside and, having a reasonable surface, it is also popular with cyclists. Along the route can also be found many of the old railway buildings and junction boxes and, in particular, Hartington station, which is now a picnic site with an information centre in the old signal box.

PARWICH

5 miles N of Ashbourne off the A515

The pronunciation of the name varies, with some people saying 'Par-rich' while others say 'Par-wich'. Most locals seem to favour the latter, but whichever way you say it, Parwich must rank as one of the most attractive villages in the southern part of the Peak District, and as it isn't on the main route to anywhere it remains relatively undiscovered.

Conspicuous amongst the stone built houses is **Parwich Hall**, constructed of brick and finished in 1747. The wonderful gardens at the Hall were created at the turn of the 20th century and it remains today a family home, though over the years it has changed hands on several occasions. Parwich Hall is a grade II* listed building and is occasionally open to the public. The **Parish Church of St Peter** is Victorian and was built between 1873 and 1874, though there are some Norman details.

Close to Parwich is Roystone Grange, an important archaeological site where, to the north of the present farmhouse, the remains of a Roman farmhouse have been excavated. To the south are an old engine house and the remains of the old medieval monastic grange. Both Roystone Grange and Parwich lie on the interesting and informative **Roystone Grange Archaeological Trail**, which starts at Minninglow car park. Some six miles long, the circular trail follows, in part, the old railway line that was built to connect the Cromford and the Peak Forest Canals in the 1820s before taking in some of the Tissington Trail.

ALSOP-EN-LE-DALE

5 miles N of Ashbourne off the A515

The old station on the Ashbourne-Buxton line, which once served this tiny hamlet, is today a car park on the Tissington Trail. The tranquil hamlet itself is on a narrow lane, east of the main road towards Parwich, just a mile from Dovedale. Alsop-en-le-Dale's **Parish Church of St Michael and all Angels** is Norman, though it was refurbished substantially during Victorian times, when the tower was completely rebuilt. The nave retains Norman features, with impressive double zigzag mouldings in the arches, but the west tower is only imitation Norman, and dates from 1883. One unusual feature, which dominates this small church, is its extraordinary 19th-century square mock-Gothic pulpit.

Opposite the church is the graceful and slender building known as **Alsop Hall**, constructed in the early 1600s for the Alsop

Viator's Bridge, Alsop-en-le-Dale

family, who were lords of the manor. Though privately owned, it is worth seeing even for its exterior, as it is built in a handsome pre-classical style with stone-mullioned windows.

Alsop makes a good base for exploring the White Peak and is also convenient for Dovedale. The renowned **Viator's Bridge** at Milldale is a mile to the west, and was immortalised in a scene in Izaak Walton's *The Compleat Angler* in which the character Viator complains to another about the size of the tiny, two-arched packhorse bridge, deeming it 'not two fingers broad'.

Surrounding the village are many Bronze Age burial sites, including **Cross Low** (north of the village), **Nat Low** (northwest of the village), **Moat Low** (southwest of the village) and **Green Low** on Alsop Moor.

NEWHAVEN

11 miles N of Ashbourne on the A515

The High Peak Trail crosses Newhaven to link up with the Tissington Trail. This charming village is also along the White Peak tourist route, though it retains a tranquil air. At Newhaven you can find Carriages Restaurant, which offers a taste of Scilly, and the meticulously-maintained Newhaven Caravan Park.

MAPPLETON

2 miles NW of Ashbourne off the A515

Mappleton can also be spelled Mapleton, as the Ordnance Survey map of Derbyshire will testify. It is a village that has existed in some form or other since before 1086, when it is recorded in the *Domesday Book*. It is a pleasant and charming village that sits almost astride the River Dove, with attractive views and a wealth of exciting natural beauty. The spectacular scenery surrounding the village includes the aforementioned Thorpe Cloud and Bunster Hill, with the famous stepping stones across the River Dove just a mile or so upstream, all of which puts Mappleton well within reach of the two million visitors each year who come to experience the natural delights of Dovedale.

The extremely small **Parish Church of St Mary** dates from 1751, and is unusual in that it has a dome rather than a tower or a steeple. There has been a church here since at least the reign of Edward I.

THORPE
3 miles NW of Ashbourne off the A515

Thorpe was mentioned in the *Domesday Book* and is one of the few villages in the Peak whose name has Norse origins, for the Danish settlers did not generally penetrate far into this area. It lies at the confluence of the Rivers Manifold and Dove, and is dominated by the conical hill of **Thorpe Cloud**, which guards the entrance to **Dovedale**. Out of interest the word 'cloud' is a corruption of the Old English word 'clud', meaning hill – a pity really as 'Thorpe Cloud' sounds like it should have a more romantic meaning than 'The hill by the Danish farm'. The summit is a short but stiff climb from any direction, but whichever way you go you are rewarded with panoramic views over Dovedale all the way to Alstonefield, Ilam and the lower Manifold Valley. Although the Dale becomes over-crowded at times, there is always plenty of open space to explore on the hill as well as excellent walking. For much of its 45-mile course from Axe Edge to its confluence with the River Trent, the **River Dove** is a walker's river as it is mostly inaccessible by car. The steep-sided valley, the fast-flowing water and the magnificent white rock formations all give Dovedale a special charm.

Dovedale, however, is only a short section of the valley; above Viator Bridge it becomes **Mill Dale** and further upstream again are **Wolfscote Dale** and **Beresford Dale**. The temptation to provide amenities for visitors, at the expense of the scenery, has been avoided, and the limestone village of Thorpe, clustered around its church, remains unspoilt and unsophisticated.

Further up the dale is the limestone crag known as **Dovedale Castle** and, on the opposite bank, is the higher promontory known as **Lover's Leap**. It's a view to gladden your hearts – not the sort of place you'd think of throwing yourself from at all. However, it was named after a young woman, who, on hearing that her lover had been killed in the Napoleonic Wars, tried to commit suicide here by jumping. However, her skirts billowed out like a parachute and she survived. The poignant end to the story is that, soon after, she discovered that her lover was very much alive, and on his way home. Other interesting natural features with romantic names found along the way include the **Twelve Apostles**, a series of limestone crags, and the **Tissington Spires**, another limestone outcrop.

Thorpe village and its surrounding area plays host to the annual **Dovedale Dash** – a cross-country race of four-and-a-half miles run by about 1200 people of all abilities. One of the main excitements is crossing the river Dove at the well-known Stepping Stones. The event was first established in 1953, and takes place on the first Sunday of November.

ILAM
4 miles NW of Ashbourne off the A52

The village of Ilam was inhabited in Saxon times and the ancient **Parish Church of the Holy Cross** still displays some Saxon stonework as well as the shrine of a much-

---

65 **THE SOUTH PEAK ESTATE**

Ilam

The estate centres around Ham Hall and within its 4,000 acres are popular visitor attractions such as Dovedale.

See entry on page 185

Ilam Hall

loved Staffordshire saint and 8th century Mercian king, Bertelin, or Bertram. Ilam has been an English pilgrim destination for over 1,300 years – ever since grief-stricken St Bertram arrived here to live as a hermit. Legend recalls that Bertram, the 'First Evangelist of the Moorlands', spent the remainder of his life here after wolves killed his wife and newborn baby, while he was out looking for food.

Now a model village of great charm on the Staffordshire side of the River Dove, Ilam was originally an important settlement belonging to Burton Abbey. Following the Reformation in the 16th century, the estate was broken up and Ilam came into the hands of the Port family. In the early 1800s the family sold the property to Jesse Watts Russell, a wealthy industrialist. He moved the village from its position near Ilam Hall and rebuilt it in its current location in 'Alpine style'. This explains both the Swiss style of the buildings and the surprising distance between them and the village church.

John Port originally built Ilam Hall in 1546, and while in the possession of the Ports, both Samuel Johnson and the playwright William Congreve stayed there. Watts Russell bought it in 1820 along with the estate and rebuilt it. As well as building a fine mansion, Watts Russell also spent a great deal of money refurbishing the village. Obviously devoted to his wife, he had the village hall rebuilt in a romantic Gothic style and, in the centre of the village; he had a cross erected in her memory. In the 1930s most of the hall had been demolished before being bought by Sir Robert McDougall, who presented it to the Youth Hostelling Association in 1934. It remains a youth

hostel to this day. The 158 acres of **Ilam Park**, on which the hall stands, is owned and managed by the National Trust.

In the valley of the River Manifold, a much-used starting point for walks along this beautiful stretch of river, the Manifold disappears underground north of the village in summer, to reappear below Ilam Hall. The village is also the place where the Rivers Manifold and Dove merge. Though Dovedale is, deservedly so, considered the most scenic of the Peak District valleys, the Manifold Valley is very similar and while being marginally less beautiful it is often much less crowded. The two rivers rise close together on Axe Edge, and for much of their course follow a parallel path, so it is fitting that they should come together eventually.

Be sure not to leave without visiting Ilam Hall's visitor centre. Jackson's Geology is a touchscreen exploration of Dovedale, explaining the geology of the White Peak through the eyes of and celebrating the work of Dr Jackson. This pioneer geologist and cave archaeologist worked in Dovedale during the 1920s-1930s.

WATERHOUSES
6 miles NW of Ashbourne off the A523

Between here and Hulme End is the Leek and Manifold Valley Light Railway, a piece of Indian engineering transplanted into Staffordshire. The Edwardian engineer who created it had recently come back from India, where he built narrow gauge railways. Sadly, it only ran from 1904 to 1934 but its track bed has been transformed into the

Thor's Cave, Waterhouses

Hamps-Manifold Trail – nine miles of gentle footpath and cycle way. The scenery of the Hamps and Manifold Valleys should be enough to tempt anyone on to this trail, which takes you through limestone gorges, woodlands and picturesque villages. Highlights along the way include **Thor's Cave**, Ecton Copper mine and Throwley Old Hall. The terminus at Hulme End has an excellent visitor centre (also see Hulme End). The trail can be reached from car parks at Hulme End, Waterhouses, Weags Bridge near Grindon, and Wetton.

WATERFALL

7 miles NW of Ashbourne off the A523

The tiny village of Waterfall is on the Staffordshire moors. It gets its name from the way that the **River Hamps** disappears underground through crevices in the ground. In the case of the Hamps, it disappears at Waterhouses and reappears again near Ilam before merging with the River Manifold.

The **Parish Church of St James and St Bartholomew** is originally Norman but was largely rebuilt in the 19th century. However, the Norman chancel has been retained.

GRINDON

7 miles NW of Ashbourne off the B5053

This unique moorland hill village stands over 1,000 feet above sea level and overlooks the beautiful Manifold Valley. Recorded in the *Domesday Book* as 'Grendon', meaning green hill, 'an ancient manor in the 20th year of the reign of William the Conqueror', Grindon is reputed to have been visited by Bonnie Prince Charlie on his way to Derby. It was once a staging post on the packhorse route from Ecton Hill and had the most productive copper mine in the country, where many of the local people would have worked. The local pub, the Cavalier, was possibly named after Bonny Prince Charlie.

The splendid isolation in which this village stands is confirmed by a look around the churchyard. The names on the epitaphs and graves reflect the close-knit nature of the communities. The Salt family, for instance,

are to be seen everywhere, followed closely by the Stubbs, Cantrells, Hambletons and, to a lesser extent, the Mycocks.

WETTON

7 miles NW of Ashbourne
between the B5053 and the A515

The village gives its name to Wetton Hill, a 'reef knoll' formed from the ancient remains of a coral reef, and Wetton Mill, on the River Manifold, both in the care of the National Trust. **Wetton Mill**, which closed down in the mid-19th-century, was sympathetically restored by the National Trust as a museum piece. There is a café on site, a very welcome sight for those walking the **Manifold Valley Trail**. There is also a car park, campsite and a picnic area for those who would rather cater for themselves.

There are many burial chambers or mounds in the area, including those on Wetton Hill itself, at Wetton Low, and at Long Low, some 2 km southeast of the village. On **Wetton Low**, 1 km south of the village, some of the burial mounds contained bones dating back to at least 1600 BC. **Ecton Hill** is covered in the remains of old lead mines worked by the Duke of Devonshire. His profits from the mine were used to build the Crescent at Buxton.

Easily accessible from Wetton is the ominous-sounding **Thor's Cave**, situated 360 feet above the River Manifold. Though the cave is not deep, the entrance is huge, some 60 feet high, a sight which is clearly visible for several miles. The stiff climb up is well worth the effort for the spectacular views, all framed by the great natural stone arch. The acoustics, too, are interesting, and conversations can easily be carried out with people far below. Ancient bones and implements have been found here dating back 10,000 years. The openings at the bottom of the crag on which the cave sits are known as **Radcliffe Stables** and are said to have been used by a Jacobite as a hiding place after Bonnie Prince Charlie had retreated from Derby.

The **Parish Church of St Margaret** is partly 14th century, though most of it dates from around 1820. In the churchyard is the grave of Samuel Carrington who, along with Thomas Bateman of Youlgreave, found evidence that Thor's Cave was occupied in ancient times. Carrington also excavated the fields close to Wetton, where he was schoolmaster in the mid 19th century, and found an abandoned village, though neither he nor his friend Bateman could put an age to the settlement.

ALSTONEFIELD

7 miles NW of Ashbourne off the A515

This ancient village, situated between the Manifold and the Dove Valleys, lies at the crossroads of several old packhorse routes and even had its own market charter granted in 1308. The market ceased in 1500 but the annual cattle sales continued right up until the beginning of the 20th century. The hamlet was also the site of England's first co-operative cheese factory, which produced a variety of Derby cheese.

Its geographical location has helped to maintain the charm of Alstonefield. There has been no invasion by the canal or railway builders (it stands 900 feet above sea level) and it is still two miles from the nearest classified road. One hundred and fifty years ago Alstonefield was at the centre of a huge parish which covered all the land between the two rivers. There has been a church here since at least AD 892, when a visit by St Oswald is recorded, but the earliest known parts of the large **Parish Church of St Peter** are the Norman doorway and chancel arch. It

was added to in the 15th century and restored in Victorian times. There is also plenty of 17th-century woodwork and a double-decker pulpit dated 1637. Izaak Walton's friend Charles Cotton, and his family, lived at nearby Beresford Hall, now unfortunately no more, but their elaborate pew, with the Cotton coat-of-arms, is still in the church.

The village also retains its ancient **Tithe Barn**, found behind the late 16th-century rectory. The internal exposed wattle and daub wall and the spiral stone staircase may, however, have been part of an earlier building.

Nearby Alstonefield you will find **Hanson Grange**, an old farmstead, and the site of an ancient burial ground. The numerous reported sounds of violent fighting and cries of anguish are thought to stem back to the murder, in 1467, of a man named John Mycock. Four people participated in his death; John de la Pole of Hartington hit him on the side of his head; Henry Vigers of Monyash stabbed him in the chest; John Harrison shot him in the back with a bow and arrow; and Matthew Bland of Hartington struck him on the head with a club staff. Witnesses were too scared to testify, so the murderers never went to trial before the king. Maybe this is why the sounds of that fateful night can still be heard as this murder most foul has gone unavenged for centuries.

ECTON

9½ miles NW of Ashbourne off the B5054

If not *'gold in them thar hills'*, there was certainly plenty of copper. In the late 1750s Deep Ecton Mine was, at nearly 1,400 feet, the richest and deepest copper mine in Europe. The copper mines here were owned by the Duke of Devonshire and it is generally accepted that the profits from the ore extraction paid for his building of The Crescent at Buxton. Work had ceased in the mines by 1900 but so impervious was the surrounding limestone that the workings took several years to flood, though now they are under water.

Hanson Grange, Alstonefield

WARSLOW

9 miles NW of Ashbourne off the B5054

Situated opposite Wetton on the other side of the River Manifold, the village is one of the main access points to this dramatic section of the Manifold Valley. Lying below the gritstone moorlands, this was an estate village for the eccentric Crewe family, who lived at Calke Abbey in south Derbyshire. The **Parish Church of St Lawrence** is a handsome building of 1820, and was formerly dedicated to St James. The village also has some pleasant 18th- and 19th-century cottages and a welcoming pub called the Greyhound, a 250-year-old coaching inn, once known as the Greyhound and Hare.

HULME END

9 miles NW of Ashbourne on the B5054

From here to Ilam, the River Manifold runs southwards through a deep, twisting limestone cleft, between steep and wooded banks. For much of its dramatic course the Manifold disappears underground in dry weather through swallow holes, which is typical of a river in a limestone area.

The village also lies at the terminus of the narrow-gauge **Leek and Manifold Valley Light Railway**, which opened in 1904. Already aware of the tourism possibilities of the Peak District by the beginning of the 20th century, the other reason for constructing the railway was to transport coal and other raw materials to the surrounding settlements. The line, however, was unable to pay its way, particularly after the creamery at Ecton, just a mile south of Hulme End, closed in 1933. The following year the railway ceased operation. The tracks were taken up and, if it had not been turned into a semi-long distance footpath, the route of the railway might have been lost forever. The old station building at the western end of the hamlet has been beautifully restored and is now an excellent visitor centre, with public toilets and a car park.

HARTINGTON

10 miles NW of Ashbourne on the B5054

People used to come to Hartington to buy the world-famous blue-veined Stilton – *'the King of English Cheeses'*. The Duke of Devonshire opened a creamery here in 1876 so that his tenant farmers could better utilise their milk but the venture failed and the business was closed in 1895. Thomas Nuttall then bought the site in 1900 and reopened it as a Stilton creamery, processing 50 gallons of milk a day. It was the last remaining cheese factory in Derbyshire and produced no less than a quarter of the world's supply of Stilton. However, it recently closed and production was moved to a site in Leicestershire though the village's Old Cheese Shop remains.

The village is very much on the tourist route and, though popular, has retained much of its village appeal. As well as the famous Old Cheese Shop, there are two old coaching inns left over from the days when this was an important market centre. One of these goes by the rather unusual name of The Charles Cotton, named after the friend of Izaak Walton. Situated in the valley of the River Dove, Hartington is an excellent place from which to explore both the Dove and the Manifold Valleys. To the south lies **Beresford**

66 **BERESFORD TEA ROOMS**

Hartington

A visit to this country side oasis is a must, to sample homemade food and a refreshing cup of tea.

See entry on page 186

67 **BIGGIN HALL COUNTRY HOUSE HOTEL**

Biggin-by-Hartington

This stunning 17th century manor house is perfect for weekends away, weddings and rustic English dinners in the heart of the Peak District National Park.

See entry on page 187

Hartington Hall

Dale, the upper valley of the River Dove and every bit as pretty as its more famous neighbour, Dovedale. It was immortalised by Izaak Walton and Charles Cotton when *The Compleat Angler* was published in 1653.

Venturing back into the annals of history, Hartington is noted at the time of the *Domesday Book* as being called 'Hortedvn'. This charming limestone village was granted a market charter in 1203 and it is likely that its spacious market place was once the village green.

Hartington Hall, built in the 17th century and enlarged in the 19th century, is typical of many Peak District manor houses and a fine example of a Derbyshire yeoman's house and farm. It is thought that Bonnie Prince Charlie stayed there on his way to Derby. It became a youth hostel in 1934, and is the oldest YHA hostel in the Peak District.

MAYFIELD

2½ miles SW of Ashbourne on the A5032

Mayfield is a large village on the edge of Ashbourne, divided into Upper Mayfield and Middle Mayfield. Though it is so close to Ashbourne, it actually lies in Staffordshire, as the border runs west of the village. Mayfield was originally a Saxon village, dating back over a thousand years and listed in the *Domesday Book* as Mavreveldt. The first Norman church was probably built about 1125 during the reign of Henry I, and the present **Parish Church of St John the Baptist** illustrates the progressive styles of architecture since that date, with a 14th-century chancel and a 16th-century tower. In

the churchyard there is an original Saxon cross. The ballad writer Thomas Moore lived at Moore Cottage, formerly Stancliffe Farm. His young daughter, Olivia, is buried in the local churchyard, her slate tombstone reading 'Olivia Byron Moore, died March 18, 1815'. Moore was friendly with Lord Byron, who visited him here.

On 7th December 1745 Bonnie Prince Charlie and his army passed through Mayfield on their retreat from Derby, terrorising the local populace. They shot the innkeeper at Hanging Bridge as well as a Mr Humphrey Brown, who refused to hand over his horse to them. Many of the terrified villagers locked themselves in the church. The soldiers fired shots through the door and the bullet holes can still be seen in the woodwork of the west door. Legend has it that many of the rebels were caught and hung from gibbets on the old packhorse bridge, whose 500-year-old grey stone arches can still be seen, even though the bridge has been rebuilt.

There is however a road out of the village, leading to the main Leek highway, marked on the Ordnance Survey map as "Gallowstree Lane", suggesting that those to be hung went their way via the bridge and Gallowstree Lane to Gallowstree Hill. Today it is a pleasant walk rewarded by a lovely view down the Dove Valley.

Mayfield Mill has been producing textiles for 200 years. The first mention of a mill occurs in 1291 when Mayfield, including its mill, belonged to the Priory of Tutbury. By 1793 there had been various owners of the site, which now included two corn mills, a leather mill and two fulling mills. Textiles were first produced in 1795. In 1806 the interior of the building and all its machinery was destroyed in a fire. The mill was

eventually rebuilt with a cast iron framework and brick vaulted ceilings, which can still be seen today.

The spinning of cotton continued in Mayfield until 1934 when it was sold to William Tatton and Company who used the mill to process silk.

LEEK

Leek advertises itself as the 'Queen of the Moorlands', and is just becoming recognised as a historical jewel in the old silk mills and Arts and Crafts heritage. Until the 19th century, this was a domestic industry with the workshops on the top storeys of the houses. Many examples of these 'top shops' have survived to this day. Leek also became an important dyeing town, particularly after the death of Prince Albert, when 'Raven Black' was popularised by Queen Victoria, who remained in mourning for her beloved husband for many years.

Leek has strong connections with the Arts and Crafts Movement because in 1873, William Morris (founder of this movement) came to Leek to investigate new techniques of dyeing and printing, staying with the Wardle family who were silk manufacturers. Lady Elizabeth Wardle founded the Leek School of Embroidery in 1879. Elizabeth Wardle, along with thirty-five members of the school and other embroiderers from the surrounding area created a full size replica of the Bayeux Tapestry in just over a year. Each embroiderer stitched her name beneath her completed panel. The tapestry toured the nation and even went to Germany and North America! It is now on display in the Museum of Reading and was first displayed here in

Nicholson Institute, Leek

1886. The imposing brick-built **Nicholson Institute** holds exhibitions on the wonderful and intricate work of the famous Leek School of Embroidery.

These days Leek is an antiques lovers' paradise with indoor and outdoor markets. Leek's first market was established by Royal Charter in 1208, and was a thriving market centre, rivaling Macclesfield and Congleton. It still runs every Wednesday in the cobbled Market Place. Leek also has a craft and antiques market on Saturday and an indoor 'butter market' on Wednesday, Friday and Saturday. Every road coming into the town seems to converge on the old cobbled Market Place and the road to the west leads down to the church. Dedicated to Edward the Confessor (the full name is the **Parish Church of St Edward's and All Saints**), the original

---

69 **THE SWAN**

Leek

The town's oldest hostelry attracts plenty of people through its doors to enjoy real ales and homemade food.

See entry on page 188

70 **RAYMONDO'S**

Leek

Lovers of fine cuisine make a bee-line for Raymondo's in Leek from all over Derbyshire, Staffordshire and Cheshire.

See entry on page 189

The Roaches, nr Leek

church was burnt down in 1297 and rebuilt some 20 years later, though the building is now largely 17th century. The timber roof of the nave is well worth a second look and is the church's pride and joy. It is boasted that each of the cross beams was hewn from a separate oak tree and, in the west part of the nave, an enormous 18th-century gallery rises up, tier on tier, giving the impression of a theatre's dress circle.

Although much has been altered inside the church, most notably in 1865 when G.E. Street rebuilt the chancel, reredos, sanctuary, pulpit and stalls, there still remains one interesting original artefact to see - a wooden chair. Traditionally this is believed to have been a ducking stool for scolds, which was used in the nearby River Churnet. Outside, in the churchyard, can be found a curious inscription on a gravestone: 'James Robinson interred February the 28th 1788 Aged 438'!

Another building worthy of a second glance is the imposing Nicholson Institute, mentioned earlier, with its copper dome. Completed in 1884 and funded by the local industrialist Joshua Nicholson, the Institute offered the people of Leek an opportunity to learn and expand their cultural horizons. The Nicholson has seen many famous people pass through its doors including the likes of Oscar Wilde, John Betjeman and D.H. Lawrence. It was recently restored and re-opened to make an enjoyable museum and art gallery. The town's **War Memorial**, built in Portland stone and with a clock tower, has a dedication to the youngest Nicholson son, who was killed in the First World War.

Leek has a famous son: it was the home of James Brindley, the 18th-century engineer

who built much of the early canal network. A water-powered corn mill built by him in 1752 (on the site of an earlier mill) in Mill Street has been restored and now houses the **Brindley Water Museum** (known as Brindley Mill), which is devoted to his life and work. Visitors can see corn being ground and see displays of millwrighting skills.

The **River Churnet**, though little known outside Staffordshire, has a wealth of scenery and industrial archaeology. It is easily accessible to walkers and its valley deserves better recognition. The river rises to the west of Leek in rugged gritstone country, but for most of its length it flows through softer, red sandstone countryside in a valley that was carved out during the Ice Age. Though there are few footpaths directly adjacent to the riverbank, most of the valley can be walked close to the river using a combination of canal towpaths and former railway tracks.

Four miles to the north of the town on the A53 rise the dark, jagged gritstone outcrops of **The Roaches**, **Ramshaw Rocks** and **Hen Cloud**. 'Roaches' is a corruption of the French word 'roches' or rocks. 'Cloud' is a local word used for high hills. Just below The Roaches there is a delightful stretch of water, **Tittesworth Reservoir**, which is extremely popular with trout fishermen.

At Winkhill is the **Blackbrook Zoological Park**, which is open all year, and which has rare birds, insects, reptiles and unusual animals. **Kiddies Kingdom**, in Cross Mill Street, is an indoor play area for children, just right for children's parties and days out.

Leek's calendar of events includes an annual Arts Festival, showcasing the wealth and range of artistic talent within Leek, and an Agricultural Show on the last Saturday of July.

Tittesworth Reservoir, Leek

Dinghy Racing on Rudyard Lake

AROUND LEEK

RUDYARD

2 miles NW of Leek off the A523

In fond memory of the place where they first met in 1863, Mr and Mrs Kipling named their famous son, born in 1865, after this village. The nearby two-mile-long **Rudyard Lake** was built in 1831 by John Rennie to feed the Cauldon canal. With steeply wooded banks, the lake is now a leisure centre with facilities for picnicking, walking, fishing and sailing. Along the west shore is also a section of the **Staffordshire Way**, the long distance footpath which runs from Mow Cop to **Kinver Edge**, near Stourbridge. This is a sandstone ridge covered in woodland and heath, and with several famous rock houses which were inhabited until the 1950s.

Back in Victorian days, Rudyard was a popular lakeside resort which developed after the construction of the North Staffordshire Railway in 1845. The **Rudyard Lake Steam Railway** uses miniature narrow-gauge steam trains to give a three-mile return trip along the side of the reservoir. Its popularity became so great that, on one particular day in 1877, over 20,000 people came here to see Captain Webb, the first man to swim the English Channel, swim in the reservoir.

RUSHTON SPENCER

5 miles NW of Leek on the A523

This pleasant, moorland village nestles under the distinctive hill called **The Cloud** (from the Old English 'clud', meaning hill or mountain) and is the ideal starting point for a walk to the summit. The church for Rushton Spencer is not in the village but up the hill to the west and is well-known for its appealing mix of styles. The '**Chapel in the Wilderness**', dedicated to St Lawrence, was originally of wood in the 14th century and later in stone. It served both Rushton Spencer and neighbouring Rushton James, and there has been a church on this site since 1206.

Trains once stopped at the magnificent Gothic station, which is now a private house. Near here is a car park that is ideally placed for those wishing to walk to nearby Lake Rudyard.

FLASH

7 miles N of Leek off the A53

At over 1,518 feet above sea level, Flash is said to be the highest village in England. The village has historical connections with cock fighting and counterfeiting money. The area around is also notable for the weirdly-shaped outcrops of gritstone that occur - Ball Stones, Gib Torr and Ball Stone Rock, for example.

Cock fighting was so popular here, that it continued long after it had been made illegal.

The men of Flash, or Flashmen, were notorious for counterfeiting coins and they found a novel way to escape punishment. The **Three Shires Head** is a local beauty spot where the three counties of Derbyshire, Cheshire and Staffordshire meet, and this meant then that the police in one county could not arrest wrongdoers in another county. So, at the Three Shires Head, Flashmen escaped capture by hopping from Shire to Shire.

CAULDON

8 miles SE of Leek off the A52

Cauldon Lowe, a lofty hill in this village, is valuable for its extensive quarries of excellent limestone, used as a building material and in iron smelting. The limestone used to be carried to the Caldon Canal and to the station at Froghall for transport across the country.

LOCATION MAP

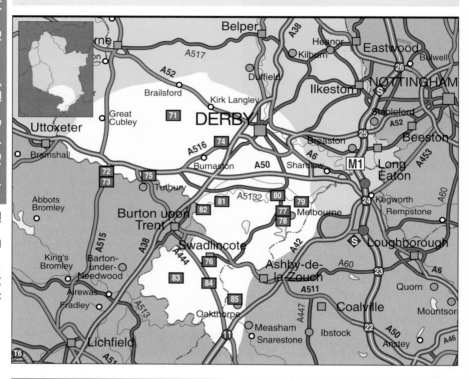

THE TRENT VALLEY

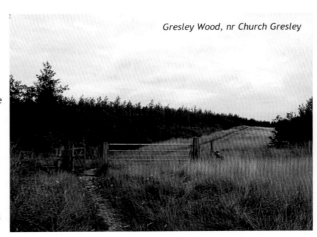

Gresley Wood, nr Church Gresley

Mention the Dark or White Peak and most people will have in mind the areas within the boundaries of the Peak District National Park. However, that boundary is a man-made line and there are some fine villages and architecture to be found outside these areas. This chapter will focus upon Derby and The Trent Valley plus the surrounding villages.

Derbyshire was at the forefront of modern thinking at the beginning of the Industrial Revolution. The chief inheritor of this legacy was Derby, and the city is still a busy industrial centre, home to engineering companies as well as a university and a cathedral. It is one of England's more recent cities, having been granted city status as late as 1977. However, it is an historic place, with a great choice of attractions. And though the county is called Derbyshire, the city is not the county town. This honour goes to Matlock, where the city council meets.

If you are interested in stately homes, it is worth leaving the Peak District and heading to the lowlands of the Trent Valley, where there are many splendid stately homes, including Kedleston Hall and the eccentric Calke Abbey. There are also lots of pleasant walks to be had in the attractive scenery around here. Truly an area of hidden places, the Trent Valley has many gems worth visiting, such as the picturesque villages of Church Gresley and Castle Gresley, the welcoming centres of Melbourne and Hartshorne, quiet Repton on the River Trent itself and the 'border' town of Swadlincote. The Trent Valley is a historically interesting area and has been a focus of human activity since early prehistory.

DERBY

A city that literally changed the world - Derby was one of the birthplaces of the industrial revolution. Derby's position, historically and geographically, has ensured that it has remained one of the most important and interesting cities in the East Midlands. Consequently, there is much for the visitor to see, whether from an architectural or historical point of view. The city's rich heritage can be seen all around - from the magnificent Cathedral with its imposing tower that can be seen for miles around, to artistic treasures at the Derby Museum and Art Gallery. There are, however, two things that most people, whether they have been to the city before or not, know of Derby: **Rolls-Royce** and Royal Crown Derby Porcelain.

When, in 1904, Sir Henry Royce and the Hon C S Rolls joined forces, and subsequently built the first Rolls-Royce (a Silver Ghost) at Derby in 1906, they built much more than just a motor car - they built a legend. Considered by many to be the best cars in the world, it is often said that the noisiest moving part in any Rolls-Royce is the dashboard clock! It is now owned by BMW of Germany, though the aircraft engine division (also based in Derby, but an entirely separate company), is a joint venture between BMW and Rolls Royce itself.

The home of **Royal Crown Derby Porcelain**, any visit to the city would not be complete without a trip to the factory and its museum and shop on Ormaston Road. The guided tours offer an intriguing insight into the high level of skill required to create the delicate flower petals, hand-gild the plates and hand paint the Derby Dwarves. You can ask questions and even try your hand at some of the skills. There are examples of some early Derby pottery preserved at the works museum, and another extensive collection is maintained in a special Ceramics Gallery at the Derby Museum. The factory shop sells both seconds and items currently in production.

There has been a church on the site of the city's **Cathedral of All Saints** since at least AD 943. It possesses a fine 16th-century tower, the second-highest perpendicular tower in England, and the oldest ring of ten bells in the country. Before 1927 it was the Parish Church of All Saints, the main church for Derby, but in that year was raised to cathedral status. In the early 18th century the nave and chancel was in a ruinous state, so they were rebuilt between 1723 and 1725 to the designs of James Gibbs. Inside is a beautiful wrought-iron screen by Robert Bakewell and among the splendid monuments is the tomb of Bess of Hardwick Hall, who died in 1607. In the late 1960s and early 1970s the building was extended eastwards and the retrochoir, baldacchino and sacristy were added, along with the screen. Only five minutes walk from the cathedral, the beautifully restored medieval **St Mary's Chapel on the Bridge** is one of only six surviving bridge chapels still in use. There is some medieval stained glass in one of the windows. In 1588 three Catholic priests, Nicholas Garlick, Richard Simpson and Robert Ludlum (the 'Padley Martyrs') were hung, drawn and quartered, and their remains hung from the chapel entrance. The bridge itself is 18th century, and straddles the River Derwent.

One of Derby's most interesting attractions is **Pickford's House Museum**, situated on the city's finest Georgian street, Friar Gate, at number 41. This Grade I listed building was erected in 1770 by the architect Joseph Pickford as a combined family home and place of work. Pickford House differs from the majority of grand stately homes in that it does not have a wealth of priceless furniture or works of art. Instead, visitors are able to gain a true insight into everyday

Pickford's House Museum

upper middle-class life – it's a time capsule of Georgian life and costume. The kitchen and servants' quarters have been re-created showing the conditions they worked under during the 1830s. Pickford House is the epitome of a late-Georgian professional man's residence. There is an exciting programme of temporary exhibitions, as well as other displays that deal with the history of the Friar's Gate area and the importance of Joseph Pickford as a Midlands architect. One special feature of Pickford House is the excellent collection of costumes, some dating back to the mid-1700s. A period 18th-century garden is also laid out at the rear of the house, and there are toy theatres from the Frank Bradley collection.

Just a short walk from Pickford House is the **Derby Industrial Museum**, also known as The Silk Mill. This is on the site of the world's oldest factories, the Silk Mills built by George Sorocold in 1702 and 1717. The foundations and parts of the tower from the 1717 mill are still visible. The displays tell the story of the industrial heritage and achievement of Derby and its people. Since 1915 Derby has been involved with the manufacture of engines, and the whole of the ground floor galleries are devoted to the Rolls-Royce aircraft engine collection, illustrating the importance played by the aero industry in the city's history. On the first floor of the building there is an introduction to other Derbyshire industries, with displays on lead and coal mining, iron founding, limestone quarrying, ceramics and brick making. There is also a Railway Research Gallery with displays covering the history of the Midland Railway since the 1840's and children will enjoy the life sized replica of an engine driver's cab. The railway industry played a large part in the life of the city, and along with Rolls Royce, British Rail Engineering Ltd (BREL) is one of its largest employers. A new swing bridge across the river provides a dramatic view of the Industrial Museum.

The **City Museum and Art Gallery** in the Strand is also well worth visiting. Opened in 1879, it is the oldest of Derby's museums and the displays relate to the social, military, and natural history of the city and county, as well as paintings by the celebrated 18th Century Derby artist Joseph Wright. This is the largest collection of the artist's work in any public gallery in the world.

The Archaeology Gallery contains local material from the Stone Age to the Middle Ages, with several fine Anglo-Saxon crosses and a splendid sarcophagus. There are also two Egyptian mummies. Derbyshire wildlife and geology feature in an exciting series of natural settings and hands-on exhibits. One section of the museum is devoted to a Military Gallery, which tells of Derby's regiments over the years. The walk-in First World War trench scene captures the experience of a night at the front. The Bonnie Prince Charlie Room tells the story of Derby's role in the 1745 Jacobite uprising, and a life-sized figure of the prince relates the sad events that led to his defeat.

The ground floor gallery houses an award-winning Ceramics Gallery, with samples of Royal Crown Derby porcelain dating to the 1750s. It is the most comprehensive collection of Derby Porcelain to be seen anywhere in the world, and includes 18th-century figurines, many interpretations of the Japanese designs for which the company is famous, the delicate 'Eggshell' China by French Art Director Desire Leroy, and examples of the Crown Derby ware commissioned for the restaurants of the *Titanic*. On the second floor of the Museum are temporary exhibition galleries. These change every three or four weeks and cover not only the museum's own collection but also host travelling exhibitions

Derby Gaol is situated in the depths of the original dungeons of the Derbyshire County Gaol, dating back to 1756, and offers a reminder of the city's grisly past. It includes a debtor's cell and a condemned cell, and was the site of the last hanging, drawing and quartering in the country, which took place after England's last revolution, the Pentrich Rebellion, in 1817. Three men were sentenced to this gruesome form of execution, while thirteen others were sent to a penal colony in Australia. The Gaol has rapidly become a popular destination for ghost hunters, serious investigators, or just the curious. Whatever your interest, this site is here to represent one of Derby's most famous places. It's only open on Saturdays, though also on Tuesdays and Thursdays during the school summer holidays. .

One of the finest buildings in Derby is St Helen's House, a Grade I listed building situated in King Street. This hidden attraction has been described by the Georgian Group of London as "one of the finest and largest eighteenth century townhouses to survive in any provincial city". Originally built about 1726 by Joseph Pickford for John Gisborne, at one time Derby School, and for a few years home to The Joseph Wright School of Art, the building unfortunately is currently disused, but it is planned to reopen the building as a hotel.

A much more modern attraction within the city's Market Place was opened in September 2008, and is called QUAD, a visual arts and media centre, cinema, café bar and workshop that anyone can use. If you're visiting it's well worth checking what films are showing or what exhibitions are on – or just call in to the popular Coors Café Bar.

Derby also has what was the first public recreational park in the country, the **Arboretum**, to the south of the city centre. The arboretum was set up by philanthropic land owner and industrialist Joseph Strutt in 1840 and its design is said to have been the inspiration for the vision of great urban parks in the USA, notably Central Park in New York City. Other major parks in Derby include **Allestree Park** to the north and **Markeaton Park** to the west. The Markeaton Park Light Railway operates within Markeaton Park, which is located next to what remains of Markeaton Village. The trains are owned by a

Allestree Hall, Derby

charitable trust and are driven and maintained by volunteers. Trains run every twenty minutes to the Mundy Play Centre; the journey is about three quarters of a mile long. At the time of writing the Railway was for sale, although still operating normally.

Further treasures including Chatsworth, Kedleston Hall and many National Trust properties are a short scenic drive away throughout Derbyshire and the Peak District.

Derby and its surrounding area host an array of annual events, whether it's the CAMRA Beer Festival, the classical music at the annual Darley Park concert or the beauty of the traditional well dressing displays.

AROUND DERBY

DARLEY ABBEY

2 miles N of Derby off the A6

Within walking distance of Derby City Centre is the tranquil village of Darley Abbey, featuring delightfully restored mill cottages. The Augustinian **Abbey of St Mary** was founded by Robert Ferrers, second Earl of Derby, around 1140 and grew to become the most powerful abbey in Derbyshire and possibly in the whole of the East Midlands. In 1538 the Abbey was surrendered to the crown as part of the Dissolution of the Monasteries. Sadly, few monasteries could have been so completely obliterated, and what is now known as The Abbey pub is the only building remaining. The layout is of a simple medieval hall house and is thought to have been used as the Abbey's guest house for travellers and pilgrims during the 13th century. During renovation, 12th-century pottery was unearthed.

Darley Park, on the River Derwent, was landscaped by William Evans and has attractive flower beds, shrubberies and lawns. It once had a hall, built in 1727 but now demolished, that for 120 years was the home of the Evans family who built the cotton mill by the river in 1783.

Pause beside the River Derwent, within sight of one of the most complete early

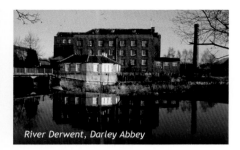
River Derwent, Darley Abbey

textile mill complexes. The mill area is quite a large complex. The oldest parts, east mill, middle mill and west mill, are five-storeyed and brick built. There is also a finishing house which has three storeys and sash windows, and an octagonal toll house in the mill yard. The Evans family built the red brick houses, still evident in the village, for the mill workers. They were typical paternalistic employers, providing subsidised rents, coal, blankets in cold weather and even arranging burials and memorials for their workers.

The **Parish Church of St Matthew** was built in the early 19th century, with a chancel added between 1885 and 1901. It is an elegant building in Gothic style, and contains monuments to the Evans family.

In the 21st century, the old village of Darley Abbey is regarded as a desirable place to live.

BREADSALL

3 miles N of Derby off the A6

Breadsall began life as a small hamlet clustered around its Norman church. It is now known primarily as a residential suburb of Derby, with new estates around the original centre.

Opposite the west end of the church can be found **The Old Hall**, which has been part of village life for over 600 years. It was originally the manor house when the village was divided into the wards of Overhall and Netherhall. In later years it has been employed as a school, farmhouse, hunting box, public house, shop, joiner's shop and post office. It currently serves as a parish hall and is used by various village organisations.

Close by is Breadsall Priory. This was originally a small 13th-century Augustinian Priory and was later converted to a large Elizabethan house. Successive owners have all left their mark on the building which is now a luxurious hotel and leisure complex. The most famous resident of Breadsall Priory was Erasmus Darwin, a respected physician, well-known poet, philosopher, botanist, and naturalist, who lived there for a short time until his death in 1802. Erasmus is one of the most remarkable and internationally important figures of the 18th century and is buried in the church graveyard. It is probably no coincidence that Charles Darwin, the grandson of such a progressive thinker, produced some of the most important work in the history of biological and social thought.

MACKWORTH

2 miles NW of Derby off the A52

Mackworth village is situated in a quiet lane and consists of a few cottages, farms, and a church, which stands alone in a field to the east of the village. The **Parish Church of All Saints** dates mainly from the 14th century and although its position is unusual, it is well worth taking a look inside to see the wealth of ancient and modern alabaster

Remains of Mackworth Castle

carving that it holds. Interestingly, it has no outside door which probably suggests it was built for defence.

A ruined 15th-century gatehouse in the village is sometimes referred to as **Mackworth Castle**, but it may have been the gatehouse for Mackworth Hall, a mansion which was never built.

KIRK LANGLEY

4 miles NW of Derby on the A52

Kirk Langley is just a five-minute drive from the city of Derby, yet the setting is truly rural and peaceful, with delightful views towards the National Trust's Kedleston Estate. Kirk Langley is bisected by the main road from Derby to Ashbourne, and actually consists of two villages: Kirk Langley and Meynell Langley, centred on the Victorian brick mansion of Langley Park, site of the Meynell Family for 800 years, since the reign of Henry I. The Poles of Radbourne have also had landed interests in this area for many years.

The **Parish Church of St Michael** is early 14th century, built on the site of an older Saxon church. There are monuments to the Meynell and Pole families, including a memorial to Hugo Frances Meynell, 'who was deprived of his life in a collision of carriages' in Clay Cross tunnel. Another one commemorates William Meynell, who was killed in the 19th century when leading the Turks against the Russians on the river Danube. The only pub is the Bluebell at Langley Common.

KEDLESTON

4 miles NW of Derby off the A52

Kedleston Hall has been the family seat of the Curzon family since the 12th century and, until it was taken over by the National Trust, it had the longest continuous male line in Derbyshire and one of the longest in the country. Nothing remains of the original medieval structure and little is known about it other than details recorded in a survey of 1657 which state that one of the doorways was over 500 years old and that there was

also a large hall and a buttery.

Since taking over the property, the National Trust has embarked on a major restoration programme and many of the stately home's rooms have been beautifully furnished with contemporary pieces; modern photographs of the family can be seen mingled with priceless paintings and other treasures such as Blue John vases. Along with the house itself and the park with its lakes, there are the boat house and fishing pavilion to explore.

One member of the family, George Nathaniel Curzon, was the Viceroy of India from 1899 to 1905. When he returned to England he brought back numerous works of art, carvings and ivories that can be seen on display in the **Indian Museum** in the hall. Though he was out in India for some time, George would not have missed his family home, as Government House in Calcutta is a copy of Kedleston Hall. Once back in England, George did not have much time to enjoy his lands: he became a member of Lloyd George's inner War Cabinet, which met over 500 times during the First World War.

The nearby **All Saints Church**, in the ownership of the Churches Conservation Trust, is the only part of the old village that was allowed to remain when the rest was moved in 1765 to make way for the landscaped park around the Hall. It dates from the 12th century, and is of an unusual design for Derbyshire in that it is cruciform in shape and the tower is placed in the centre. Inside are Curzon monuments dating from 1275 to the present day, some designed by Adam. The only brass in the church is to

Kedleston Hall

Richard Curzon, who died in 1496. Perhaps the most magnificent tomb is of Mary, wife of George Curzon, Viceroy of India. It was built within a magnificent memorial chapel by her husband between 1907 and 1913, and is of white marble. The church has an unusual east-facing sundial. Because of its orientation, the dial only catches the sun between the hours of 6am and 11am. The hour lines are parallel with each other, with half hour lines in between. The gnomon is in the form of a letter "T", the top bar of which casts a shadow across the dial. The inscription above the dial is "Wee Shall", which cryptically links to sundial (soon die all) to make a sombre message. This is reinforced by the carvings on top of the dial, showing a skull between two hour glasses.

Entrance to Ednaston Manor

BRAILSFORD

8 miles NW of Derby on the A52

Brailsford is a pretty, red-brick village bisected by the A52. It is mentioned in the Domesday Book as having a priest and 'half a church': this curious tale refers to the shared ownership of its church with Ednaston, to the north. The **Parish Church of All Saints** is set in a delightful location, about half a mile from the village, down a long country lane. The carved Saxon cross in the churchyard dates from the 11th century, though the church itself is an interesting mix of the 11th and 12th centuries, with much Norman work and an ashlar-faced diagonally buttressed tower.

There are many fine houses in the district, which includes two 20th-century country homes, Brailsford Hall, built in 1905 in Jacobean style, and Culland Hall. On the first Wednesday in October an annual ploughing match takes place in Brailsford.

EDNASTON

7 miles NW of Derby off the A52

This is a small ancient manor and was recorded, in the *Domesday Book* of 1086, as being in the ownership of Henry de Ferrers of Duffield Castle. The present manor house, **Ednaston Manor** on Brailsford Brook, was

built in a Queen Anne style by Sir Edwin Lutyens between 1912 and 1914. It is a Grade I listed building, and although the house, grounds and plant nursery used to be open to the public, now it is a private house and access is not permitted.

LONG LANE

6 miles NW of Derby off the A52

You won't find Long Lane village on most maps – it is truly a hidden place! But it can be reached by heading for the village of Lees and then following the sign for Long Lane. It is set on the old Roman road bearing the same name and is not much more than a cluster of cottages, a school, a church and a pub. The **Parish Church of Christ Church** dates from the 1860s, as does the school. The church is a plain structure of brick and consists of chancel, nave, south porch and a belfry containing 3 bells.

LONGFORD

8 miles W of Derby well south of the A515

Longford lies very much off the beaten track, but it is well worth finding as the village has

---

71 **THE THREE HORSESHOES**

Long Lane, nr Ashbourne

This traditional eighteenth century inn offers delicious English cuisine, real ales, roaring log fires and acoustic music nights on weekends.

See entry on page 189

the distinction of being the home of the first cheese factory in England. Opened on the 4th May in 1870, its first manager bore the memorable name Cornelius Schermerhorn. Derbyshire, with its excellent rail and canal links, was an ideal centre for the mass production of cheeses for foreign markets.

Longford Hall

The ancient and spacious mansion of **Longford Hall** was the family seat, first of the Longford family and then of the Cokes. The Longfords settled here in the 12th century and the church, which is close to the hall, was built then. The **Parish Church of St Chad**, surrounded by magnificent lime trees, still retains many Norman parts, though the tower was added in the 15th century. There are some fine monuments to both the Cokes and the Longfords.

NORBURY

14 miles W of Derby off the B5033

Norbury lies on the River Dove and was recorded in the *Domesday Book* as Norberre or Nordberie, the 'norther' defence on the Dove. The 14th-15th century **Parish Church of St Mary and St Barlok** is one of the most significant churches to be found in Derbyshire because of the outstanding quality of the stained glass in the chancel. This dates from 1305 and was restored by Holywell Glass in 2004. Much of the original expense of the current church building was met by Nicholas Fitzherbert, who died in 1473. You will find his magnificent tomb in the chancel. Like many churches in Derbyshire, this is another church with literary connections. Those

familiar with the works of George Eliot will feel much at home in this part of the county. Eliot's real name was Mary Anne Evans. The characters Adam and Seth from her famous novel *Adam Bede* were based on her father, Robert Evans, and his brother, and many scenes from the book are set in this village. Members of Eliot's family are buried in the churchyard. The church is generally kept open. Unfortunately though, there are no tourist facilities in the village.

DOVERIDGE

15 miles W of Derby off the A50

As its name suggests, this village is situated on the banks of the River Dove, and more specifically its name stems from having a bridge over the River Dove (i.e. Dove[B]ridge). Although there is a fair amount of modern housing, Doveridge still retains a rural atmosphere and like many of Derbyshire's old villages was mentioned in the *Domesday Book* as having a parish church and a water mill. Today the church remains, but the mill was demolished in the 1970's after being left in disrepair for many years. The **Parish Church of St Cuthbert**, dating essentially from the 13th century, contains memorials to the Cavendish family. Approaching St Cuthbert's by the main path you enter a 'tunnel' of branches formed by an ancient yew tree, reputed to be some 1,200 years old. According to legend, Robin Hood was betrothed to his lady under its boughs.

BOYLESTONE

10 miles W of Derby off the A515

The church at Boylestone, dedicated to **St John the Baptist** is famous for an incident during the Civil War. Two hundred Royalist troops spent the night in the local church on their way to Wingfield Manor. Rather foolishly they set no watch, and in the morning found themselves surrounded by Cromwell's men. The Royalists surrendered, were disarmed, and quietly filed out of the building. This later became known as the bloodless battle of Boylestone. The priest's doorway through which the Royalist troops emerged is still there. The church itself is mainly 14th century, and has an unusual pyramidal roof. The unusual tower dates from 1846, and was added after a fire. Today the heart of the village is based around the Rose & Crown, a welcoming 17th-century pub with real ales.

CHURCH BROUGHTON

10 miles W of Derby off the A50

Church Broughton is a quiet village which was, until the early part of the 20th century, part of the Duke of Devonshire's Derbyshire estates. The **Parish Church of St Michael**, built in the 14th century, is a handsome building benefiting from a sturdy west tower topped with a small spire and Victorian pinnacles. Interestingly there are also gargoyles and a long 14th-century chancel.

One of the first police houses in the country, now called Peel House, was established here in 1855 due to the amount of rowdy locals. The **Old Hall** (private) in Hall Lane is a 16th-century timber-framed building. The Holly Bush is the only pub in the village and together with the village shop and tennis club, it forms the main daily focus of activity in Church Broughton.

SUTTON-ON-THE-HILL

8 miles W of Derby off the A516

Despite its name, this is a sheltered spot, with only the church standing on the hill. The **Parish Church of St Michael** has a 14th-century tower with a spire that was rebuilt in 1841. A few other parts are 14th century, but mostly the church was rebuilt in 1863. It contains an unusual monument to Judith Sleigh, who died in 1634. It is a standing coffin with handles carved in black stone.

A cheese factory was built here in 1875, as in other local villages, but closed down due to competition and the building is now private housing. There was also a water mill, again now private housing.

Cricket fans will take special pleasure in visiting Sutton-on-the-Hill, as it was the family home of G. M. and R. H. R. Buckston, both of whom captained the Derbyshire cricket team.

Sudbury Hall

SUDBURY

12 miles W of Derby off the A50

This is the estate village to **Sudbury Hall**, home of a branch of the Vernon family who lived at Haddon Hall. It was built in the late 17th century by George Vernon in red brick and gifted to the National Trust in 1967. The house and gardens are open to visitors and the hall offers many specialised tours too. The lavish interiors boast elaborate decorative plasterwork, woodcarving by Grinling Gibbons, murals throughout, including painted ceilings by Louis Laguerre. The long gallery and staircase are among the grandest in any English country house. Perhaps you will recognize it from the BBC's

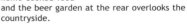

72 **THE SWAN**

Draycott-in-the-Clay

This traditional village pub serves freshly prepared home cooked food and the beer garden at the rear overlooks the countryside.

See entry on page 190

73 **THE ROEBUCK INN**

Draycott-in-the-Clay

A delicious selection of dishes and real ales are served at this superb public house.

See entry on page 190

Pride and Prejudice.

Of particular interest is the **Museum of Childhood**, which is situated in the servants' wing and provides fascinating displays telling the story of what it was like to be a child in England from the 18th century to the present. Displays range from a wealthy family's nursery and an Edwardian schoolroom to a 'chimney climb' and coal tunnel for the adventurous. The formal gardens and meadows lead to the tree-fringed lake. Wildlife abounds, including kestrels, grey herons, grass snakes, dragonflies, newts, frogs, toads, little and tawny owls and woodpeckers. Special events are held throughout the year.

ETWALL

5 miles SW of Derby off the A516

Well-Dressing, Etwall

This charming place has a fine range of Georgian buildings including some almshouses known as the **Port Hospital Almshouses**, built by Sir John Port, the founder of nearby Repton College. The almshouses, fronted by wrought iron gates made by Robert Bakewell of Derby, were rebuilt in 1681 and recently restored again. Until the 1960s, almsmen and women wore special hats or bonnets and a dark blue cloak with a silver clasp.

The original site of **Etwall Hall**, where Sir John lived, is now the site of a large comprehensive school, which bears his name. For a village that derived its name from 'Eata's Well', it seems strange that Etwall only took up the custom of well-dressing recently and by chance. To mark the centenary of the village primary school, the teachers dressed a token well while the Women's Institute, with the help of people from two villages within the Peak District,

dressed the only true well in Etwall, Town Well. This was in 1970 and the event, in mid-May, was so successful that it is now an annual occasion and a total of eight wells are decorated.

As there is no long-standing tradition of well-dressing in the village, the themes for the dressings are not the more usual Biblical subjects but have covered a wide range of stories and ideas, including racial unity and the life and times of Sir John Port. Etwall is also the most southerly village to take part in the custom of well-dressing and its position, well below the harsh uplands of Derbyshire's Peak District, has ensured that there is always a good supply of flowers, even though the dressing takes place late in spring. Etwall Well Dressings is a popular event. There are eight well-dressing sites around the village to visit plus a 'Have-a-go' tent, where visitors can try their hand at making a well-dressing. The event also includes a variety of family entertainment like traditional dancing, musical entertainment, puppet shows, a dog show competition, a scarecrow competition, a hog roast, 'village fete' stalls, an owls display and much more.

The **Parish Church of St Helen** has some stonework of the 13th century and earlier,

---

74 THE MASONS ARMS

Mickleover

A few miles from the centre of Derby is this quality pub serving a range of real ales and superb food too.

See entry on page 191

though the building was largely rebuilt in the mid-16th century after a great storm damaged it. It was restored in 1881 and has a monument to Sir Arthur Cochrane, who died in 1954 and was the Clarenceux King of Arms, an officer of the College of Arms who looked after the armorial bearings for the south of England.

HILTON

8 miles SW of Derby off the A5132

As with other ancient settlements, Hilton, like Breaston and Borrowash, has undergone rapid expansion during the 20th century with the construction of new housing estates to serve the city of Derby. Though most of the buildings are new, it has a few points of interest such as the Old Talbot Inn, the Wesleyan Chapel and Wakelyn Hall. The Old Talbot Inn dates back to the 15th century. The old gravel works are now a bird sanctuary and a nature reserve. **Wakelyn Hall** is an unusual half-timbered house dating from the 17th century. When the Wakelyn family left in 1621, the building became The Bull's Head Inn. Supposedly Mary, Queen of Scots stopped here briefly on her way to imprisonment at Tutbury Castle.

SWADLINCOTE

Here at the extreme edge of Derbyshire, well south of the River Trent, Swadlincote is known to its inhabitants simply as "Swad" and shares many characteristics with Staffordshire. It is South Derbyshire's largest town, with a population of about 36,000. Historically more a collection of villages, though officially an urban district, it retains a rural feel that is charming and worth

exploring. The **Parish Church of Emmanuelle** was built in 1846: the year Swadlincote became a parish in its own right. Modern attractions in Swadlincote include Sharpe's Pottery Museum, Swadlincote Ski Slope, the Conkers amusement park and the Swadlincote Woodlands Forest Park.

NORTH OF SWADLINCOTE

HARTSHORNE

1 mile NE of Swadlincote off the A514

One of this lovely village's most renowned sons was George Stanhope, who grew up to be a famous preacher, a bold critic and a brave writer during the reign of Queen Anne.

As in many villages there are certain buildings in Hartshorne that are very old, have unique historical value or just have distinctive character. The **Parish Church of St Peter** was rebuilt in 1835, and only the tower remains of the original church, although the font is believed to be 14th century and two of the five bells pre-date the Reformation. A fine altar tomb shows the alabaster figures of Sir Humphry Dethick of 1599 and his wife, along with relief carvings of their six children. The Dethicks paid long and loyal service to the Royal family of their day - one of the Dethicks went to Cleves to find a fourth wife for Henry VIII. His son Sir William is said to have laid a pall of rich velvet on the coffin of Mary, Queen of Scots.

CALKE

5 miles NE of Swadlincote off the B587

Calke village barely exists but the main focus of interest here is the hall known as **Calke**

---

75 THE SALT BOX CAFE

Hatton

This bustling cafe is well known for its generous portion sizes. The dishes are made from locally sourced produce and freshly cooked to order.

See entry on page 191

76 NUMBER 10 CAFE BAR RESTAURANT

Swadlincote

Number 10 is the hub of life in Swadlincote. The restaurant has been beautifully refurbished and is proving popular with diners.

See entry on page 192

Calke Abbey

Abbey. In 1985 the National Trust bought Calke Abbey, a large Baroque-style mansion built between 1701 and 1704 on the site of an Augustinian priory founded in 1133. However, it was not until 1989 that the Trust was able to open the house to the public, because this was no ordinary building. It was called 'the house that time forgot', as since the death of the owner, Sir Vauncy Harpur-Crewe in 1924, nothing had been altered in the mansion. In fact, the seclusion of the house and also the rather bizarre lifestyle of its inhabitants had left many rooms and objects untouched for over 100 years. There was even a spectacular 18th-century Chinese silk state bed that had never been unpacked.

Today, the Trust has repaired the house and returned all 13,000 items to their original positions so that the Abbey now looks just as it did when it was bought in 1981. The attention to detail has been so great that none of the rooms have been redecorated. Visitors can enjoy the display of silver and trace the route of 18th-century servants along the brew house tunnel to the house cellars. The house stands in its own large park with gardens, a chapel and stables that are also open to the public. There are three walled gardens with their glasshouses, a restored orangery, vegetable garden, pheasant aviaries and the summer flower display within the unusual 'auricular' theatre. Calke is home to lots of wildlife including fallow deer, weasels, stoats, barn owls, little owls, tawny owls, woodpeckers, common toads, butterflies and beetles.

MELBOURNE

6 miles NE of Swadlincote off the B587

This small town, which gave its name to the

rather better-known city in Australia, is a fascinating little place. A famous son of Melbourne, who started his working life in one of the market gardens, was Thomas Cook, who was born here in 1808. He went on to pioneer personally-conducted tours and gave his name to the famous travel company.

Full of Georgian charm, Melbourne has a wealth of historic buildings which includes one of the finest examples of Norman ecclesiastical architecture in the country, the **Parish Church of St Michael and St Mary.** It sits on the site of an earlier Saxon church, and seems rather a grand church for this modest place. It is a large, very lavish mid-12th century cruciform building, often described as a "miniature cathedral". In the 12th century, when the Bishopric of Carlisle was formed, the bishops needed a place of safety for the clergy when Carlisle was being raided by the Scots. This church was therefore built many miles south at Melbourne and, while Carlisle was subjected to raids and violence, the Bishop retired to Melbourne and continued to carry out his duties. The church was built between 1133 and 1229 and, in 1299, the then Bishop built a palace on land that is now home to **Melbourne Hall**, which is another fine building in this area. Originally a rectory for the Norman Parish Church, it became the home of Sir John Coke in 1628 and has been

inherited by subsequent members of the family till the present day, and is now home to Lord and Lady Ralph Kerr and their young family. Melbourne Hall gardens are the place to visit if you are seeking a relaxing thoughtful stroll. The walks, vistas and statuary, much favoured in the early 18th century, have been restored in the influential, Dutch/French formal style of the time. The most notable feature is a beautiful wrought-iron birdcage pergola, built in the early 1700s by Robert Bakewell, a local blacksmith from Derby. Bakewell lived in Melbourne for a time at the house of a widow named Fisher and her daughters. However when one daughter became pregnant, he moved hurriedly to Derby. Unfortunately the house is only open to the public in August (except for the first three Mondays), but the splendid and famous formal gardens are open from April through to September, and are well worth a visit.

There was also once a substantial castle in the town, but it fell into disrepair in the 17th century. **Melbourne Castle**, located in the village centre, was built by the Earl of Lancaster in the early 14th century, and later became a royal castle when it came into the possession of Henry IV. The castle was bought from the crown by the Earl of Huntingdon, who demolished it in 1637. Remnants of it can be seen in Castle Farm by prior appointment.

SWARKESTONE

9 miles NE of Swadlincote off the A5132

The ancient village of Swarkestone originated at a crossing point of the River Trent. This small village has also been, quite literally, a turning point in history. The **Swarkestone Bridge**, with its seven arches and three-quarter-mile long causeway, is the longest

Swarkestone Bridge

stone bridge in England and holds Grade I listed building status. In 1745, during the second Jacobite Rebellion, Bonnie Prince Charlie and his army reached Derby and made arrangements for the capture of the strategically important Swarkestone Bridge. It was the only bridge on the River Trent between Burton and Nottingham. Had they managed to cross it at this point, they would have faced no other natural barriers on their 120-mile march to London. As it transpired, the army retreated and fled north. If the march had continued, it would probably have been successful and the whole course of British history could have changed. In memory of this important event, a cairn has been erected at Swarkestone Bridge to mark the southern most point reached by Bonnie Prince Charlie's army.

The tiny **Parish Church of St James** was so heavily restored between 1874 and 1876 that little now remains of the original church, apart form the southwest tower and the Harpur Chapel. The chapel contains tomb chests of Richard Harpur (1573), who was one of Queen Elizabeth's judges, and Sir John Harpur, who died in 1627. Close to the parish church are the scanty remains of old Harpur Hall (the precursor of Calke Abbey) which

---

79 YE OLDE PACKHORSE

Kings Newton

A fantastic country inn offering the best in olde worlde hospitality, well-kept ales and quality cuisine.

See entry on page 194

---

80 IVY HOUSE FARM B&B & WOODLAND HILLS COURT

Stanton-by-Bridge

If you are after an unwinding break or just after a nights stay, this traditional farmhouse accommodation ensures relaxation in an idyllic setting.

See entry on page 195

includes a Jacobean grandstand (now a Landmark Trust property) to a bowling green or bull-baiting ring. Most of the Hall remains date to about 1630.

Excavations in the village of Swarkestone, at Lowes Farm, led to the discovery that the district was occupied in the Bronze Age and also in Saxon times. Iron Age remains were found here when the A50 was constructed.

BARROW-ON-TRENT

8 miles NE of Swadlincote off the A514

Barrow-on-Trent, as its name tells us, stands on the River Trent, between the river and the Trent and Mersey Canal. An interesting feature of this attractive village is that during the 18th century a row of parish cottages was built by parish levy, and first rented for £1.50 a year, and the parish council still maintains them.

The **Parish Church of St Wilfrid's** is a beautiful medieval building overlooking the Trent valley, and dates mainly from the 13th century. The Church, at one time, was an outpost for the Knights Hospitallers of St John and has many interesting features, old and new. The north arcade, with its original columns, is one such notable feature. The plain glass windows lend the church a light and airy atmosphere. The base of the square tower and the north aisle date from the 1300s; there is also a Georgian east window.

The Derbyshire-born artist George Turner (1841-1910) was such an accomplished landscape painter that he has been dubbed 'Derbyshire's John Constable'. Turner's favourite painting haunt was around this village, and it is where he met his first wife, Eliza Lakin of Walnut Farm. They were married in the village in 1865 and took up residence at The Walnuts.

BRETBY

2 miles N of Swadlincote off the A50

Now a leafy rural backwater, Bretby was first mentioned in the *Domesday Book* as an agricultural settlement around a green. The name means *"dwelling place of Britons"*. There was once a castle in this quiet village until it was demolished during the reign of

James l, and the stones used to build a mansion house. In the 18th century that too was demolished, and **Bretby Hall** was built in 1813 by Sir Jeffrey Wyatville, the designer of the 19th-century extension at Chatsworth House. Only the Hall and lakes remain.

One of the owners of the estate was Lord Carnarvon, the Egyptologist, who sold the property to finance the famous expedition in search of the tomb of Tutankhamun, the boy king. The present Bretby Hall now comprises luxury private apartments.

MILTON

5 miles N of Swadlincote off the A514

Milton is a small village, established over 1,500 years ago. It was once owned by the Burdett family, who built the nearby church of St Saviour. Although the village has seen many changes in the last century, it still has a very rural character with its one main street and the many paths, initially used for the movement of cattle and sheep, have become public footpaths and bridle paths to provide pleasant walks for residents and visitors. The village has an original classic red phone box on main street which was given a Grade II listing in January 2005.

REPTON

5 miles N of Swadlincote off the B5008

This village, by the tranquil waters of the River Trent, is steeped in history. The main core of Repton village was designated as a Conservation Area in 1969, and extended in 1982. There are some forty buildings listed as being of historical and architectural interest. However, the village is not just about its historical past, it is a vibrant community with many clubs, societies, shops and pubs.

81 THE SWALLOW'S REST

Repton

Guests return time and time again to this intimate b&b with quality accommodation.

See entry on page 196

Foremark Hall, Repton

The first mention of Repton came in the 7th century when it was established as the capital of the Saxon Kingdom of Mercia. A monastery, housing both monks and nuns, was founded here sometime after AD 653 but the building was sacked by the Danes in AD 874. Three Mercian kings were buried here - Merewahl in AD 686, Aethelbald in AD 757 and Wiglaf in AD 839, as well as St Wystan, who was Wiglaf's grandson. He is supposed to have been interred alongside his grandfather. A battle-axe, now on display in the school museum, was excavated a little distance from the church. It had apparently lain undisturbed for well over 1,000 years.

The **Parish Church of St Wystan** is famous for its distinctive Anglo-Saxon stonework, which can be admired from both inside and outside the church. Sir Nikolaus Pevsner wrote: "...the chancel....and the crypt form one of the most precious survivals of Anglo-Saxon architecture in England." When the chancel and part of the nave were enlarged in 1854, the original Anglo-Saxon columns were moved to the 14th-century porch. The crypt claims to be one of the oldest intact Anglo-Saxon buildings in England and was rediscovered by chance in 1779 by a workman who was digging a hole for a grave in the chancel floor.

To read an interesting tale, turn right before you reach the south porch, go up to the stone wall and look at the headstones against it. One slate memorial is dedicated to a Samuel Marshall, aged 21. He was murdered in 1786, and his killer was caught but acquitted at trial for the lack of witnesses. If you examine the headstone, you will see it depicts a tree with five branches, one of which has been cut off with an axe, representing the dead man, and the others his surviving brothers.

The ancient but restored **Cross**, still at the central crossroads in the village, has been the focal point of life here for centuries and it has also stood at the heart of the Wednesday market. Right up until the late 19th century a Statutes Fair, for the hiring of farm labourers and domestics, was also held here at Michaelmas.

Parts of an Augustinian priory, founded in 1170, are incorporated in the buildings of **Repton College**, itself founded in 1557. Sir John Port had specifically intended the college to be a grammar school for the local poor children of Etwall, Repton and Burnaston. These intentions have somewhat deviated over the passing years and now Repton is one of the foremost public schools in the country. Interestingly, two of its headmasters, Dr Temple and Dr Fisher, went on to become Archbishops of Canterbury, while Dr Ramsey was a pupil at the school under Dr Fisher's guiding light. Film buffs will recognise the 14th-century gatehouse and causeway, as they featured in both film versions of the popular story *Goodbye, Mr Chips*.

Just to the west of the village is **Foremark Hall**, built by Robert Adam in 1762 for the Burdett family. It is now a preparatory school for Repton College.

---

82 THE UNICORN INN

Newton Solney

An outstanding village inn which provides an ideal place to stay for visitors to Derbyshire or users of East Midlands Airport.

See entry on page 196

SOUTH OF SWADLINCOTE

CHURCH GRESLEY

2 miles SW of Swadlincote off the A514

This former mining village has a distinguished history dating back to the time of the

Augustinian monks who settled here in the 12th century and founded a priory. The village's name, like that of nearby Castle Gresley, recalls the great Gresley family, said to have been the only Derbyshire family to have retained their lands from the time of the *Domesday Book* up until the 20th century.

The **Parish Church of St Mary and St George** has a link with this illustrious past, as the tower and two internal arches are all that remain of the priory church. It became run-down after the Dissolution of the Monasteries, and remained in a sad state of disrepair up until 1872, when a new chancel was built. Remains of the priory have been found, including fragments of painted glass, stone coffins and medieval tiles. An impressive alabaster monument of 1699 depicts Sir Thomas Gresley, surrounded by arms showing the marriages of his ancestors dating back to the time of William the Conqueror. The church's treasures, though, are the ten large and wonderfully carved 17th-century stalls.

In around 1800 the pottery Mason Cash was established here. Mason Cash has become a much-loved English pottery, producing traditional ceramic mixing and baking ware.

CASTLE GRESLEY

3 miles SW of Swadlincote on the A444

Just like Church Gresley, Castle Gresley, unsurprisingly, is also named after the Derbyshire family of Gresley, which has owned land in the area since before the *Domesday Book*. But where is the castle? Unfortunately, nothing is left of the castle built by William de Gresley in the mid-14th century - apart from the grassy mound, or motte, on which it stood, still known as **Castle Knob**.

LINTON

2 miles SW of Swadlincote off the A444

Linton is a charming and restful village, within the National Forest, which is mainly agricultural since the closure of the Coton Park colliery. This place is celebrated for its cheese and cattle.

ROSLISTON

5 miles SW of Swadlincote off the A444

Rosliston was recorded in the Domesday Book as Redlauseton, an Anglo-Saxon name meaning 'farm of Hrolf', this Hrolf probably being a Norseman. Rosliston is part of the National Forest and in the **Rosliston Forestry Centre** there are way-marked walks, a wildlife hide and children's play equipment. On summer evenings bats may be seen at dusk - several different species make this area their home.

The **Parish Church of St Mary the Virgin** is mainly 19th century but the 14th-century tower with its broach spire still remains. Except for the later Victorian furnishings the interior is quite unaltered and well worth a visit.

COTON IN THE ELMS

6 miles SW of Swadlincote off the A444

Until around 60 years ago, Coton in the Elms had elm trees bordering every road into the village, but they all succumbed to Dutch Elm disease. The **Parish Church of St Mary** dates from 1846. It replaced an earlier church which stood behind the Shoulder of Mutton pub in the village. The bells from this older church were removed when it was pulled down and hung in the nearby church at Lullington. It is said that when the wind is in the right direction, the villagers of Coton-in-the-Elms can still hear their original bells.

Nearby is Grangewood Farm Forestry, which has 100 acres of new woodland adjoining the ancient woodland of Grange Wood. The site includes laid out trails, camping facilities, horse riding and fishing. Coton in the Elms also has the distinction of

83 THE PLOUGH INN

Rosliston

This pretty village inn attracts a wide range of customers eager to sample the home cooked food and well kept ales on offer.

See entry on page 197

being the furthest place away from the sea in the British Isles. The exact point, according to Ordnance Survey, is near Church Flatts Farm, roughly one mile southeast of the village centre.

NETHERSEAL

6 miles S of Swadlincote off the A444

Netherseal is a picturesque village on the banks of the river Mease, overlooking Leicestershire. The village was once part of the district of Seal, which included quite a few settlements, many of which now form Netherseal and Overseal. 'Seal' suggests the area was once heavily forested and Netherseal was recorded in the *Domesday Book* as a wooded area on the edge of the Ashby Woulds. It was once a mining community with a two-shaft colliery and several related industries. The mining industry has long gone and the centre of Netherseal village is now a conservation area with many listed buildings, including the 17th-century almshouses.

The **Parish Church of St Peter** was built in the 19th century, though it looks much older, and has some medieval fragments, including the tower. It stands on the site of an earlier church dating from the 13th century. The churchyard is the final resting

place of Sir Nigel Gresley, who designed the famous Mallard locomotive.

DONISTHORPE

3 miles SE of Swadlincote off the A444

Donisthorpe is a famous old mining village right on the Derbyshire-Leicestershire border. The River Mease, which marks the border, runs right through it. Its inhabitants are justly proud of the village's industrial and historical heritage. The old colliery, the pit railway and the old British Rail line had all closed down by the 1960s. Left behind is a proud history and a tranquillity unknown in the days of the mines.

MOIRA

6 miles SE of Swadlincote off the A444

Moira is actually just over the border in Leicestershire, and close by is the award winning attraction called **Conkers**, at the heart of the National Forest. It is a mix of indoor and outdoor experiences where you can watch the effect the four seasons have on a forest. There are over 1,000 interactive exhibits.

Another legacy of the area's industrial heritage is the **Moira Furnace**, a restored 19th-century blast furnace. Today it is a museum with interactive displays and information on how the furnace worked, and its influence on the local economy and the lives of the workers. There is also a restored section of Ashby Canal near the site so you may wish to enjoy a boat trip. The furnace adjoins a 50acre newly-planted Woodland Park. The furnace site also includes craft workshops and a small nature reserve.

84 **THE NAVIGATION INN**

Overseal

This quality inn is renowned for its excellent facilities for families with play areas, excellent home cooked food and guest accommodation.

See entry on page 197

85 **THE SHOULDER OF MUTTON**

Oakthorpe

Fine food, real ale, good music – all under one roof at the warm and welcoming Shoulder of Mutton.

See entry on page 198

Moira Furnace

LOCATION MAP

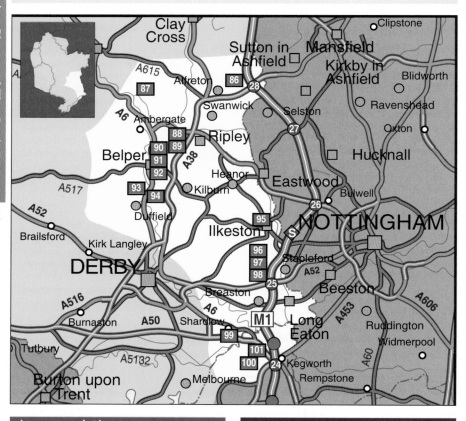

Accommodation

94	The Spotted Cow Inn, Holbrook	*pg 112, 203*

Food & Drink

86	The Devonshire Arms, South Normanton, Alfreton	*pg 102, 199*
88	Eagle Tavern, Heage	*pg 107, 200*
90	The Railway Tea Rooms, Belper	*pg 110, 201*
91	Cross Keys, Belper	*pg 110, 201*
92	The Tavern, Belper	*pg 110, 202*
93	Angelo's Restaurant at the New Inn, Milford	*pg 112, 202*
94	The Spotted Cow Inn, Holbrook	*pg 112, 203*
95	The Coffee House, Ilkeston	*pg 113, 204*

Food & Drink

97	The Old Schoolhouse Deli Café, Stanton-by-Dale	*pg 116, 205*
98	The Seven Oaks Inn & Restaurant, Stanton-by-Dale	*pg 116, 206*
99	The Old Crown Inn, Shardlow	*pg 119, 205*
100	The Cross Keys, Castle Donnington	*pg 120, 207*
101	The Jolly Sailor, Hemington	*pg 120, 208*

Places of Interest

87	Crich Tramway Museum, Crich, Matlock	*pg 104, 199*
89	Heage Windmill, Heage	*pg 108, 200*
96	All Saints Church, Dale Abbey, Stanton-by-Dale	*pg 115, 204*

THE AMBER VALLEY AND EREWASH

This area encompasses the Amber Valley and the eastern part of the area known as Erewash. These two regions cover the eastern and south eastern parts of Derbyshire respectively. The Rivers Amber, Derwent and Trent run through this part of the county. With such spectacular scenery, it's no surprise that the area abounds with excellent walks and trails, many of which are drawn together in the annual Amber Valley and Erewash Walking Festival. Taking place each September, the festival attracts walkers from around the area and includes guided walks by experienced guides as well as numerous self-guided trails.

Amber Valley

There's plenty to discover in the towns, villages and landscapes of the Amber Valley and Erewash - whether you're exploring the area's rich industrial heritage and historical connections, visiting one of the area's numerous attractions or simply absorbing the views on foot, by bike or on horseback, there's something for everyone.

The landscape of the area is one shaped both by nature and by entrepreneurs, and it's a landscape rich in history and nostalgia. Originally small farming communities, many of the villages expanded at the time of the Industrial Revolution and they can, in many cases, be characterised by unflattering rows of workers' cottages. And while a lot of the area did not escape from the growth of Derby and Nottingham, there are still some interesting and unique buildings to be found in this corner of the county. The Grade II listed Heage Windmill, built in 1797, is the only stone-towered, multi-sailed windmill in England and many of its original wooden mechanisms are still in place – offering a nostalgic glimpse back to the past. Crich Tramway Village is home to The National Tram Museum, a superb collection of running trams, set in a beautifully-restored period townscape, the buildings of which have been brought in from around the UK, restored and reconstructed brick by brick! Alternatively you could get all steamed up on a seven-mile steam train ride through the countryside at the Midland Railway. The ruined Dale Abbey is another of the region's attractions, founded here by Augustinian monks in the 13th century. However, unlike the area to the west, there are no great stately mansions, except for one, Elvaston Castle, which, along with its extensive grounds, is an interesting and delightful place to explore.

The area's villages and towns like Belper and Alfreton also provide great places to explore and offer regular markets.

ALFRETON

This historic town dates back to Saxon times and, despite local legends to the contrary, Alfred the Great was not immortalised in the naming of the place, nor, as legend tells us, did he live in a house on what is now King Street. Instead the town belonged to a Saxon nobleman called Alfred, and was named 'Aelfredingtune', which, in the *Domesday Book*, is recorded as 'Elstretune'.

This attractive former coal-mining town stands on a hill close to the Nottinghamshire border, and benefited from the philanthropy of Robert Watchorn, a local pit boy made good, who emigrated to America and became Commissioner of Immigration in the early 19th century. This highly respected man never forgot his roots and gave the town a substantial amount of money. Several buildings including the Watchorn Memorial Church, a school, a manse, cottages, sports ground, pavilion and the Lincoln Library were all built by him.

Along the charming High Street can be found the George Hotel, a fine Georgian building that looks down the length of the street. Also on the High Street you can find plenty of shops, and there are a great many restaurants, pubs and other places to visit, including a number of splendid 18th-century stone-built houses that add real character to a stroll along this High Street.

Further historical points of interest in Alfreton include the **Parish Church of St Martin**, which contains monuments to the Morewood family and dates from the 13th century. The south arcade is 14th century, and the north arcade was rebuilt in 1868. Its impressive fine western tower dates from the 15th century, and rises from an earlier base. Also of interest is an old lock-up, known as a 'house of confinement' dating from 1820, which can be found at the bottom of King Street. It was built to house lawbreakers and drunkards. The close confines of the prison, with its two cells, minute windows and thick outer walls, must have been a very effective deterrent.

The market at Alfreton was granted in 1251 to Robert de Latham and Thomas de Chaworth, to be held on a Monday, together with a fair for three days at the Feast of St Margaret. There is still a bustling market and Alfreton attracts visitors from a wide radius to its busy town centre. The **Alfreton Heritage Centre** in Rodgers Lane is housed in an old chapel with the municipal cemetery, and contains a collection of material relating to Alfreton and its hinterland including photographs, maps, etc. **Alfreton Park** on the edge of the town was once part of the Palmer-Morewood estate and their home, Alfreton Hall, is now a wedding and conference venue and the surrounding land is an attractive public park.

AROUND ALFRETON

SOUTH NORMANTON

2 miles E of Alfreton off the B6109

The origin of South Normanton is uncertain. Early evidence suggests that the first settlement was Celtic although other evidence points to the name Normanton having an Anglo-Saxon derivation, meaning 'the farm of the north men' or 'Northwegans'. However, it is certain that following the Norman Conquest of 1066, South Normanton was granted by William the Conqueror to his bastard son William Peveril. In common with much of the rest of the country the main activity of the village in medieval times was that of agriculture, though by 1881 the county had been overtaken by 'coal fever'.

The village was transformed after the opening of 'A Winning' colliery in 1871 and 'B

---

86 THE DEVONSHIRE ARMS

South Normanton

Good company, good food, good beer and good times, guaranteed at the Devonshire Arms.

See entry on page 199

Winning' in 1875, by the Blackwell Colliery Company. By the 1880s 'A Winning' had the largest output of coal in Derbyshire, but with the pits came the insatiable demand for miners. Many people came to South Normanton from depressed agricultural areas and this migration was helped by the Erewash Valley railway extension, which reached Alfreton in 1865. Terraced houses were built to accommodate the growing population, which doubled in the ten years from 1871 to 1881. Like many Victorian industrialists, the Blackwell Colliery Company took a paternalistic attitude to its workforce, providing a reading room, library, tennis courts and playing fields, as well as a cottage hospital. In February 1937 the South Normanton Mining Disaster killed eight miners due to an underground explosion. South Normanton Colliery closed in 1952, B Winning in 1964 and A Winning in 1969.

Today South Normanton is a large, busy, industrial village, but it has definitely cleaned up its act since the early part of the 20th century when it was known as the dirtiest village in Derbyshire. The **Parish Church of St Michael** dates from around the 13th century but most of the present building is 19th century. It contains a monument to a Robert Ravel who lived at the nearby Carnfield Hall, an early 17th-century stone mansion built by the Revell family.

The most famous person to come out of South Normanton was Jedediah Strutt, who, along with Rickard Arkwright, founded the Derbyshire cotton industry; he was born in the village in 1726. Its former centre, around the old market place, has moved to a new market area and a mass of housing covers the site of Jedediah Strutt's birthplace next to the Shoulder of Mutton pub.

OAKERTHORPE

1 mile W of Alfreton off the B6013

Tucked away in a narrow valley lies **Oakerthorpe Nature Reserve**. Its size and location make it easy to miss, yet this patch of land supports a variety of species and habitats. There is a short circular walk around the reserve, with a pond-dipping

platform which is an ideal location to spot frogs, toads and common newts - and you may be lucky enough to come across a grass snake. These harmless reptiles are now rare in Derbyshire, and Oakerthorpe is one place where they are still seen regularly.

SOUTH WINGFIELD

2 miles W of Alfreton on the B5053

As Derbyshire emerged from the Dark Ages and towns with markets like Chesterfield began to attract a population of artisans and traders during the early Middle Ages, prosperous merchants and churchmen became attracted to the county. One of the most eminent of these was Thomas Cromwell, at one time the richest and most powerful man in England, who built **Wingfield Manor.**

Wingfield Manor

The evocative and hauntingly beautiful ruins of Wingfield Manor stand proudly atop a rocky hill above the village of South Wingfield, with the tall chimneys and gaunt towers rising resolutely to two hundred feet above the valley floor, and dominating the surrounding pastoral landscape. High up in the tower can also be seen a single archer's slit, built the opposite way round so that only one archer was needed to defend the whole tower. A wander around the remains reveals the large banqueting hall with its unusual oriel window and a crypt which was probably used to store food and wine. Whatever its use, it is a particularly fine example and rivals a similar structure at Fountains Abbey.

This was the romantic setting for scenes from the films, *The Virgin & the Gypsy* and

Zefferelli's adaptation of *Jane Eyre*. The ruins have also been featured in the TV series, *Peak Practice* - but most famously, the manor house was used as Mary, Queen of Scots' prison on two separate occasions in 1569 and 1584 when she was held under the care of the Earl of Shrewsbury. The local squire, Anthony Babington, attempted to rescue the Queen and lead her to safety but the plot failed and, instead, led to them both being beheaded. Though still a ruin, the house is now owned by English Heritage and open to the public at certain times of the year for pre-booked guided tours only. It can be reached by a farm track half a mile to the south of the village.

East of the village is the **Parish Church of All Saints**, which dates originally from the 13th century. At the same time as building Wingfield Manor, Cromwell refurbished the church and built a new tower, while also preserving the arcades on both sides of the nave.

CRICH

6 miles W of Alfreton off the A6

Probably better known as the village of Cardale in the TV series *Peak Practice*, Crich (pronounced 'Cry-ch' and meaning 'hilltop'), with its church and market cross, is also the home of the **Crich Tramway Village**, which is the National Tram Museum. Referring to itself intriguingly as 'the museum that's a mile long', it offers a wonderful opportunity to enjoy a tram ride along a Victorian street. The signposts, stone flags and gas lamps are all original and come from such diverse places as Liverpool, Oldham and Leeds. Today, in many towns and cities, trams are making a come-back, but here the museum

Crich Stand

gives visitors the opportunity to view tramways of the past. As well as those shuttling up and down the mile-long scenic route, there is an exhibition, which contains not only trams but also much more besides, including some wonderfully colourful fairground organs. Throughout the year the museum holds many special events and, with their policy of no hidden extras, this is a great place to take all the family for a fun day out. Started in 1959, it now has over 50 trams, with a third of them being in full working order. It stands on the site of a quarry that was owned by the great engineer George Stephenson, who also owned the railway that carried the stone down the steep incline to his lime kilns alongside the Cromford Canal.

This large, straggling village was also a flourishing knitting centre at one time, and the telltale 18th-century cottages with their long upper windows can still be seen. The **Parish Church of St Mary**, with its tall spire, dates back to around 1135, but is now mostly 14th century. Although there is evidence of 'Norman' influence inside the Church. It sits on a hilltop, and contains a built-in stone lectern, which, though common in Derbyshire, is rare elsewhere in the country.

Also situated on a hilltop, 1,100 feet above sea level is **Crich Stand**, an operational lighthouse and memorial tower, complete with flashing beacon. Built in 1923, it is dedicated to the memory of the 11,409 men of the Sherwood Foresters who died during the First World War. The memorial also honours those who died in the Second World

---

87 CRICH TRAMWAY VILLAGE

Crich

Crich Tramway Village offers a family day out in the relaxing atmosphere of a bygone era.

See entry on page 198

War and other conflicts, up to the year 1970. There is another part to the Memorial, which is not generally known. This was the provision of two books in which are inscribed the names of all the men of the Regiment who were killed in the Great War of 1914-1918. One book is deposited at The Sherwood Foresters Museum Gallery in Nottingham Castle and the other is deposited in the Derby City Museum and Art Gallery. They are commonly known as the Roll of Honour, or Books of Remembrance.

The hill on which it is set has been used as a signalling point for centuries - including during the Spanish Armada in the 16th century, and is often used as a site for celebratory beacons to this day. The spiral staircase with fifty-eight steps takes the visitor to a viewing gallery, where there are splendid views in all directions. It's said that on a clear day you can see eight counties from here. Open all year, there is a short walk and seating available round the site.

WHATSTANDWELL

4 miles W of Alfreton off the A6

On Burdett's Map of 1791 Whatstandwell is shown as "Hottstandell Bridge", probably a literal spelling of the local dialect. A mid-19th century Ordnance Survey map shows it as "Whatstandwell Bridge" which was the name given to the railway station. This tiny village, of which it has been said 'the loveliness of the English countryside is always here,' was once owned by the monks of Darley Abbey and nestles in the valley of the River Derwent. To the south and on the west bank of the Derwent are the **Shining Cliff Woods**, and along the steep lanes lie grey stone cottages and farmhouses, built of stone from local quarries, which merge gently into the background of woods and cliff. The area supports an abundance of wildlife and because of its value as a natural habitat, it has been designated a Site of Special Scientific Interest. Florence Nightingale knew and loved the village, and took a keen interest in its people. Ellen MacArthur, the round-the-world yachtswoman, was brought up in the village.

Ruins of Fritchley Windmill

FRITCHLEY

3 miles SW of Alfreton off the A610

During the 19th and early 20th centuries, this quiet hamlet had an active body of Quakers, and a flourishing community survives today. The traditional 'chapel' design, brick-built **Meeting House** of 1897 is in the centre of the village. Here also can be seen the remains of a pre-Stephenson tramway that was built at the end of the 18th century to carry stone to the lime kilns at Bull Bridge.

AMBERGATE

6 miles SW of Alfreton off the A6

Ambergate stands where the River Amber joins the Derwent, and is on the route of the National Heritage Way, a 55-mile walk along the Derwent Valley. The village itself is surrounded by deciduous woodland, including the fine Shining Cliff Woods, an important refuge for wildlife (see Whatstandwell). Before 1840 and the building of Ambergate station for the North Midland Railway, there was no village here at all, though there was a tollhouse for the recently constructed turnpike road, opened in 1817. Not surprisingly, Ambergate is the product of the 19th century, and it's probably from the tollhouse that it got its name. The railway, road and canal here are all squeezed into the tight river valley, and the railway station, standing 100 feet above the road, had a triangular layout of platforms, due to the configuration of the lines. It was an important junction, and in its heyday employed over 50 men. Now there is just one platform.

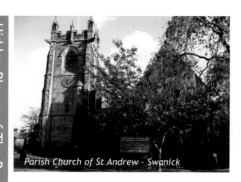
Parish Church of St Andrew - Swanick

SWANWICK

2 miles S of Alfreton off the A38

Swanwick is a large and lively village, which grew into a thriving industrial centre during the 18th and 19th centuries. Coal mining and stocking manufacture had provided work for centuries, but it was the arrival of the Butterley Company, the largest coal, iron and engineering concern in the East Midlands in the late 18th century, that changed the face of Swanwick.

The **Parish Church of St Andrew**, a substantial and attractive stone building, was completed in 1860, with the tower being added 43 years later. Swanwick Hall was once the home of the Wood family, local landowners in the area, but was opened as a school in 1922.

RIDDINGS

2 miles S of Alfreton on the B6016

Riddings was first recorded in the 12th century as 'Ryddynges', meaning 'a clearing in the grove'. Now a tranquil village, Riddings has twice been the scene of important discoveries. In the mid-18th century, 800 precious Roman coins were uncovered here. The second time was in the mid-19th century, when the world's first paraffin wax candle was produced. The story of its discovery begins with James Oakes, a colliery proprietor and ironmaster, who discovered a mysterious liquid flowing in one of his coal mines. He called in the assistance of his brother-in-law, Sir Lyon Playfair, one of

the most brilliant practical scientists of his day. Playfair found the liquid to be petroleum, then a product with no commercial value, although it had been known as naphtha, 'salt of the earth', from Biblical times.

Playfair summoned the help of his Scottish friend, James Young, who, soon after he came to Riddings, approached Playfair in dismay to show him that the oil was in a thick, contaminated condition. Playfair recognised at once the presence of paraffin, and instructed Young to extract enough paraffin to make two candles - the first paraffin-wax candles ever produced.

With one candle in his left hand and the other in his right, Playfair illuminated a lecture he gave at the Royal Institution. From these small beginnings date the enormous petroleum industry and the rich trade in paraffin and its by-products. Young, known thereafter as Paraffin Young, earned himself a fortune, and when the knowledge of his work spread about, a worldwide search for petroleum began.

RIPLEY

Ripley may not be the largest tourist Mecca in the world but, acre for acre, it probably has more to offer the curious and the casual caller than most other towns in the county. This old industrial town is mentioned in the *Domesday Book*. Ripley was originally called Ripelie. Once a typical small market town, Ripley expanded dramatically during the Industrial Revolution when great use was made of the iron, clay and coal deposits found nearby. The town's Butterley ironworks, founded in 1792 by a group of men which included renowned engineer Benjamin Outram, created the arched roof for London's St Pancras Station. Outram's even more famous son Sir James enjoyed an illustrious career that saw him become Bayard of India, and earned him a resting place in Westminster Abbey. Butterley Hall, which was built in the 18th century, is the headquarters for the Derbyshire Constabulary.

Interestingly, according to a study of

people's names, the town of Ripley is the most English. The research, which classified the ethnic background of Britain's 42.2 million adult voters according to the origin of their names, found that 88.5 per cent of Ripley's inhabitants were ethnically English. The study, carried out by Professor Richard Webber, of University College London, was on behalf of OriginsInfo marketing.

AROUND RIPLEY

PENTRICH

1 mile NW of Ripley off the A38

Mentioned in the *Domesday Book* as Pentric, this hilltop village with its brownstone gabled houses is very charming. Some Pentrich houses still stand exactly where medieval cottages were shown in maps of the 16th and 17th centuries. Its sturdy **Parish Church of St Matthew** is approached via a picturesque flight of 48 steps. It dates back to the 12th century, with much rebuilding and alterations being carried out in the 15th century. A striking stained-glass War Memorial window created in 1916 depicts the warrior saints of England and France and a figure of St Michael.

Pentrich is probably most famous for the **Pentrich Revolution** of 1817. A small band of half-starved weavers, labourers and stockingers - no more than 200 or 300 men - met and marched towards Nottingham, where they expected to meet up with more men before marching on London. However, the uprising was soon quelled, with a resultant trial of 50 of the insurgents in Derby that lasted 10 days. The men were accused of high treason, and a few were pardoned, 11 sent to Australia for life and three to Australia for 14 years. Three of the men, however, were executed at Derby Gaol. The poet Shelley witnessed the scene and described the despair of the relatives and the disturbance of the crowd as the men were beheaded. So restless and angry was the crowd watching the executions that the executioners were masked and their names

kept secret. The execution block is still to be seen in Derby Prison.

The history of Pentrich almost stopped with the revolution. The 1821 census recorded a decrease of a third in the population of the parish because the Duke of Devonshire's agents destroyed many of the houses after the insurrection. Wives and children were put out of their tenancies and years later could be traced in other parts of the country, still scraping a livelihood after their disgrace. The village became smaller and less important in succeeding years.

LOWER HARTSHAY

2 miles W of Ripley off the A610

Lower Hartshay sits on what was Ryknield Street, an important Roman military and trade route from the Fosse Way in Gloucestershire to the north. The line of Ryknield Street through Ripley, Pentrich and Lower Hartshay can still be seen and makes a pleasant walk with splendid views. Lower Hartshay was still on a main route for traffic until the 1970s. Now by-passed by the major trunk roads, it is a pleasant and tranquil backwater.

HEAGE

1 mile W of Ripley on the B6013

Heage, from the Anglo-Saxon word 'heegge', meaning 'high', was on the ancient packhorse route from Derby to Chesterfield, and the old turnpike road passed through here. The village has no obvious centre and is scattered along the roads and lanes. The village is still split into two main parts, High Heage and Low or Nether Heage. The main occupations for centuries were farming and coal mining.

88 EAGLE TAVERN

Heage

This family run public house offers the very best in real ales, freshly cooked food and top quality service.

See entry on page 200

Heage Windmill

In fact, Morley Park has been worked for coal and ironstone since 1372, and the remains of bell-pits were discovered during recent open cast mining. On Morley Park are the remains of two cold blast coke iron furnaces built by Francis Hurt in 1780 and the Mold Brothers in 1818. The older furnace was probably the first of its kind in Derbyshire. Other local industries included framework knitting and weaving.

The oldest domestic building in the village is Heage Hall Farm, once the home of a branch of the Pole family. Crowtrees Farm was built in 1450 with three good cruck beams and was refurbished in 1712. An interesting feature of the village is its postbox, in the wall of the post office. It is one of the few in the country bearing the name of Edward VII, who abdicated in 1936.

The **Parish Church of St Luke** was originally constructed of wood, and during a great storm in June 1545 it was destroyed. It was then rebuilt in stone in 1661, and subsequently enlarged in 1836.

---

89 HEAGE WINDMILL

Heage

Heage Windmill stands in a very striking position overlooking the village of Nether Heage.

See entry on page 200

Heage Windmill is situated west of the village between High Heage and Nether Heage. It is a Grade II listed tower mill and the only one in Derbyshire to retain its six sails, fan tail and machinery. Standing on the brow of a hill, overlooking Nether Heage, it is built of local sandstone and is over two hundred years old. It has been restored to full working order and is open to the public at weekends and bank holidays. There was a small stone building, built some years after the mill itself, alongside the mill which was used as the kiln. This kiln has been rebuilt and provides the Visitor Centre and shop selling souvenirs, flour and light refreshments.

DENBY

2 miles S of Ripley off the A38

Denby was mentioned in the *Domesday Book* as Denebi, which means village of the Danes. Ryknield Street, a Roman road, runs through the village.

Denby Pottery, to the north of the village, is one of the biggest attractions in Derbyshire, and has a fascinating history. Derbyshire has a long tradition of stoneware pottery, closely associated with the natural clay deposits of the county. When a seam of clay was discovered in Denby in 1806 while constructing a road, a local man, William Borne, recognised its quality and thus Denby Pottery was born. Production of salt-glazed pottery began in 1809, with Bourne's son Joseph in charge. Soon the company was known world-wide for its containers and stoneware bottles. Soon the company diversified into kitchen and tableware. By the 1930s, classic ranges such as Imperial Blue orient ware, which was brown, had established the company as one of the premier stoneware potteries in the world, introducing its 'oven to tableware' in the 1970s.

Open all year, Denby Visitor Centre is next to the working pottery, set in a cobbled courtyard with award winning home, garden, cookery and gift shops. There are two Pottery Tours to choose from: both include a video presentation, and the opportunity to have fun! A factory shop for Dartington Crystal can also be found at this superb attraction.

A mile from the pottery visitor centre, in Denby's oldest part, is the little **Parish Church of St Mary**, set amid a lovely churchyard filled with trees. The church's round arches and pillars date from the late 12th century, while the chancel with its sedilia, piscina and aumbry is from the 14th century. The altar table is 17th century, while the tower, spire, porch and eight-sided font are from the 20th century.

As well as clay, tarmacadam was also first made here by accident at the start of the 20th century and it revolutionised road building. The history of Tarmac is itself interesting. As if by chance, the county surveyor of Nottingham, Edgar Purnell Hooley, noticed that a barrel of tar had fallen from a dray and burst open. To avoid a nuisance, someone from the ironworks had thoughtfully covered the sticky black mess with waste slag from nearby furnaces - and the world's first tarmacadam surface was born. Hooley noticed that the patch of road which had been unintentionally re-surfaced was dust-free and hadn't been rutted by traffic. So he set to work and by the following year, 1902, Hooley obtained a British patent for a method of mixing slag with tar, naming the material Tarmac.

CODNOR

2 miles SE of Ripley on the A610

The village of Codnor has been a major crossroads for over a thousand years: roads meet on the market place from Ripley, Alfreton, Langley Mill and Heanor. The village itself probably dates back to Saxon times, and is mentioned in the *Domesday Book* of 1086 as Cotenovre. Following the Norman Conquest, the land around Codnor fell under the jurisdiction of William Peveril.

The surrounding fields and woods make it easy to forget the coal and iron which made this part of Derbyshire famous. Once it was a great park of nearly 2,000 acres, the centrepiece being the mighty **Codnor Castle**, the scant ruins of which still stand. The castle itself was a stone 'keep and bailey'

Codnor Castle

fortress, with a three-storey keep and a strong curtain wall and ditch, flanked by round towers. It was the home of the influential de Grey family, the most famous member being Richard de Grey, who was one of Henry III's loyal barons. Edward II visited another Richard de Grey here after fighting the rebels at Burton-on-Trent. All that survives of the castle today is a length of the boundary wall from the upper court, parts of the dividing wall and the defending towers, as well as the odd doorway, window and fireplace.

HEANOR

3 miles SE of Ripley off the A608

Heanor sits across the valley from Eastwood in Nottinghamshire, the town made famous by writer D.H. Lawrence and so is often described in his novels. The River Erewash passes through the area at Langley Mill and visitors are able to enjoy the restored boats, which travel to and from the 200-year-old canal basin.

Heanor's hub is the market place, where the annual fair is held, as well as a twice-weekly market, which takes place on Fridays and Saturdays. To the south of Heanor is the **Shipley Country Park**, on the estate of the now-demolished Shipley Hall. In addition to its magnificent lake, the country park boasts over 600 acres of beautiful countryside, which should keep even the most enthusiastic walker busy. In 2008 Shipley Country Park Visitors Centre went 'green' and is now being powered by the wind after the installation of a wind turbine. Well-known as both an educational and holiday centre, there are facilities for horse riding, cycling and fishing. Near the park is **Shanakiel House**, built in the early 1900s for Dr E.V. Eaves.

This medieval estate was mentioned in the *Domesday Book* and, under the Miller-Mundy family, it became a centre for farming and coal-mining production during the 18th century. Restoration over the years has transformed former railways into wooded paths, reservoirs into peaceful lakes, and has re-established the once-flowering meadows and rolling hills, which had been destroyed by the colliery pits.

The ancient **Parish Church of St Lawrence** dates back to the 12th century, though little of the old church remains after rebuilding in 1868. The 15th-century tower is still intact.

BELPER

Belper is a small, attractive market town eight miles north of Derby. Until Jedediah Strutt came to Belper in 1776, it was a small town well known for producing quality nails that were used throughout the world. If your surname is Naylor then it is most probable that your family originate from Belper. The town grew rapidly at the beginning of the 19th century due to the industrial development of cotton mills. However, the origins of the town go back much further than the Industrial Revolution. It was mentioned in the *Domesday Book* as 'Beau Repaire', the beautiful retreat; in 1964 the remains of a Roman kiln were found here.

Now famous for its cotton mills, the town is situated alongside the **River Derwent** on the floor of the valley. In 1776 Jedediah Strutt, the wheelwright son of a South Normanton farmer, set up one of the earliest water-powered cotton mills here to harness the natural powers of the river. With the river providing power and fuel coming from the nearby South Derbyshire coalfield, the valley has a good claim to be one of the cradles of the Industrial Revolution. Earlier, in 1771, Strutt had gone into profitable partnership with Richard Arkwright to establish the world's first water-powered cotton mill at Cromford. In 1780 another mill was built at Milford. Over a period of almost 30 years, a collection of six mills were built. Great benefactors of the town for 150 years, the Strutt family provided housing, work, education and even food from the model farms they established in the surrounding countryside.

Today only the North and East Mills remain, and the historic **North Mill** on the River Derwent is one of the oldest surviving examples of industrialised water-powered cotton spinning mills in the world. The original North Mill was destroyed in a fire in 1803 and was rebuilt by Strutt's son William, though the new mill was built of iron and bricks so that it was fire proof. The North Mill is open to the public and well worth a visit. The massive **East Mill** was built by the English Sewing Cotton Company in 1912. It

91 THE CROSS KEYS

Belper

This traditional inn is perfect for ale lovers stocking five on rotation, holding regular beer festivals and live music events throughout the year.

See entry on page 201

90 THE RAILWAY TEA ROOMS

Belper

Home-cooked treats for lovers of trains and cakes in the heart of Belper.

See entry on page 201

92 THE TAVERN

Belper

This inn offers a jovial atmosphere for all and specialises in great real ale, showing all the best sporting events throughout the week.

See entry on page 202

East and North Mill, Belper

FARNAH GREEN

1 mile W of Belper on the A517

Farnah Green is a charming hamlet on the outskirts of Belper, near to the village of Hazelwood. It has no shops but has a pleasant old country pub which serves food.

SHOTTLE

2 miles W of Belper off the A517

Shottle is a picturesque hamlet of a few farms, houses, the **Parish Church of St Lawrence**, and a chapel, surrounded by little lanes and footpaths. Unlike most of the nearby villages it appears little changed since the 19th century. Shottle was the birthplace of Samuel Slater, the apprentice to Jedediah Strutt, who left Belper for the USA and built the first water-powered cotton mill there; his original Slater Mill at Pawtucket is now a museum. American President Andrew Jackson called him the 'Father of American Manufactures', and his technological contribution and unique management style made him one of the most successful New England entrepreneurs of his era.

IDRIDGEHAY

10 miles NW of Derby off the B5023

This pleasant village is pronounced 'Ithersee' by the locals and it lies in the valley of the River Ecclesbourne. Formerly a working rural village, it is now purely residential. The area is also part of a conservation scheme including the half-timbered building, **South Sitch**. The date above the door, 1621, may refer to alterations carried out to a much older building. The apparent Elizabethan mansion, **Alton Manor**, was in fact built by Sir George Gilbert Scott in 1846, when he moved from Darley Dale because of the coming of the railway.

Idridgehay's most prominent building is the **Parish Church of St James**, built in the early 1840s and consecrated in 1845. George Turner the Victorian landscape painter from

closed as a mill in the late 20th century and now houses a number of small industrial units, but remains largely empty.

The **Derwent Valley Visitor Centre** tells the story of the cotton industry and the great influence the Strutt family had on the town. It also tells of Samuel Slater, Strutt's apprentice, who emigrated to America in 1789, built a mill, and became the father of the American cotton industry. The centre is housed in the oldest surviving mill, the two-storey North Mill at Bridgefoot, near the magnificent crescent-shaped weir in the Derwent and the town's main bridge.

Less than two minutes stroll away from North Mill are **The River Gardens**, offering a wonderful place for a picnic, somewhere to play or simply a sit-down. Rowing boats can be hired for a trip along the Derwent. The gardens are a favourite with the film industry, having been used in Ken Russell's *Women in Love*, as well as television's *Sounding Brass* and *In the Shadow of the Noose*. The riverside walk through the meadows is particularly rich in bird life.

The **Chapel of St John the Baptist** in The Butts was the chapel of the original village of Belper. It consists of nave and chancel only, and dates from 1250. The **Parish Church of St Peter** with its pinnacled west tower dates from 1824. It contains a monument to George Brettle, who built **George Brettle's Warehouse** in Chapel Street, a distinctive and elegant building in the classical style.

Barrow on Trent is buried here, as is Sir Peter Hilton, a former incumbent of the manor house.

MILFORD

1 mile S of Belper off the A6

Milford was a quiet hamlet until the cotton mills came. The power of the River Derwent brought Jedediah Strutt and Richard Arkwright to Milford, where he built the mill which gave the village its name around 1780. It was only a year later that their partnership dissolved and both industrialists went their separate ways to forge individual empires. The majority of the mill was demolished around the middle of the last century. What does remain of the mill is now filled with a shop and small businesses.

HOLBROOK

2 miles S of Belper off the A6

The Saxon name for Holbrook was Hale Broc meaning 'badger hill'. The ancient Roman Portway (which the Romans surfaced with coal) runs through the village and one of the toll houses for the turnpike road still stands in the village. In the early 1960s two Roman kilns were discovered here. Holbrook was once a busy industrial village well known for

framework knitters, who supplied stockings for royalty. It is now a pleasant place, with some attractive old houses, serving mainly as a commuter area for the nearby towns of Belper and Derby.

The **Parish Church of St Michael** was built in 1761 as a private chapel to Holbrook Hall. It was rebuilt as the parish church in 1841, but still retains the elegant classical lines of its predecessor. Holbrook Hall was built in 1681 although it looks later, it is Grade II* listed and is now a residential home for the elderly.

DUFFIELD

2 miles S of Belper off the A6

This ancient village is a charming place, with Georgian houses and cottages lining the banks of the River Ecclesbourne. For such a cosy place, it seems odd that the **Parish Church of St Alkmund** is situated in isolation down by the river. However, as it stands on the site of a Saxon one, it is thought that the river was used to baptise converts. The saint to whom it is dedicated was a Northumbrian prince who was murdered in AD 800 at nearby Derby by bodyguards supposed to be protecting him. They were sent by King Eardulf, who was trying to claim the Northumbrian throne. Alkmund's sarcophagus is now in a Derby museum.

The church has a 14th-century east tower with a recessed spire. It was much restored in the 19th century. Inside the Church there is an impressive monument dating from 1600, dedicated to Anthony Bradshaw, his two wives and their 20 children. He had 23 children in all, with the 22nd being called 'Penultima'. Bradshaw was a barrister and the deputy steward of Duffield Firth, a former hunting forest between Duffield and Wirksworth. His great nephew went on to officiate over the court, which called for the execution of Charles I.

Located in the centre of Duffield, **Duffield Castle** is an 11th-century stone motte and bailey fortress, founded by Henry de Ferrers, Earl of Derby. In 1886 and 1957, excavations on the large low motte and wide bailey ditch uncovered the foundations of a magnificent

93 ANGELO'S RESTAURANT

Milford

Fine European dining is found at Angelo's, inside the old stone New Inn.

See entry on page 202

94 THE SPOTTED COW

Holbrook

Known best for its delicious, modern English menu and luxury accommodation, this historic alehouse is must for weekends away in Derbyshire.

See entry on page 203

square Norman keep, with a forebuilding and a deep well. Sadly the keep, one of the largest in England, is only five courses of sandstone ashlar high, after being taken and destroyed in 1266 by the Royalist forces of Henry III. The site is owned by The National Trust and is freely accessible in daylight hours, by steep steps from Milford Road.

Duffield Hall is situated at the southern edge of the village. It is an Elizabethan building, enlarged in 1870 and once used as a girls boarding school. It is now the headquarters of the Derbyshire Building Society.

ILKESTON

With a population of just over 37,000, Ilkeston is the third largest town in Derbyshire. It received its royal charter for a market and fair in 1252, and the market and fair continue to flourish to this day. The market place is brought to life every Thursday and Saturday offering an excellent range of goods, from toys, confectionery and greeting cards to electrical goods, books and clothes. The **Charter Fair**, held in October each year, is one of the oldest and largest in Europe and an event not to be missed. The history of the town, however, goes back even further to when it was an Anglo-Saxon hilltop settlement known as Tilchestune.

Once a mining and lace-making centre, a history of the town's industrial past is told in the award-winning **Erewash Museum**, housed in a fine Georgian house with Victorian extensions on the High Street. It was a family home and then part of a school before becoming a Museum in the 1980s. Many original features survive including a restored

Edwardian kitchen and wash house. The garden has unrivalled views across the Erewash Valley. Other fine examples of elegant 18th-century houses can be found in East Street while, in Wharncliffe Road, there are period houses with art nouveau features. Despite the town's industrial outlook, parks, trees and flower beds are a feature of the community and there is some pleasant countryside around the town.

The **Parish Church of St Mary** has undergone many changes since it was first erected in the 12th century. It is particularly notable for its window tracery, especially in the six windows in the older part of the church. A former tower and elegant spire were destroyed by storm in 1714. Only the tower was rebuilt, to be succeeded by another on the old foundations in 1855. This tower was then moved westwards in 1907, at which time the nave was doubled in length. One intriguing feature it has retained throughout all these changes is its 13th-century archway. The organ is also distinguished, in that it originally came from a London church and is known to have been played by the great Mendelssohn himself.

AROUND ILKESTON

MAPPERLEY

2 miles NW of Ilkeston off the A609

Although Mapperley is an agricultural village with half a dozen working farms, any stroll from the village centre will take the walker past industrial remains. To the south of Mapperley is the former branch line of the Midland Railway, which served Mapperley Colliery, as well as the old raised track which is all that remains of an old tramway, and ran from the Blue Fly Shaft of West Hallam Pit to the **Nutbrook Canal** further east. The canal, which opened in 1796, carried coal from the pits at Shipley to the ironworks at Stanton and beyond. Only just over four miles long, the canal had some 13 locks but it fell into disuse after the Second World War and much of it has now been filled in.

95	THE COFFEE HOUSE

Ilkeston

In Ilkeston centre, the perfect place to stop for breakfast, lunch or just a cup of tea.

See entry on page 204

Nutbrook Canal, Mapperley

This historic village was first granted a market charter in 1267 and, though its old church was demolished due to mining subsidence, the modern church has some interesting stained glass windows. Opposite the church are the village stocks.

WEST HALLAM

2 miles W of Ilkeston off the A609

West Hallam stands on a hilltop and its **Parish Church of St Wilfrid**, set between the great expanse of **West Hallam Hall** and the rectory, is approached via a lovely avenue of limes. The church is over 700 years old and has a very handsome tower, with a blue clock with gilt hands and figures. The rector's garden has a glorious lime tree, and looks out over the valley to a great windmill with its arms still working as they have done since Georgian times.

One of the premier attractions in the area, **The Bottle Kiln** is a handsome and impressive brick-built former working pottery, now home to a fine art gallery with a new exhibition every month. Visitors can take a leisurely look at both British studio ceramics and contemporary painting in the European tradition. Two shops filled with jewellery, cards, gifts, objects d'art, soft furnishings and household items with an accent on style, design and originality can also be found here. At the Buttery Café visitors can enjoy a wide choice of freshly-prepared and hearty food, along with a tasty selection of teas, coffees and cakes. All this is in an attractive landscaped setting with a Japanese-style tea garden and a unique

renovated bottle-necked kiln.

West Hallam also has a well-dressing ceremony each year, normally held during the second week of July.

HORSLEY

6 miles W of Ilkeston on the A609

Horsley is a charming little village, complete with traditional village green and spreading chestnut tree. Walking is a popular activity for locals thanks to the beautiful surrounding countryside. Horsley boasts one of the most attractive village churches in the county, sitting on a hill, set amongst flowers and trees. The **Parish Church of St Clement and St James** is a real gem dating back to the 13th century with later additions. It has a broach spire, mid-15th century battlements and a pretty porch with a medieval crucifix. The interior is much restored but there are some scraps of ancient glass in one window.

The village pillar box is one of the most unusual in England, as it is made of stone. The village also has three wells, called Blanche, Sophie and Rosamund. They were given to the village in 1824 by the local vicar, Reverend Sitwell.

There once was a castle, but few traces of it remain today. Horsley Castle, also known as Horston or Horeston Castle, was a Norman earthwork motte and bailey fortress, built in the 12th century with a rectangular great tower which was in ruins from the late 16th century. It was owned by the Crown from 1268 to 1514. The site has a dense cover of trees and is best viewed in winter.

MORLEY

4 miles SW of Ilkeston off the A608

Morley is essentially a rural village with working farms around it. There are four parts to the village: Brackley Gate and the Croft, the Smithy and Brick Kiln Lane, Almshouse Lane and Church Lane.

Brackley Gates has some disused quarries and marvellous views to the north. It is now a wildlife reserve owned by the Derbyshire Wildlife Trust. The Croft has a cluster of 17th- and 18th-century cottages. The 17th-century **Almshouses** in Almshouse Lane were originally provided by Jacinth Sitwell, then Lord of the Manor of Morley for 'six poor, lame or impotent men'.

The **Parish Church of St Matthew** has a Norman nave, with the tower, chancel and north chapel being late 14th/early 15th century. It is perhaps best known for its magnificent stained glass windows dating from medieval times. Originally in the Abbey Refectory at Dale, the windows were acquired by Sir Henry Sacheverell in 1539. There are monuments and brasses to important local families like the Sacheverells and the Sitwells, including one to John Sacheverell, who died at Bosworth Field in 1485, and the beautifully-carved tomb chest of Henry Sacheverell, who died in 1558 and his wife Katherine Babington, who died in 1553.

DALE ABBEY

3 miles SW of Ilkeston off the A6096

The village takes its name from the now-ruined abbey that was founded here by Augustinian monks in the 13th century. Beginning life in a very humble manner, local legend has it that a Derbyshire baker had a vision of the Virgin Mary, which told him to come to Dale Abbey and live the life of a hermit. He accordingly came to the area in 1130, carved himself a niche in the sandstone and devoted himself to the way of the hermit. The owner of the land, Ralph FitzGeremunde, discovered the baker and was so impressed by the man's devotion that he bestowed on him the land and tithe rights to his mill in Borrowash. In about 1200 the Augustinian canons founded **Dale Abbey** on the site, which lasted until the Dissolution of

the monasteries in 1538.

The sandstone cave and the romantic ruined 40-feet-high window archway (all that now remains of the original Dale Abbey) are popular attractions locally and a walk around the village is both an interesting and pleasurable experience. Nearby **Hermit's Wood** is an ancient area of woodland with beech, ash, oak and lime trees. It is wonderful at any time of year, but particularly in the spring when the woodland floor is covered with a carpet of bluebells.

STANLEY

3 miles SW of Ilkeston off the A609

Stanley is a pleasant little rural village, whose main industry was coal mining until the closure of Stanley colliery in 1959. The remains of the pits can still be seen on the outskirts of the village.

Stanley's church, the **Parish Church of St Andrew**, dates originally from the 12th century, though all that remains of this Norman building nowadays is the south door. Some of the buttresses and a small lancet date from the mid-13th century. The font dates back to the 14th century and the pulpit to the 17th century. A brass tablet on the floor by the pulpit is dedicated to Sir John Bentley of Breadsall, who was buried here 20 years before the Civil War.

STANTON BY DALE

2 miles S of Ilkeston off the A6096

The village of Stanton by Dale retains its unspoilt charm and peace and quiet of days gone by, and is mentioned in the *Domesday Book* having derived its name from the nearby stone quarries. The houses in the village are mainly 18th and 19th century brick or stone. The village pump, erected in 1897 to commemorate Queen Victoria's jubilee, had fallen into a sad state of dilapidation. It is now repaired, completely renovated and returned to its original green and gold.

The **Parish Church of St Michael and All Angels** is 13th century in origin but there is a fine modern stained glass window depicting Stanton Ironworks. At the bottom of the path

96 ALL SAINTS CHURCH

Dale Abbey

Little altered since 1650, this fascinating little church has some interesting features and still holds regular services.
See entry on page 204

Middlemore Almshouses, Stanton by Dale

leading to the church, on the right are the **Middlemore Almshouses**; the row is named after Mrs Winifred Middlemore, who gave the four houses nearest the church for occupation by 'eight poor people'.

SANDIACRE

4 miles S of Ilkeston off the B5010

Sandiacre is situated on the border with Nottinghamshire. The name Sandiacre is usually thought to refer to a sandy acre, though another theory is that it is derived from the name of Saint Diacre. Although it has been all-but incorporated into the ever-expanding Nottingham conurbation, it maintains many village features including the picturesque 14th-century **Parish Church of St**

---

97 THE OLD SCHOOLHOUSE DELI

Stanton by Dale

Celebrity cake-maker's own café and deli with some of the finest cakes in the county.

See entry on page 205

---

98 THE SEVEN OAKS INN AND RESTAURANT

Stanton by Dale

This historic public house, with its superb gardens, offers fine food and a succulent Sunday roast.

See entry on page 206

Giles, situated up a narrow lane at the top of a hill. In the churchyard, four stones commemorate the remarkable Charlton family. One was an MP as far back as 1318, Sir Richard was slain on Bosworth Field, Sir Thomas was Speaker in 1453 and Edward was a commissioner in the Civil War.

The Erewash Canal passes through the centre of Sandiacre and situated next to the canal is Springfield Mills, which was built in 1888 and acts as a reminder of Sandiacre's industrial heritage. Examples of lace making, engineering and furniture-making can still be found here today.

RISLEY

4 miles S of Ilkeston on the B5010

Risley consists of no more than a small group of old buildings, but they are unique and well worth a visit. **Risley Hall** is a gorgeous manor house dating back to the 15th century. However, nothing now remains of the original Risley Hall, home of the Willoughbys, except an Elizabethan gateway. The present one

All Saints Church, Risley

dates from the late 17th century.

In 1593, Sir Michael Willoughby started to rebuild the **Parish Church of All Saints**. Although small, even by the standards of the day, it is charming and essentially Gothic in style.

OCKBROOK

4 miles SW of Ilkeston off the A52

This attractive village close to, but hidden from, the busy main road between Derby and

Nottingham, has managed to retain much of its charm and at least a reasonable level of peace and quiet. There is evidence of human activity in Ockbrook as far back as 10,000 BC (the Mesolithic) in the form of two bifacial cores of flint. A small greenstone axe head attests to Neolithic activity. There are two distinct parts to the village. The old part of Ockbrook was established by Occa, an Anglo-Saxon, around the 6th century. Alongside it is the Moravian settlement, a product of the 18th century, with its delightful terrace of red-brick Georgian buildings and handsome **Moravian Chapel**.

This is farming country and many of the ancient hedgerows remain, sustaining all manner of wildlife that has disappeared from many other areas. Several old farm buildings also remain, including an impressive 17th-century timber-framed building at Church Farm. Little but the ground floor however, remains of **Ockbrook Windmill**, one of only 10 windmill sites still existing in Derbyshire.

BORROWASH

6 miles SW of Ilkeston off the A6005

Pronounced 'borrow-ash', this now quiet village has lost its railway station and canal, which was filled in during the early 1960s. However, thanks to the efforts of the Derby and Sandiacre Canal Society, the Derby Canal is currently undergoing restoration. The Borrowash Bottom lock is beginning to look like a canal lock again too.

P H Currey designed the small redbrick **Parish Church of St Stephen** in 1899. The interior features a low, 18th-century ironwork chancel screen, believed to be the work of Robert Bakewell of Derby.

SPONDON

5 miles SW of Ilkeston on the A6096

This village, with its many Georgian brick houses, is now almost engulfed by Derby, but the older parts can still be picked out. The **Parish Church of St Werburgh**, damaged by fire in 1340, was completely rebuilt and has also undergone restoration work in 1826 and again in the 1890s. Nearby is **Locko Park**, the

privately owned ancestral home of the Drury-Lowe family since 1747, when it was purchased from the Gilberts by John Lowe. In 1790 it passed to William Drury, who changed his name to Drury-Lowe. The present hall was built by Francis Smith in the 18th century, and since then it has been given an Italian appearance. Today, the hall houses one of the largest private collections of Italian paintings in Britain. The chapel is earlier than the hall, having been built in 1669. Way back in medieval times a leper hospital stood here, and indeed the word 'Locko' comes from the Old French 'loques', meaning rags.

BREASTON

5 miles S of Ilkeston on the A6005

On the southern borders of the county, close to Nottinghamshire and Leicestershire, Breaston occupies the flat countryside near the point where the River Derwent joins the River Trent. Of particular note in the village is the 13th-century **Parish Church of St Michael**, with its recently-restored soaring spire, spotted for miles around and which tops a short square clock-face tower. This ancient building occupies a peaceful setting and has many treasures from the past that are well worth seeing.

The church also boasts the 'Boy of Breaston' - a small, chubby-faced child, immortalised in the 13th century by the mason of the nave arches. He has smiled down on worshippers and visitors for the past seven centuries. The story has it that this boy would come in and watch the masons at work while the church was being built. The master mason decided to make the child part of the church, so that he could always have a good view of it.

For visitors who chance to be this way Breaston's fine **Millennium Sensory Garden** is worth spending time in, as is the delightful Butterfly Garden.

DRAYCOTT

7 miles S of Ilkeston on the A6005

The uninformed visitor might at first sight be forgiven for believing that this village,

Victoria Mill, Draycott

nestling on the banks of the River Derwent, has little to offer historically and that there is little of interest for the casual visitor, but that's far from being the case. The best-known landmark in Draycott is **Victoria Mill**, built in 1888 and established as one of the most important lace factories in the world. When it was completed in 1907, it was the largest manufacturing mill in Europe. The four-storey building, with its green-capped ornamental clock tower, still dominates the Draycott skyline though it is now the home of an electrical component manufacturer. **Draycott House**, designed by Joseph Pickford, was built in 1781. It remains a private residence.

Draycott also boasts the beautiful St Chad's Water, a 12-acre Nature Reserve sitting peacefully beside St Chad's Church (records of which go back to the 7th century).

ELVASTON

8 miles SW of Ilkeston on the B5010

Elvaston Castle Country Park opened to the public in 1970. It was the first of its kind in Britain and spans more than 200 acres of woodland, parkland and fascinating formal gardens. At the heart of the park is the **Elvaston Castle** which, despite its name, is really a country house. Today, due to its need for restoration, the castle is only occasionally open to the public. The magnificent Gothic castle seen today was designed by James Wyatt and built about 1817 for the 3rd Earl of Harrington. It is now owned by Derbyshire County Council, who are considering turning it into a hotel and golf complex, though

there is a campaign to stop this happening and keep the castle in public hands.

Though the building itself is strikingly handsome, it is, perhaps, the grounds which make Elvaston Castle famous. They were originally laid out and designed for the 4th Earl by William Barron. Barron, who was born in Berwickshire in 1805, started work in 1830 on what, at first, appeared to be an impossible task. The 4th Earl wanted a garden 'second to none', but the land available, which had never been landscaped, was flat, water-logged and uninspiring with just two avenues of trees and a walled kitchen garden (but no greenhouses or hot houses). First draining the land, Barron then planted trees to offer shelter to more tender plants. From there the project grew.

In order to stock the gardens, Barron began a programme of propagation of rarer tree species and, along with the tree-planting methods he developed specially to deal with Elvaston's problems, his fame spread. The gardens became a showcase of rare and interesting trees, many to be found nowhere else in Britain. Barron continued to work for the 5th Earl, but resigned in 1865 to live in nearby Borrowash and set up his own nursery.

As well as fine formal gardens and the walled kitchen garden, there are gentle woodland walks and, of course, the man-made lake. However, no visit to Elvaston would be complete without a walk down to the **Golden Gates**. Erected in 1819 at the southern end of the formal gardens, the gates were brought from the Palace of Versailles by the 3rd Earl of Harrington. Little is known of the gates' history, but they remain a fine

Elvaston Castle

118

monument and are the symbol of Elvaston. Around the courtyard of the castle can be found a restaurant as well as an information centre and well-stocked gift shop. All manner of activities take place from the castle, which can provide details. Elvaston Country Park is at present open to the public from dawn to dusk. Admission is free though a small car parking fee applies.

SHARDLOW

9 miles SW of Ilkeston off the A6

Shardlow is located just within the Derbyshire border. There was a settlement here at the time of the *Domesday Book*, when the area belonged to the Abbey of Chester and the village was known as Serdelov. Shardlow was once an important port on the River Trent and a horse-drawn ferry was used to cross the river. This was replaced in 1760 by a toll bridge and the stone giving the toll charges can still be seen on the roadside approaching the modern Cavendish Bridge. This replaced the old bridge, which collapsed in 1947.

After 1777, when the **Trent and Mersey Canal** was opened, Shardlow became a canal port, one of only a few in the country. With

Canal Moorings, Shardlow

---

99 **THE OLD CROWN INN**

Shardlow

Whether you want fine ales or fine food, find the Old Crown in Cavendish Bridge and you'll find the best of both.

See entry on page 205

Liverpool, Hull and Bristol now linked by water, the warehouses here were quickly filled with heavy goods of all descriptions that could be carried at half the cost of road transport and with greater safety. Many of the homes of the canal carriers and their warehouses survive to this day and the port is now a modern marina, linked to the River Trent, and filled with all manner of pleasure barges.

Many of the old cottages in Shardlow were swept away by 1960s development but some were saved when much of the canalside was designated a conservation area in 1978. There are still some fine houses remaining that were built by the wealthy canal merchants. **Broughton House**, built in the early part of the 19th century is just one example. The **Shardlow Heritage Centre** is housed in the earliest of the old canal warehouses, the Old Salt Warehouse, and has exhibitions and displays about Shardlow's heyday as a canal port. The outstanding **Shardlow Marina** covers 46 acres, of which the Marina itself is 12 acres, all set in beautiful rolling countryside. The marina has moorings for up to 365 boats, with berths available for up to 70-feet narrow and wide-beam boats.

The **Parish Church of St James**, though it looks much older, dates only from 1838 and sits on land given to the village by the Sutton Family of Shardlow Hall.

ASTON-ON-TRENT

9 miles S of Ilkeston off the A50

It won't come as a suprise to learn that Aston-on-Trent stands on the River Trent, marking the border between Derbyshire and Leicestershire. Aston's **Parish Church of All Saints** is mainly Norman, though there is plenty of evidence of Saxon masonry, notably in the northeast corner of the nave. There is an octagonal font dating from the 13th century inside the church, and a moving, early 15th century alabaster tomb chest of a husband and wife holding hands, she with a small dog at her feet.

Aston Hall dates from 1753; much enlarged over the centuries, it was originally a fine Georgian mansion with no fewer than five bays and central Venetian windows. Ashton Lodge stands close to the heart of the village and was once the home of the Bowden family, who were lace makers. The main part of the house was dismantled and transported to the United States, while the rest was converted into flats.

CASTLE DONINGTON

10 miles S of Ilkeston off the A50

Castle Donington (pronounced Dunington) is just over the Leicestershire border on a hill above the Trent River. As the name suggests, there was once a Castle in the area. It was built in the 11th or 12th century, demolished in 1216, rebuilt later that century and was finally demolished in 1595. All that is left of the castle now is a mound in the actual location.

Today the village is a pleasant blend of the old and new, with modern shops standing alongside dignified Georgian and Regency houses. Several timber-framed houses dating from the 17th century and earlier survive along the main road. The oldest part of the **Parish Church of St Edward, King and Martyr**, dates back to 1200 but it was probably built on the site of an older Saxon church. The spire, rising to a height of 160

feet, is a landmark for miles around.

Donington Hall with its park was the home of members of the Hastings family from 1595 until the death of Lord Donington in 1895. The old hall was replaced by the present building in 1793 by Earl Moira, later 1st Marquis Hastings. The Hall is of the 'Strawberry Hill Gothic' style, first made fashionable by Walpole. The hall and park were developed between the wars into what would today be known as a Country Club with accommodation, golf, boating and other amusements, the most notable of which was the racetrack, which developed from humble beginnings using the park driveways to a Grand Prix circuit. Today the racetrack is open again and it is possible to see something of its pre-war glories in the **Donington Park Museum**. Vehicles on show include Ascari's Ferrari, Jim Clark's Lotus 23 and Nigel Mansell's Williams. The Hall is now the headquarters of British Midland Airways who have carefully restored it to much of its former glory. The medieval Deer Park survives and is designated a Site of Special Scientific Interest.

Close to the village stands **Nottingham East Midlands Airport**, originally a Royal Air Force base. It was purchased in the 1960s and soon became the main airport for the nearby conurbations of Derby, Nottingham and Leicester.

LONG EATON

7 miles SE of Ilkeston off the A52

Long Eaton, straddling the Derbyshire and Nottinghamshire border, has a history that goes back earlier than the 7th century. Lying close by the River Trent, the name came from the Anglo-Saxon 'Aitone' meaning town by the water. Visited by the Romans and settled by the Danes, the medieval village remained undisturbed for centuries. A national census of 1801 recorded that only 504 people lived here.

The **Parish Church of St Lawrence**, according to local legend, dates from the time of King Canute, though it is more likely to be Norman in origin. At one time it was only a 'chapel of ease' for the main parish

---

100 THE CROSS KEYS

Castle Donington

A friendly village pub close to Donington Park Racetrack and East Midlands Airport, and noted for its real ales, filling snacks, and welcoming atmosphere.

See entry on page 207

---

101 THE JOLLY SAILOR

Hemington

For lovers of real ale and good food alike, tucked away in a pretty little village near the Nottinghamshire border.

See entry on page 208

Trent Lock, nr Long Eaton

church in Sawley, but in 1868, when the church was largely rebuilt, it became a parish church in its own right.

It was not until the Industrial Revolution and the 19th century that Long Eaton awoke from its long slumbers to become a centre for quarrying, lace making and other industries, all boosted by the coming of railways and canals. The arrival of the railway in 1847 triggered the expansion, and the hosiery and lace-making factories, escaping the restrictive practices in nearby Nottingham, brought employment for many and wealth for some. By the 1870s the population was recorded at over 3,000, doubling over the following 10 years. In 1915 construction began on the National Shell Filling Factory, just over a mile away from Long Eaton's ancient market place. A staggering 19 million large shells were filled to aid the war effort, and it was not until there had been 19 explosions at the plant, the worst with a death toll of 140, that the operation ceased.

The lace industry, forever associated with this area, gave way to furniture, narrow fabrics and electrical wiring manufacture, which reflected the interests and activities of a stream of entrepreneurs drawn to the town. The most famous of these men was Ernest Tehra Hooley – lace maker, property dealer, builder, benefactor and company director. Hooley was responsible for the flotation of such well-known names as Dunlop, Raleigh, Humber and Bovril before he went bankrupt.

Trent Lock, an easy stroll from the town, is a centre for sailing and boating and there are plenty of other sporting facilities available.

SAWLEY

8 miles SE of Ilkeston off the B6540

Up until the 19th century, Sawley was the most important village in the area, an extensive ecclesiastical parish which included Breaston, Draycott, Hopwell, Long Eaton, Risley, Wilne and Wilsthorpe. The old English name for Sawley village was Sallé, meaning 'hill where willow trees grow' and the early development of the village was due to its command of a river crossing.

Over 1,000 years ago a small collective of monks boated down the Trent from Repton to the green meadows of Sawley, where they built the **Parish Church of All Saints**. Much of the church we see today is 14th century, with a 15th-century tower and spire and much 15th-century timbering. The chancel arch is Saxon. The interior boasts an impressive group of monuments, a 600-year-old font, a 500-year-old screen, a Jacobean pulpit and a 17th-century altar table.

In the late 15th century the Bothes (or Booths) settled at Sawley in a house of which some of the timbers remain in the cellars of **Bothe Hall**, near the church. Sawley's most noted son was John Clifford. Born here in 1836, he became one of the most powerful voices of nonconformity, known as 'the greatest Free Churchman of his day'.

Sawley Marina, with over 600 moorings, has been described as the 'most sophisticated' marina on the inland waterways network, sitting as it does at the junction of four cruising routes. You can cruise from here all the way to the North Sea.

For the canal enthusiast, the Trent and Mersey Canal starts just two miles from Sawley, near the historic canal village of Shardlow. Less well known, but some argue the better for it, is the quiet and intriguing Erewash Canal, providing a mixed cruising experience for those who love industrial heritage and exploring the 'out of the way'.

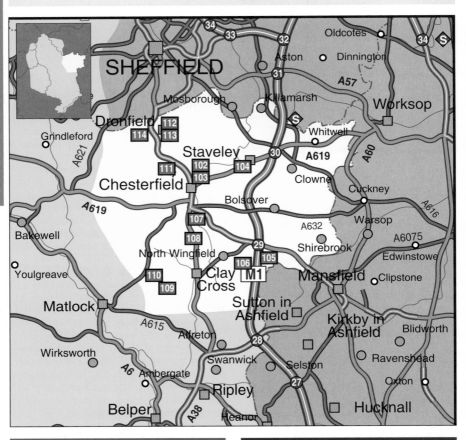

Accommodation

111 The Peacock Inn, Cutthorpe,
     Chesterfield   *pg 136, 215*
113 The Manor House, Dronfield   *pg 137, 217*

Food & Drink

102 Cock & Magpie, Old Whittington,
     Chesterfield   *pg 125, 209*
103 The White Horse, Old Whittington,
     Chesterfield   *pg 125, 210*
104 The Victoria Inn, Staveley, Chesterfield   *pg 127, 211*
105 The Hardwick Inn, Hardwick Park,
     Chesterfield   *pg 130, 212*

Food & Drink

106 The Famous Shoulder, Hardstoft,
     Chesterfield   *pg 131, 213*
107 Telmere Lodge, Hasland, Chesterfield   *pg 132, 214*
108 The Barley Mow Inn, Wingerworth,
     Chesterfield   *pg 132, 213*
109 The White Horse, Woolley Moor,
     Alfreton   *pg 134, 215*
110 Kelstedge Inn, Kelstedge, Ashover   *pg 134, 216*
111 The Peacock Inn, Cutthorpe,
     Chesterfield   *pg 136, 215*
112 Coffee Central, Dronfield   *pg 137, 217*
113 The Manor House, Dronfield   *pg 137, 217*
114 The Miners Arms, Dronfield Woodhouse   *pg 137, 218*

DERBYSHIRE COALMINES

Ashover Show

A landscape of rolling hills, meadows and moorland, rippling river valleys and sleepy villages, North East Derbyshire is a varied area that's still surprisingly unspoilt. While the urban crowds escape en masse to the Peak District and the Derbyshire Dales, the north eastern corner of the county centred on the coal mining town of Chesterfield, remains a largely undiscovered jewel - boasting some of Derbyshire's best views within easy reach of the M1 motorway.

The clangs of pick and shovel have echoed down through the centuries, as this was heart of the county's coal mining area, and many of the towns and villages reflect the prosperity the mines brought in Victorian times. It was George Stephenson, a pioneering railway engineer, who discovered the important coal reserves under the hamlet of Clay Cross during the building of the North Midlands Railway between Derby and Chesterfield in the early 1840s. Sadly, the traditional industries have waned in recent years and an era finally came to an end with the closure of the last colliery at Renishaw in 1989.

Despite the fact that many of the places in and around Chesterfield only date from the Industrial Revolution, the area is rich in history. From medieval times this has been an area of trade, and the weekly markets were an important part of the local economy. Though some have been lost over the years, most of these traditional centres and meeting-places remain.

There are also many new and interesting sights and attractions to discover, as well as many superb walks and specially designed trails throughout the area. But there's nothing like a carnival and, between Spring and Autumn, most villages in the area have either a carnival, gala or fair – Barlow, Dronfield, Grassmoor and Wingerworth, to name but a few. For a real country experience, the Ashover Show is held every August and is a great day out for all the family.

The ancient custom of well-dressing is just as popular and well-executed here as elsewhere in the county, plus there are curiosities such as a castle that isn't a castle despite its battlements, a church clock that has sixty-three minutes in an hour and an Italian-style garden in the grounds owned by a famous English family. The area boasts several exceptional Norman churches, most notably at Steetley (near Creswell) and Ault Hucknall.

CHESTERFIELD

Situated just three miles from the eastern boundary of the Peak District National Park, Chesterfield is a medieval market town with a history and treasures of its own. It is Derbyshire's largest town (Derby itself being a city), although the county town of Derbyshire is Matlock in the Derbyshire Dales. The *Domesday Book* calls the town 'Cestrefeld', meaning 'open field', which points towards its success as a market town. The market, established over 800 years ago and claiming to be England's largest outdoor market, still remains a bustling area of the town itself, running on a Monday, Friday and Saturday, with an antique/bric-a-brac market on Thursday. More than 250 stalls crowd into the town centre, enabling the visitor to purchase almost anything.

The town centre has been conserved for future generations by a far-sighted council, and many buildings have been saved, including the Victorian **Market Hall** built in 1857. The traditional cobbled paving was restored in the Market Place, and New Square was given a complete facelift. It's worth taking a walk down the narrow streets off the Market Place into the **Shambles**, an area of old, narrow streets featuring the Royal Oak, one of Chesterfield's oldest public houses, first mentioned as an inn in 1722 formerly being a rest house for the Knights Templar band of Crusaders.

Visitors to the town are drawn to a peculiarly graceful spire on top of the **Parish Church of St Mary and All Saints**. Twisting and leaning, it is totally confusing to the eye, and gives Chesterfield its identity. Built, along with much of the rest of the church, in the 14th century, it was straight for several centuries before it began to twist. Its 228-foot spire stands on the skyline like a question mark: how did it happen? Superstition surrounds it and, sadly, the real story of its unusual appearance has been lost over the years. The truth probably lies in the wake of the Black Death during the 14th century when many fell to the plague and, among them, skilled craftsmen who knew how to correctly cross-brace and season wood. However, legends say a magician persuaded the Bolsover blacksmith to shoe the Devil. Shaking with fear, he drove a nail into the Devil's foot. Howling in pain, the Devil took flight towards Chesterfield. Skimming over the church he lashed out in agony, caught the spire and twisted it out of shape. It now leans over 9 feet to the south, twisting 45 degrees from its true centre and is still moving. It is eight-sided, but the herringbone pattern of the lead slates trick the eye into seeing 16 sides from the ground. The spire is open for guided tours throughout the day; the church, the largest in Derbyshire, is open all year, Monday to Saturday 9am to 5pm (9am to 3pm January and February), and Sundays at service times only.

The church itself is also impressive since it is the largest in Derbyshire and has seen Civil War, fire, revolution and World Wars, but it still survives as a symbol of Chesterfield.

Opposite the church is **Chesterfield Museum and Art Gallery**. The museum is home to exhibitions depicting the story of the town, from the arrival of the Romans to the first days of the market town, the industry of the 18th century and the coming of the 'father of the railways', George Stephenson. Take a look round the Art Gallery as well, where the works of local artist, Joseph Syddall, are on show (Syddall lived at nearby Whittington).

Perhaps surprisingly, Chesterfield is home to one of the earliest canals in the country, the **Chesterfield Canal**. The canal was surveyed by James Brindley and linked the town to the River Trent. At the cutting edge of technology in its day, it had the longest tunnel in the country at Norwood, and one of the first multiple staircase lock flights. It was 2,884 yards long, 9 feet 3 inches wide and 12 feet high. The entire canal was officially opened in 1777.

All the working boats on the Chesterfield Canal were horse-drawn until, by 1962, virtually all the boat traffic had gone. The whole length of the canal is in the process of restoration and is open to walkers and, though some sections border onto busy roads,

Chesterfield Canal

much of the waterway runs through quiet and secluded countryside. The Chesterfield Canal Trust runs boat trips on the canal, and one of their two boats has wheelchair access.

Apart from the famous Crooked Spire and medieval market, Chesterfield is also worthy of note for Queen's Park, the Tapton Lock Visitor Centre (where you can go for a ride on a narrow boat), the Pomegrante Theatre, the Winding Wheel Concert and Exhibition Centre and The Revolution House (see Whittington). The fine **Queen's Park** has delighted locals and visitors alike since it was opened to celebrate Queen Victoria's Golden Jubilee, in 1893. There are gardens, a boating lake, children's play area, Victorian Bandstand and occasionally it is used for county cricket. The Pomegranate is a Grade II listed Victorian 546-seater proscenium arch theatre offering a wide range of professional touring and local amateur productions. The Winding Wheel is a Grade II listed building situated on the edge of the town centre; a former cinema, it was restored in the late 1980s by Chesterfield Borough Council to provide a much-needed multi-purpose venue. The venue plays host to many of Chesterfield's popular exhibitions and shows, such as the annual fashion show put together by students from Chesterfield College. To find out more about the attractions in and around Chesterfield, the Tourist Information Centre can be found in a new building, beside the church in Rykneld Way. It is open all year, Monday to Saturday.

Finally, although the custom of tap-dressing took place in Chesterfield in the 19th century, it was not until 1991 that the tradition, this time of well-dressing, was revived. Initially with help from local

experts from Holymoorside, the Chesterfield dressers are developing their own styles and customs.

AROUND CHESTERFIELD

SHEEPBRIDGE

3 miles N of Chesterfield off the A61

Dunstan Hall, below Newbold Moor, was built in the 17th century and extended in the 18th century. In an excellent parkland setting, the Gothic-style park railings mirror the Gothic Revival details that were added to the hall in 1826.

WHITTINGTON

3 miles NE of Chesterfield off the B6052/A61

This village changed the face of English history. Travel back to the late 17th century, when James II is on the throne but there is unrest throughout England. It was here in Whittington in 1688 that three local noblemen - the Earl of Devonshire, the Earl of Danby and John D'Arcy - met to plan the downfall of James II in favour of his daughter Mary and her husband, William of Orange. As planned, the North and Midlands rose in

102 COCK AND MAGPIE

Old Whittington

This Georgian, family-run pub is popular with locals and visitors for its wide selection of delicious, home cooked dishes.

See entry on page 209

103 THE WHITE HORSE

Old Whittington

Traditional British pub with real ales but with an unusual international flavour to their menus, from Portugal, Spain and South Africa.

See entry on page 210

support and James fled to France. The Glorious Revolution was over.

More specifically, the men met in an alehouse called the 'Cock and Pynot' ('pynot' being the local dialect word for magpie) and on the 250th anniversary of the Glorious Revolution this modest house was turned into a museum, and named **Revolution House**. The national importance of the 16th-century former 'Cock & Pynot Inn' is signified by its designation by English Heritage as a Grade I listed building. Both the 100th and the 200th anniversaries of the revolution were keenly celebrated here.

Revolution House is now open to the public and features period furnishings and a changing programme of exhibitions on local themes. A video relates the story of the revolution and the role which the house played in those fraught and dangerous days.

ECKINGTON

6 miles NE of Chesterfield off the A616

This large, sprawling village built of local Derbyshire stone lies close to the Yorkshire county border. The name Eckington is of Saxon origin, meaning the township of Ecca. Eckington was once an agricultural settlement but, as a result of coal beneath and around it, it was transformed into a village dependent on the collieries. Since the decline of coal mining in the late 20th century, several light industries have become established and much farmland has been lost.

The village has a fascinating church, the **Parish Church of St Peter and St Paul**, which dates from 1100 and still retains the original Norman doorway. In a field at the back of the church, near the river, stands the Priest's Well where the parish priest used to draw water, as did the travelling people who used the field as a camp until the 1930s.

D.H. Lawrence is said to have used the village of Eckington and Renishaw Hall as inspiration for his most famous novel *Lady Chatterley's Lover*.

The area to the west of Eckington, once known for its sickle and scythe industry, is today a sanctuary for wildlife. A two-mile circular walk, 'Old Eckington Explored',

highlights the history of this delightful Derbyshire town. Other circular walks of varying length take in all aspects of the Moss Valley.

RENISHAW

6 miles NE of Chesterfield off the A616

Renishaw is a large industrial village, whose industry long pre-dates the Industrial RevolutionL the Sitwell family founded an ironworks here in about 1640. To the east lies **Renishaw Hall and Gardens**, overlooking the pleasantly situated Renishaw Park Golf Club. Renishaw Hall was for four centuries the home of the idiosyncratic Sitwells and famed for the unmatchable four-acre Italianate garden laid out by the eccentric Sir George Sitwell. The Sitwell family and, in particular, Dame Edith, Sir Sacheverell and Sir Osbert, have over the years become one of the most famous literary families in England.

The Hall is also said to be haunted by a number of ghosts. In particular there is the little boy in pink, known as the Kissing Ghost because this is just what he likes to do to any guests at the Hall. The grounds of the village rectory, a handsome late-Georgian building, are also worth seeing. Though not laid out by the Reverend Christopher Alderson, he set about improving them in the late 18th century. A magazine of the time said that the Reverend 'was so renowned as a garden improver that he was employed at Windsor as well'. Renishaw Hall is open to the public from April to September.

Renishaw village also marked the end of an era for the traditional industries of the area,

Renishaw Hall & Gardens

when the last colliery closed here in 1989.

STAVELEY

4 miles NE of Chesterfield off the A619

Staveley lies to the south of the great **Staveley Iron Works** and has its fair share of large 20th-century housing estates. However, this is not altogether a modern village and has some fine earlier structures, including the **Parish Church of St John the Baptist**, dating originally from the 13th century. In the north aisle is a rare example of a medieval Easter Sepulchre. The name of Frecheville is one that crops up from time to time in this part of Derbyshire, and the church has a selection of tombs and monuments to the family. As well as the tomb-chest of Peter Frecheville, dating from around 1480, there is also an early 16th-century monument to Piers Frecheville. In the Frecheville Chapel is a memorial to Christina Frecheville, who died in childbirth in 1653. Another fine building in the village is **Staveley Hall**, built in 1604 and now the District Council Offices.

BARLBOROUGH

7 miles NE of Chesterfield off the A619

Lying close to the county borders with both Nottinghamshire and Yorkshire, this village still retains its manor house. Lying just north of the village centre, **Barlborough Hall** (now a school) was built in 1584 by Lord Justice Francis Rodes to plans drawn up by the designer of Hardwick Hall, Robert Smythson. Those who visit both houses will notice the strong resemblance. As well as building houses, Rodes was also one of the judges at the trial of Mary, Queen of Scots. The Hall is supposed to be haunted by a grey lady, said

to be the ghost of a bride who received the news of her groom's death as she was on her way to the village church. Barlborough Hall should not be confused with **Barlborough Old Hall**: this is an easy mistake to make as Barlborough Old Hall is actually the younger of the two! Built in 1618, as the date stone over the front door states, the Old Hall is of a large H-plan design and has mullioned windows. Today it is a private residence.

Although there is a lot of new development, particularly around Barlborough Links, the village also boasts some fine old stone houses with pantile roofs. The **Parish Church of St James** dates from the beginning of the 13th century, though it was heavily restored in 1899. Among the medieval work extant is the four-bay north arcade. The church contains the effigy of a grieving woman, said to be Lady Furnival, who died in 1395. The monument was probably brought here from Worksop, where she is buried.

The **Market Cross**, which stands in the High Street, bears testimony to the fact that this was an important place at one time - a centre of trade for the surrounding area.

CLOWNE

7½ miles NE of Chesterfield off the A616

The village derives is name from 'Clun', a Celtic river name. This small village started off as an ancient settlement but grew up around the county's coal mining industry. The **Parish Church of St John the Baptist** in Clowne is nearly a mile away from the centre and one explanation for its location is that the church stands close to an ancient ridgeway, once the site of a monastery. The church is believed to have been built in 1130, with the two side chapels not added until 1955, one of them dedicated to the memory of those lives lost in the Creswell Colliery disaster and in other coal mines (see also Creswell). The village is now mainly residential, but retains its own identity and sense of community. It is well-known locally for its dazzling Christmas lights display.

Clowne is only a few minutes away from Creswell Crags, the UK's only verified example of Palaeolithic cave art.

104 THE VICTORIA INN

Staveley

A traditional local pub with good beer and a warm welcome from the friendly family hosts.

See entry on page 211

CRESWELL

9 miles E of Chesterfield on the A616

Once a sleepy hamlet nestling amid peaceful farming country, the character of Creswell was irreversibly changed at the end of the 19th century. It was then that Creswell Colliery was opened, and now the village is one of the biggest in the county. There is also a village within a village here as, between 1896 and 1900, a model village of houses and cottages was built around an open space called Creswell Green, part of which is now known as Fox Green. The **Model Village** was built by the Bolsover and Creswell Colliery Company in 1896 to house the workforce at the Creswell Colliery, and everybody who lived on the Model worked in the coal mine. It remained as housing for miners until the mid-1980s when they were let on the open market. The houses were neglected, repairs were not done and the area became run down. Now with the help of a lottery grant, the central park has been almost restored to its original Victorian state with newly planted trees and shrubs, seating and play areas. The restored Model Village is an excellent example of Victorian social housing for

working families.

Lying close to the Derbyshire-Nottinghamshire border, the limestone gorge of the **Creswell Crags** is well worth seeing. Here are caves, some of the oldest once-inhabited caves in the world, certainly the furthest north that have been discovered. Used by Neanderthal man as shelters while out hunting, tours can be taken from the visitor centre, where there is also a display of artefacts found in the area. The largest cavern, Church Hole Cave, extends some 170 feet into the side of the gorge; it was here that hand tools were found. An impressive new Visitor Centre was opened in 2009 by TV presenter David Attenborough, and this was followed by a new museum, creating the UK's first National Center for the Ice Age in this important spot.

WHALEY

8 miles E of Chesterfield off the A632

The **Whaley Thorns Heritage Centre**, situated in a disused school, tells the story of human activity in the area from the Stone Age to the present day. In particular there are displays illustrating the history of coal mining in this region of Derbyshire and, since the decline of the industry, the efforts that have been made to restore the area to its natural state.

BOLSOVER

7 miles E of Chesterfield off the A632

The approach to Bolsover from the north and east is surrounded by some splendid dramatic scenery, and the town has a significant amount of historical importance, with the main tourist attraction being **Bolsover Castle**. A castle has stood here since the 12th century, though the present building is a fairytale 'folly' built for Sir Charles Cavendish during the early 1600s on the site of a ruined castle. By the mid-18th century much of the building had been reduced to the ruins seen today, though thankfully the splendid keep has withstood the test of time.

Pevsner remarked that not many large houses in England occupy such an impressive

Cresswell Crags

Bolsover Castle

position as Bolsover Castle, as it stands on the brow of a hill overlooking the valley of the River Rother and Doe Lea. The first castle at Bolsover was built by William Peveril, illegitimate son of William the Conqueror, as part of his vast Derbyshire estates. Nothing remains of that Norman building. Now owned by English Heritage, visitors can explore the Little Castle, or Keep, which is decorated in an elaborate Jacobean celebration with wonderful fireplaces, panelling and wall paintings. The series of remarkable rooms includes the Vaulted Hall, the Pillar Room, the Star Chamber, the Elysium and the Heaven Room. Sir Charles' son, William, was responsible for the eastern range of buildings known as the Riding School, an impressive indoor area built in the 17th century, and the roofless but still impressive western terrace. The ruins of the state apartments are also here to be discovered. The whole building later descended to the Dukes of Portland, and it remains a strangely impressive place. However it is threatened by its industrial surroundings. The legacy of centuries of coal mining beneath its walls is subsidence. Bolsover Castle regularly hosts historic and cultural events throughout the year and the site is ideal for family picnics.

One building in Derbyshire no longer in need of restoration is Bolsover's Cundy House. It's recently been restored using money from English Heritage and is open for visitors at any reasonable time of day. Hundreds of years ago, Cundy House was built to provide water for Bolsover Castle.

Naturally, the **Parish Church of St Mary's** in Bolsover holds many monuments to the

Cavendish family, but it seems amazing that the church has survived when its recent history is revealed. Dating from the 13th century, the church's monuments include two magnificent tombs: one to Charles Cavendish, who died in 1617, and the second to Henry Cavendish, who died in 1727. Destroyed by fire in 1897, except for the Cavendish Chapel, St Mary's was rebuilt, only to be damaged again by fire in 1960. It has since been restored. Buried in the churchyard are John Smythson and Huntingdon Smythson, the 17th-century architects probably responsible for the design of the rebuilt Bolsover Castle.

SCARCLIFFE

8 miles E of Chesterfield off the B6417

Scarcliffe, recorded as Scardeclif in the *Domesday Book*, takes its name from the escarpment of magnesium limestone on which the village stands. It was settled in Roman times, evidenced by the collection of Roman coins found near the village in 1876. The skyline of this tiny village is dominated by the **Parish Church of St Leonard**. This Norman church contains a magnificent monument of a woman holding a child in her arms, which roughly dates from the 12th or 13th century. The effigy is probably that of Constantia de Frecheville, who died in 1175 and is known in Scarcliffe as Lady Constantia. A bell is tolled here in her memory around Christmas time. During the industrial revolution, coal mining was the main industry and the Lancashire, Derbyshire and East Coast Railway cut through the previously agricultural land. It included a tunnel between Scarcliffe and Bolsover. The

Poulter Country Park, Scarcliffe

Langwith Colliery closed in 1978 and the railway has long gone.

Poulter Country Park, created from the old colliery spoil heaps, provides scenic walks with excellent views of the surrounding countryside. Also to the east of the village are two large wooded areas, Langwith Wood and Roseland Wood.

HEATH

5 miles SE of Chesterfield off the A617

In the Domesday Book of 1086, two settlements are recorded around the present location of the village of Heath; they were called 'Lunt' and 'Le Hethe'. The two villages probably combined during the 12/13th centuries. However, relatively little change has taken place since then, and maps from as long ago as 1609 show the village in almost its present layout.

There many places of interest close to Heath, including to the north the ruins of what was one of the grandest mansions in Derbyshire, **Sutton Scarsdale Hall**. Built in 1724 for the 4th Earl of Scarsdale, to the designs of Francis Smith, the stonework of the previous Tudor manor house was completely hidden behind the Baroque splendour of the new hall. At the beginning of the 20th century Sutton Scarsdale was owned by a descendent of Sir Richard Arkwright, the famous industrialist. It is this gentleman that D.H. Lawrence is supposed to have chosen as the inspiration for his character of Sir Clifford Chatterley in the controversial novel *Lady Chatterley's Lover*. The hall is said to have many ghosts.

Stainsby Mill is also a short distance away, as is Hardwick Hall. With its machinery now restored to illustrate the workings of a 19th-century water-powered corn mill, Stainsby Mill is well worth a visit. Open between March and 21st December, however the particular days vary, please check opening times. Details can be found online at www.nationaltrust.org.uk.

AULT HUCKNALL

6 miles SE of Chesterfield off the A617

Known locally as the 'smallest village in England', a claim which can't be proved, Ault Hucknall was much larger in the Middle Ages than it is today. Its most significant building is the magnificent Tudor house, **Hardwick Hall**. 'More glass than wall', it is one of Derbyshire's Big Three stately homes alongside Chatsworth and Haddon, all three glorious monuments to the great land-owning families who played so great a role in shaping the history of the county. Set in rolling parkland, the house, with its glittering tiers of windows and crowned turrets, offers quite a spellbinding sight. Inside, the silence of the chambers strewn with rush matting, combined with the simplicity of the white-washed walls, gives a feeling of almost overwhelming peace. The letters E S can be seen carved in stone on the outside of the house: E S, or Elizabeth of Shrewsbury, was perhaps better known as Bess of Hardwick. This larger-than-life figure had attachments with many places in Derbyshire, and the story of her life makes fascinating reading.

She was born in the manor house at Hardwick in 1520. The house stood only a little distance from the present-day hall and was then not much more than a farmhouse.

---

105 THE HARDWICK INN

Hardwick Park

Ancient inn serving some of the best food and drink in Derbyshire, with outstanding gardens too.

See entry on page 212

Sutton Scarsdale Hall, Heath

Hardwick Hall, Ault Hucknall

The young Bess married her neighbour's son, Robert Barlow, when she was only 12. When her young husband, himself only 14, died a few months later she naturally inherited a great deal of property. Some 15 years later she married Sir William Cavendish and, when he died in 1557, she was bequeathed his entire fortune. By this time she was the richest woman in England, save for one: Queen Elizabeth I.

The Gallery at Hardwick Hall, with its gorgeous lavender-hued tapestries, has, in pride of place, a portrait of this formidable woman. It depicts a personage who could be mistaken for Queen Elizabeth, and indeed they were both forceful, independently-minded women. Bess began the building of the house in 1590, towards the end of her life and after her fourth lucrative marriage to George Talbot, sixth Earl of Shrewsbury. It stands as a monument to her wealth and good taste, and is justly famous for its magnificent needlework and tapestries, carved fireplaces and friezes, which are considered among the finest in Britain. She died in 1608, and now lies within Derby Cathedral.

Though Bess is the first person that springs to mind with regard to Hardwick Hall, it was the 6th Duke of Devonshire who was responsible for the hall's antiquarian atmosphere. He inherited the property in 1811 and, as well as promoting the legend that Mary, Queen of Scots stayed here, he filled the house with furniture, paintings and tapestries from his other houses and from Chatsworth in particular.

As well as viewing the hall, there are some wonderful grounds to explore. To the south are the formal gardens, laid out in the 19th century and separated by long walks lined with yew. One area has been planted as a Tudor herb garden and is stocked with both culinary and medicinal plants used at that time. Down in the southeast corner of the garden is the small Elizabethan banqueting hall, used as a smoking room by the 6th Duke's orchestra, as they were not allowed to smoke in the hall itself. There is also, to the back of the house, a lake and lime avenue. Owned by the National Trust, Hardwick Hall is a must for any visitor to Derbyshire . The parkland, which overlooks the valley of the Doe Lea as well as the M1, is home to an impressive herd of Longhorn cattle among the stag-headed oaks. The ruins of Hardwick Old Hall (English Heritage) also stand in the grounds, and are the remains of Bess's former Tudor mansion.

Another interesting building here is the **Parish Church of St John the Baptist**, which is Grade I listed and dates back to Saxon times. The yew tree in the churchyard is variously aged between 2,000 and 4,000 years old but, again, this can't be proved. Overlooking Hardwick Hall's beautiful parklands, with the square towers of Bess of Hardwick's great house in the distance, the battlemented church exterior does not prepare visitors for its dark, mysterious interior, which reveals the church's much earlier origins. Though dating originally from Saxon times, there are many Norman features, including the north arcade, nave and the narrow arches holding up the rare crossing tower. There is more Norman work in the plain capitals of the north arcade.

There are several interesting tombs in the church, such as the large and detailed wall monument just below the east window to the first Countess of Devonshire, dating from 1627. On the floor in front is a simple black slab commemorating the influential and renowned philosopher, Thomas Hobbes - author of *The Leviathan* and *De Mirabilibus Pecci: Concerning the Wonders of the Peak* (the latter being one of the first accounts of the Seven Wonders of the Peak) - who died at Hardwick. A much simpler table in the north aisle commemorates Robert Hackett, a keeper of Hardwick Park who died n 1703. It reads: 'Long has he chas'd/The red and fallow deer/But death's cold dart/At last has fix'd him here.'

WINSICK

2 miles S of Chesterfield off the A617

This charming hamlet is just a short drive from the centre of Chesterfield but retains a tranquil rural feel.

GRASSMOOR

3 miles S of Chesterfield on the B6038

Whilst Grassmoor is mentioned in the *Domesday Book*, as 'Grey Copse', there is little else worthy of historic note. The present village of Grassmoor owes its existence to the seams of coal upon which it stands but has since expanded and developed, now having a golf course, driving range and country park. The country park is on the site of the old Grassmoor Colliery and marks the start of a pleasant walk called the **Five Pits Trail**, a popular trail running between Grassmoor and Tibshelf, with miles of traffic-free walking and cycling. There are many picnic sites along the way past the sites of the old pits, along the line of some of the old railways.

WINGERWORTH

3 miles S of Chesterfield off the A61

The village was settled in Anglo-Saxon times, and is recorded in the Domesday Book as a community of fourteen households. It is today an attractive residential area set amidst undulating wooded countryside providing enjoyable walks. Smithy Pond is a pleasant area for visitors to relax.

The Hunlokes were the dominant family in Wingerworth from the reign of Queen Elizabeth I until 1920, acquiring nine-tenths of the land in the parish and becoming lords of the manor. The grand mansion of Wingerworth Hall, which they built in the early 18th century, was demolished in the 1920s. Olave, Lady Baden-Powell, first Chief Guide, was born here in 1889.

Standing at one of the highest points of the village is the **Parish Church of all Saints**, and although it retains some Norman and 13th century work it has had many additions over the centuries. A tower was added around 1500 and a substantial extension in 1963.

PILSLEY

5 miles S of Chesterfield off the B6014

As mentioned earlier in Chapter Two, there are two Pilsleys in Derbyshire, this one in North East Derbyshire and the other near the Chatsworth Estate Village. This Pilsley is actually comprised of two smaller villages, Lower Pilsley and (Upper) Pilsley, but most locals class the two as just one, fairly large village. Mary, Queen of Scots, whilst in captivity in Derbyshire, is said to have enjoyed riding through the leafy lanes of the village.

The Herb Garden in Pilsley, featured on the BBC TV programme *Country Gardens*, is

---

107 TELMERE LODGE

Hasland

With superb gardens, children's play area, well rested ales and delicious food on offer, this popular establishment is not to be missed.

See entry on page 214

---

108 THE BARLEY MOW INN

Wingerworth

Traditional inn serving real ales and delicious food on the edge of lovely Derbyshire countryside.

See entry on page 213

one of the foremost herb gardens in the country. Consisting of four display gardens, the largest is the Mixed Herb Garden, boasting an impressive established parterre. The remaining three gardens are the Physic, the Lavender and the Pot Pourri, each with its own special theme and housing many rare and unusual species. Areas of native flowers and wild spring bulbs can be enjoyed from March to September (Wed-Sun and Bank Holiday Mondays). On the grounds there is also a lovely tea room serving such delicacies as lavender cake, rosemary fruit slice and cheese and herb scones.

TIBSHELF

6 miles S of Chesterfield on the B6014

Stretching from Tibshelf north to Grassmoor, the **Five Pits Trail** follows an undulating off-road route between former coal mines, at Tibshelf, Pilsley, Alameda, Williamthorpe and Grassmoor, transformed into peaceful lakes and parks. Suitable for walkers, cyclists and horse riders, the trail is lovely, and offers some splendid views. The **Tibshelf Ponds picnic site**, a popular place with locals and fishermen, is a picturesque mix of wooded glades, meadows and ponds where Tibshelf Colliery stood. It also provides several opportunities for short walks.

The village stretches for about a mile along a main street that was once part of the Mansfield-Matlock turnpike road. There are fine views all round. Westwards you look across to the hills around Ashover with Crich Stand on the horizon. Eastwards the view is to what is left of Sherwood Forest, and a

Tibshelf Ponds

couple of miles northwards Hardwick Hall sits grandly on its own hilltop. Within the village, the **Parish Church of St John the Baptist** has been extensively restored over the centuries but it still retains an impressive 14th-century tower.

CLAY CROSS

5 miles S of Chesterfield off the A61

At the beginning of the 19th century Clay Cross was mainly a rural area, but railway pioneer George Stephenson changed that. During the building of the North Midlands Railway between Derby and Chesterfield, he found massive deposits of coal and iron ore that persuaded him to stay in North East Derbyshire and launch the Clay Cross Company in 1840. Subsequently, the hamlet grew from a small farming community into an industrial town dominated by the Clay Cross Company. The Company also provided schools, churches and housing. An impressive monument consisting of two large wheels with the inscription "In memory of all North East Derbyshire miners who lost their lives working to keep the home fires burning and the wheels of industry turning", takes pride of place in the High Street.

The **Parish Church of St Bartholomew** dates from 1851, though it looks much older. The land on which it stands was gifted to the church by George Stephenson and Company.

The **Clay Cross Countryside Centre** is one of three bases for the Countryside Service working throughout the north east of the county. Regular exhibitions are held and there is a shop stocking many free leaflets, local maps, guides, gifts, educational toys and a variety of books including walking, cycling, local and natural history. The Five Pits Trail (see Tibshelf) is managed from the Clay Cross Countryside Centre. To discover more about Clay Cross you can follow the Heritage Trail on a one-hour walk around the area's industrial heritage.

In 1972 the town earned the title "the Republic of Clay Cross" when left wing councillors, including David and Graham Skinner, both related to Dennis Skinner, MP for Bolsover, would not implement the terms of the Tory Housing Finance Act. The Clay Cross Rebels, as they became known, refused to put up council house rents by £1 a week. After a bitter dispute with the Government, which divided the community, they were surcharged, bankrupted and disqualified from office.

STRETTON

6 miles S of Chesterfield on the A61

First mentioned in 1002, Stretton is situated on the old Roman road known as Ryknield Street. Stretton village lies close to **Ogston Reservoir**, which covers an area of over 200 acres and is a favourite place for sailing. An old railway line lies at the bottom of the reservoir, as well as a pub and many other buildings that were also lost when the Reservoir was created in 1958. The man-made lake is overlooked by the romantic **Ogston Hall**, which dates from the 16th century and was the ancestral home of the Turbutt and Revell families. The house was altered extensively in 1768, and then modernised and 'medievalised' during Victorian times.

Ogston Reservoir, Stretton

BRACKENFIELD

7 miles S of Chesterfield off the A615

This village was known as Brackenthwaite in the Middle Ages, a name that means 'clearing in the bracken'. Like Clay Cross, Brackenfield is known today primarily for its proximity to the Ogston Reservoir, created in 1958 by damming the River Amber at the south end of the valley. The site of the former Ogston Mill was submerged under the rising waters.

Hidden in the surrounding trees is the ruin of the former **Trinity Chapel**, built around 1500. A pilgrimage from the village to this chapel is still held on Trinity Sunday to commemorate its historic place in the community. This church was abandoned when the new **Parish Church of the Holy Trinity** was built in 1856. It contains the 15th-century screen from the ruined church.

ASHOVER

6 miles SW of Chesterfield off the B6036

Ashover contains plenty of historical connections, including the site of a Druid temple on one of the surrounding hills. There is plenty of evidence of its past heritage of local industries, which include lead mining and nail making amongst many others. For visitors who chance to be this way, Ashover's splendid **Parish Church of All Saints** dating in parts from the 13th century is worth a visit.

Viewed from the southern rocky ridge known as **The Fabric** (apparently because it provided the fabric for much of the local building stone) and with the monolith of **Cocking Tor** in the foreground, Ashover can be seen as a scattered village filling the pleasantly wooded valley of the River Amber. The name of this village means 'ash tree

---

109 THE WHITE HORSE

Woolley Moor, nr Clay Cross

A hidden gem serving superb food and surrounded by scenic views of Derbyshire countryside.

See entry on page 215

---

110 KELSTEDGE INN

Kelstedge

With quality food, real ales and traditional values, this 18th century country inn is everything an English pub should be.

See entry on page 216

Ashover Village

slope' and though there are, indeed, many ash trees in the area, other varieties, including oak and birch, also flourish. Ashover was a flourishing industrial town in the past. As well as lead mining, which dated back to Roman times, there was nail making, lace, ropes, stocking weaving and malting. The ropes were said to be the longest and strongest in the country.

One part of the village is called the Rattle because of the sound of the looms rattling in the making of stockings. The industries, with the exception of quarrying and fluorspar have all died out and the work is now chiefly farming. Ashover lies just outside the boundary of the Peak District National Park but it still captures the typical character of a Peak village. At the heart of the largest parish in northeast Derbyshire, the village is chiefly constructed from limestone and gritstone, which were both quarried locally. The ruined shell of **Eastwood Hall**, once a large fortified Elizabethan manor house, also lies in the village. Owned over the years by several prominent Derbyshire families, including the Willoughbys, the house was blown up by the Roundheads during the Civil War.

The **Parish Church of All Saints**, with its 15th-century tower, is a prominent landmark in the valley. It houses the alabaster tomb of Thomas Babington and his wife, said by many to be the best tomb in Derbyshire. There are also some handsome brasses. What is surprising is the lead-lined Norman font, described by Pevsner as 'the most important Norman font in the country'. It is the only lead-lined font in an area that is so well-known for its mining. The Crispin Inn, next to the church, claims to date from the time of Agincourt, 1415. However, it is far more likely that, like many other buildings in the parish, it dates from the 17th century. The inn's name reflects one of Ashover's traditional trades: St Crispin is the patron saint of shoemakers and cobblers.

HOLYMOORSIDE

3 miles SW of Chesterfield off the A619

Holymoorside was once a thriving industrial centre, with three cotton thread mills dominating the village. Nothing remains now except the dam and the mill pond, which is now a popular recreation spot. Surrounded by the attractive moorland of Beeley Moor and Eastmoor, and lying in the picturesque valley of the River Hipper, this scattered village has now become a much-sought-after place to live in the 21st century.

Hipper Hall, an early 17th-century farmhouse with an even older tithe barn, is probably the oldest building in the village. It contains later additions and has some interesting internal features including an oak partition.

The **Stone Edge Cupola**, in a remote spot beside the B5057, is Britain's oldest free-standing chimney. Dating from 1770, it is a

Chimney, nr Holymoorside

testimony to the lead mining industry that survived here until the 19th century.

OLD BRAMPTON

3½ miles W of Chesterfield off the A619

Situated on a quiet road above a wooded valley, Old Brampton is well-known locally for its most unusual church clock that actually has sixty-three minutes in the hour! Just over the road from the Norman church is the George and Dragon pub, where the painter of the clock might have spent too long since he painted only four minutes between twelve and one, then six minutes between one and two. The mainly 13th-century **Parish Church of Saints Peter and Paul** is also of interest for its battlemented walls, short octagonal spire, and Norman doorway and window. Opposite the Norman church is **Brampton Hall**, a 12th-century building of immense historical interest with cruck oak beams reputed to have come from the earlier village. Also worthy of note is the large cruck barn, probably the largest in Derbyshire, to be found at **Frith Hall Farmhouse**.

CUTTHORPE

4 miles W of Chesterfield off the B6050

Cutthorpe does not have its own parish church as it is part of the parish of Old Brampton, but the village does have two historic halls. These are the Old Manor House (1625), once the property of the Sitwell family, and Cutthorpe Hall (1675), a former residence of the Heathcote family.

The land of Walter de Linacre is listed in the *Domesday Book*. Linacre Hall was situated at Cutthorpe on land which now contains the three **Linacre Reservoirs**. Built

Linacre Reservoir, Cutthorpe

between 1855 and 1904, until recently they supplied water to Chesterfield. Today the area is home to many species of fish, waterfowl, mammals and plant life, and is considered one of the most important ecological sites in the area. There are very pleasant walks, nature trails and fishing, and a scenic picnic area.

Before the Second World War the well-dressings in this village, which take place on the third Friday in July, had no religious links. After the war the custom died out, but was revived again by three people from nearby Barlow, in 1978. The three dressed wells are blessed during a service of thanksgiving for the pure water.

BARLOW

3 miles NW of Chesterfield on the B6051

Over a century ago there were at least 14 coal mines and as many open cast sites in and around Barlow. Now the mining industry has gone completely, though it helped, over the years, to shape the village. It is mentioned in the *Domesday Book*, and was the home of Robert Barlow, the first of Bess of Hardwick's four husbands. Although situated outside the limestone area, Barlow has been dressing its main well for longer than most. It is not known for certain when the custom began in the village, though it is known that, like Tissington, the well here provided water throughout the drought of 1615, which may have marked the start of this colourful practice.

---

111 THE PEACOCK INN

Cutthorpe

Home of great beer, food and entertainment, and with stunning views as well.

See entry on page 215

Another theory suggests that the tradition in Barlow could date back to the days of Elizabeth I's reign, as the church register of 1572 states that the festival of St Lawrence was celebrated. Whatever the origins of the well-dressings in the village, it is known that they have continued unbroken, even through two World Wars, throughout living memory. The wells are dressed during the second week of August every year.

HOLMESFIELD

4 miles NW of Chesterfield off the B6054

An ancient manor with the **Parish Church of St Swithin** standing on the highest point of the village, overlooking fine moorland scenery with spectacular views both north and south. Well-dressings are held in July.

DRONFIELD

5 miles NW of Chesterfield off the A61

Possessing an interesting blend of old and new buildings within a town centre Conservation Area, Dronfield hosts a bustling weekly market that has since developed industrially. The prosperity of Dronfield in the early years of the Industrial Revolution was such that an unexpectedly large number of mansions were built in and around the town, leaving a legacy of many beautiful 17th- and 18th-century listed buildings. **Chiverton House**, built in 1712, and **Rose Hill**, dating from 1719, are fine examples.

In the town centre, in front of the early 18th-century **Manor House** (now the home of the town library), the **Peel Monument**, dating from 1854, stands on the site of the former town cross and stocks, as a tribute to Sir Robert Peel's efforts in repealing the Corn Law in 1846. **The Cottage**, close to the monument, dates from the 16th century, and is reputed to have been owned by Lord Byron, though he never visited it. The **Parish Church of St John the Baptist** has a fine perpendicular tower, though much of it is 14th century. South of the church is a fine **Cruck Barn**. **The Hall** is also worth seeing as it has an attractive balustrade and a fine Queen Anne façade.

112 COFFEE CENTRAL
Dronfield

The aroma of homemade cooking oozes from this fabulous coffee shop. It is definitely worth checking out.

See entry on page 217

113 THE MANOR HOUSE
Dronfield

A recent transformation has attracted plenty of people through the doors of this Grade 2 listed hotel, cafe and bar.

See entry on page 217

114 THE MINERS ARMS
Dronfield Woodhouse

Whether you like the traditional Sunday Carvery, steaks, curries, vegetarian meals or a good children's menu, the Miners Arms caters for everyone – and with a range of real ales too.

See entry on page 218

Accommodation, Food & Drink and Places to Visit

The establishments featured in this section includes hotels, inns, guest houses, bed & breakfasts, restaurants, cafés, tea and coffee shops, tourist attractions and places to visit. Each establishment has an entry number which can be used to identify its location at the beginning of the relevant county chapter.

In addition full details of all these establishments and many others can be found on the Travel Publishing website - www.findsomewhere.co.uk. This website has a comprehensive database covering the whole of the United Kingdom.

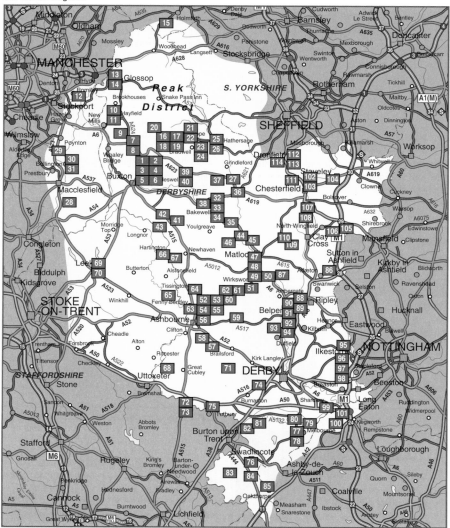

1 CHESHIRE CHEESE

37-39 High Street, Buxton, Derbyshire SK17 6HA
Tel: 01298 212453
e-mail: steven.marples@sky.com

With a central location in the market town of Buxton,
Cheshire Cheese is definitely worth a visit. The former
coaching inn dates back in parts to the 18th century and
attracts plenty of customers of all ages through its doors
despite the large number of pubs and restaurants in Buxton.

Sue and Steven have years of experience in the trade and
took over here in July 2009. Cheshire Cheese is open from
10am every day (except Christmas day) and serves two or
three fine real ales. Greene King IPA and Speckled Hen are
the regulars and there is also a rotating guest ale to sample.

The Sunday roast dinners here are very popular with diners
and homemade cottage pie is a traditional favourite. There
are plenty of other choices on the printed menu with
additional options on the daily specials board.

A quality beer garden is located to the rear of this child friendly public house and parking is not
a problem.

Cheshire Cheese is always bustling with locals and visitors, especially on evenings where there
is entertainment. Open mic night is held on Wednesday from 8pm, live bands can be seen every
Saturday from 9pm and on Sunday there is karaoke from 7pm.

2 THE DEVONSHIRE ARMS

North Road, Buxton, Derbyshire SK17 7EA
Tel: 01298 22148
e-mail: devonshirearms@hotmail.com
website: www.thedevonshirearms.org.uk

On the edge of Buxton and by the golf club, the **Devonshire
Arms** under its new hosts is back on the map. Joanne
Hallworth and her mother Moira Fenton are the new tenants,
with Joanna cooking the food in the kitchen. Traditional
favourites like Fish and Chips, Scampi, Steak and Lasagne are
on the menu alongside more unusual offerings such as Rabbit
and Bacon Sausages, and daily specials too. These might
include Rabbit Stew, Devonshire Arms Sausage with Mash and
Onion Gravy, or Sweet and Sour Pork.

Joanne will even try to cater to individual requests,
provided she has the time and the ingredients. There are also
special promotions to watch for, like kids eating free on a
Sunday, which keep people coming back for more.

Fine food at good prices isn't the only focus, with
occasional guest ales available alongside the regular Greene King IPA. For those who want to stay
and enjoy the attractions of Buxton and the surrounding countryside, the Devonshire Arms has six
attractive ensuite rooms offering Freeview TV, free wireless internet and a hearty cooked
breakfast. The pub is open all day, every day, with food available Tue-Fri noon-2pm and 5-8pm, Sat
noon-8pm and Sun noon-6pm.

3 NAT'S KITCHEN

9-11 Market Street, Buxton, Derbyshire SK17 6JY
Tel: 01298 214642
e-mail: natskitchen@btconnect.com
website: www.natskitchen.co.uk

Todd and Nicola took over what is now known as
Nat's Kitchen in February 2009. Together they have
built an enviable reputation in the local and
surrounding areas for fine food and hospitality. Todd
has been a professional chef for over twenty years,
and his experience really shows. Nat's Kitchen is a
popular place to dine for young and old, offering
high standards delivered in a warm and friendly
way.

The premises itself has a modern farmhouse feel
to it with contemporary lighting, sofas and seating,
but with the relics of a more traditional building
adding character with stone walls and beautiful
wooden floorboards. It's light and breezy décor is
aided by a large wall to wall window at the front of
the property, adding space and sunshine to any
meal here.

Todd and Nicola open for food and drink all day
from Tuesday to Saturday and on Sundays for a
traditional lunch. Booking is recommended at
weekends as it can get very busy at times. The
restaurant was awarded an AA rosette for the
quality of its cuisine and some of the dishes
available have featured in the Good Food Guide,
offering dishes inspired from all over the world. An
a la carte menu is available for lunch and dinner,
with a breakfast menu also operating throughout
the morning. Todd uses mainly local suppliers for
his food in a bid to beat the competition by
offering real freshness in his dishes, but also to do
his bit for lowering his carbon footprint – however
he believes nobody makes cheese quite like the
French so all cheeses are bought in separately.

Starters include clam, cockle and fine herb
risotto, seared scallops, rabbit and foie grass
terrine and apple jelly and a classic chicken and
bacon Caesar salad. Main courses continue the luxurious theme with dishes like curried hake on
creamed mussels and potato, rack of lamb Babagnoush with roasted vine tomatoes, guinea fowl
with vegetable macedoine, and confit of pork belly with chorizo and sautéed potatoes. Desserts
are also not to be missed with sticky toffee pudding and crème fresh, hot chocolate fondant cake
and an espresso crème brulee. Sandwiches, sides and lighter bites are also available for those with
a smaller appetite.

Accommodation is also available at Nat's, with five decadently furnished three star en suite
rooms to choose from. Ideal for couples and families wanting a slice of luxury without pretences
in the heart of Derbyshire.

4 THE TRADEMAN'S ENTRANCE

13 Scarsdale Place, Buxton, Derbyshire SK17 6EF
Tel: 07950 530654

The Tradesman's Entrance is quickly becoming the place to dine during the day in the Georgian town of Buxton, which rivals Ambleside for the title of the highest town in England. Carolyn and Jo are firmly in charge here and opened the cafe and sandwich bar to the public in July 2010.

Business is increasing week on week and The Trademans Entrance is forever bustling with people eager to sample what is on offer. It is open seven days a week from 7am – 4pm and serves a wide range of dishes and refreshments. All of the dishes are freshly prepared and cooked to order and local produce is used. Hot baguettes, baked potatoes, and freshly made sandwiches are always popular with diners here and fresh and speciality salads provide a healthy option.

For customers with a larger appetite there is always the cafe's homemade burger or chilli burger to have or one of the many breakfasts which are served throughout the day. The portion sizes are very generous and this might explain why the breakfasts are a favourite with visitors here. The reasonable prices definitely help!

Located in Buxton, which is the largest settlement within the boundaries of the Peak District National Park, there is plenty for visitors to see. The town is surrounded by some of the most glorious countryside in the area and after a morning exploring The Tradesmans Entrance provides an ideal resting spot.

Carolyn and Jo are always ready to welcome customers here, be they local or visitors. They are helped by Carolyn's mum Mo and one of their friends, Kerry. The Tradesman's Entrance is busy regardless of what time in the day it is and it has built up a good reputation since it opened in the summer of 2010. If you are visiting Buxton take heed from the locals and pay a visit to this up and coming cafe.

Carolyn is also the licensee at The Bull in Fairfield Road, Buxton, which is a drinkers pub offering two real ales.

5 ALPINE LODGE GUEST HOUSE

1 Thornsett, Hardwick Mount, Buxton,
Derbyshire SK17 6PS
Tel: 01298 26155
e-mail: info@alpinelodgebuxton.co.uk
website: www.alpinelodgebuxton.co.uk

Alpine Lodge Guest House is located just a short walk from the centre of historic Buxton. It was originally built as a retreat for the local mill owner in 1850, and retains much of that 19th century charm. Alpine Lodge's owner only took over in August 2010, finally fulfilling her dream of entering the hospitality trade. Jean takes pride in welcoming guests into her home which she keeps bright and airy, beautifully decorated with handsome furnishings.

   Jean offers five guest bedrooms, each of which has modern en-suite facilities and decadently comfortable beds. Rooms come in a range of sizes and styles, ideal for small families, singles or couples who are looking for a weekend away.   Alpine Lodge's location affords guests ample opportunity for exploring Buxton and the nearby towns, as well as enjoying the abundance of walking trails in the surrounding countryside, with something for all abilities. Delicious breakfasts are more than enough to keep you going for the day with generous portions, cooked with great locally sourced produce. Guests return time and time again for the hospitality here, allowing them to fully re-charge their batteries in this beautiful part of the country.

6 BUXTON MUSEUM AND ART GALLERY

Terrace Road, Buxton, Derbyshire SK17 6DA
Tel: 01298 24658 Fax: 01298 79394
e-mail: buxton.museum@derbyshire.gov.uk
website: www.derbyshire.gov.uk

Explore the Wonders of the Peak through seven time zones. Discover when sharks swam in warm 'Derbyshire' seas; when lions and sabre tooth cats terrorised mastodons. Meet the Roman Legionaries, and the scientists unravelling the history of Earth. An audio tour, 'Time Moves On', helps to enhance your visit. For art lovers, enjoy intricate Ashford Black Marble inlay and Blue John ornaments, and a regular programme of exhibitions, featuring work by national and local artists, photographers and craftworkers. Activities for all the family accompany the exhibitions.

Garden Centres and Nurseries

www.fiNdSOMEWHERE.co.uk
For people who want to explore the United Kingdom

7 IN A PICKLE

31 Market Street, Chapel-en-le-Frith, High Peak,
Derbyshire SK23 OHP
Tel: 01298 816555
website: www.inapickleuk.co.uk

In a Pickle is one of Derbyshire's most prized family businesses, found in the heart of picturesque Chapel-en-le-Frith. The mouth watering aroma of home baked goods lures in many guests each day; some who come to shop and some who come to dine in themselves.

It is run by charming mother and daughter team Dorothy and Sara who have been here for the past two and a half years. Their warm and friendly approach to hospitality means that each guest receives the warmest of welcomes, something that ensures they see many repeat visitors from both the local village and those further afield. Open from 8am-4pm Monday to Friday and on Saturdays from 8am-2pm, they offer eat in, deli and takeaway services.

Breakfast is served throughout the morning, with plenty of light snacks and lunches available the rest of day ranging from filled jacket potatoes, salads, sandwiches, Panini's and oatcakes. Each day freshly homemade cakes, scones, quiches and other pastries are proudly shown in the display counter. A selection of sweets are also on show to tempt you including homemade chocolate brownies. All produce served here is sourced locally, including fresh bread delivered from a nearby bakery in Buxton. Sara and Dorothy also offer a buffet catering service for a variety of events. Cash only please.

8 THE ROEBUCK INN

9 Market Place, Chapel-en-le-Frith,
Derbyshire SK23 OEN
Tel: 01298 812274
e-mail: info@roebuck-inn.co.uk
website: www.roebuck-inn.co.uk

The beautiful 17th-century **Roebuck Inn** stands in the centre of Chapel-en-le-Frith and is everything a good pub should be. It is superbly run by Angie Thomas and her mother, Pat, who is the Queen of the Kitchen. Pat produces an impressive array of dishes, and locals look forward to her Pie of the Day. There are inexpensive lunch menus with dishes ranging from the old favourites like fish, chips and mushy peas through to Thai fishcakes drizzled with sweet chilli sauce. In the evenings you could enjoy a gammon steak or a tasty spinach and wild mushroom lasagne. Pat's desserts are always tempting, with such treats as hot chocolate fudge cake or sticky toffee pudding.

At the Roebuck the beer is as important as the food, and there are four real ales to be sampled, with regulars including Tetley's and Black Sheep. There are also five affordable ensuite bedrooms, with a 3-star rating from Visit England, and coming with TVs, tea and coffee facilities, Egyptian cotton towels and a full cooked breakfast.

9 THE LAMB INN

Hayfield Road, Chinley, High Peak, Derbyshire SK23 6AL
Tel: 01663 750519
website: www.goodfoodpeakdistrict.co.uk

If you are looking for a great country pub to enjoy real ales and good food in the Peak District then look no further than **The Lamb Inn**. Owned by David and Fiona Asquith the establishment dates back to 1769 where it was formerly three cottages. It was a beer house by 1830 and an inn by 1839 when it was known as The Board Inn.

Today, it provides an ideal place to visit for those wanting to sample quality food and real ales in Derbyshire. The Lamb Inn is a traditional inn with 2 ft thick stone walls, woodburning stoves, low beamed ceilings, amazing views and a large outside seating area. The inn is renowned for its well stocked bar, fine food and first class service. David and Fiona use only the best ingredients, which are sourced locally for a greater taste and to support local farmers.

The two experienced chefs that work here are well regarded in the region and serve up a delicious selection of home cooked dishes with a wide selection of tasty starters to begin your meal.

To follow, there is a good selection of lamb dishes using Glossop Mooreland lamb, vegetarian dishes, fish dishes using locally caught trout, chargrilled steaks and regularly changing traditional favourites which include more elaborate dishes according to the season such as fish and game.

Monthly specials are listed on a blackboard and there is a good variety of salads and sandwiches to enjoy of a lunchtime.

Food is served between noon and 2.15pm, and 6pm – 9pm every week day and between 12 noon and 9pm on Saturday and Sunday.

If your visit is on a Friday you have a 50/50 chance of catching the popular fortnightly quiz. Ring for accommodation details. The inn is close to walkways leading to Kinder Scout and Cracken Edge.

10 THE SPORTSMAN

Kinder Road, Hayfield, High Peak, Derbyshire SK22 2LE
Tel: 01663 741565
e-mail: info@thekindersportsman.co.uk
website: www.kindersportsman.co.uk

Found high up on the hills in the heart of the glorious Derbyshire countryside is **The Sportsman**. Occupying an unrivalled location that commands stunning views across the hills, and is at the foot of Kinder Scout. The inn has become famous amongst both locals and visitors to Derbyshire not only for the scenery but for the quality of service within.

Their knowledge and love of the surrounding area and the inn makes for friendly and approachable landlords for whom nothing is too much trouble.

The inn is open all day every day apart from the evening of Christmas day. A variety of real ales are always available, with two to three rotating ales to sample at all times. Thwaites Original and Wainright's are the regular brews, although a good range of other beers, lagers, wines and spirits are also on offer.

The inn is particularly well known for its restaurant, which opens from 12-3pm and 6-9pm Monday to Thursday, 12-9pm on Saturdays and from 12-7pm on Sundays. The restaurant is usually busy, owing to its excellent reputation locally, necessitating booking on weekends to avoid disappointment. The menu has been especially created for the Sportsman by its own professional chefs it employs. Dishes range from simple snacks and elegant light bites to succulent mains and 'home comforts' pub style. Starters often include the inn's speciality homemade soup, Thai salmon rostis, fried black pudding with spicy apple puree and smoked mackerel pate. Main dishes include braised lamb Henry with wholegrain mustard mash, wild mushroom stroganoff and a hearty rib eye steak. For those who fancy something a little closer to home, the menu also provides with a selection of homemade pies, burgers and other tasty dishes like butcher's trio of sausages, freshly battered fish and chips and chilli nachos with all the toppings – perfect to share. On Sunday, roast dinners are also available with a choice of meats and delicious vegetables. Children are welcome to dine at any time from either the main menu in half portions or from a separate children's menu.

Guests who want to get to know Derbyshire a little better are welcomed to stay at the Sportsman which houses five guest bedrooms with their own separate entrance. Three rooms have full en suite facilities, and two have partial en suites, although all are wonderfully comfortable. The tariff includes a delicious home cooked breakfast, taken in the restaurant between 8.30-10am.

11 THE PACK HORSE

3-5 Market Street, Hayfield, Derbyshire SK22 2EP
Tel: 01663 740074
e-mail: info@thepackhorsehayfield.com
website: www.thepackhorsepayfield.com

In the foothills of Kinder Mountain lies **The Pack Horse**. Found within the idyllic village of Hayfield, this traditional pub and restaurant has recently undergone intense renovation, revealing a stylish and modern twist on the typical sleepy village inn. It's owned by Simon Woodall who took over here in June 2009. Together with his Executive Head Chef Kurt Thomas and manager Josh Unsworth, Simon is able to offer

something patrons describe has 'a cut above the rest' in terms of not only facilities, but decor and cuisine.

The team open to the public all day every day, offering guests their choice of a well stocked bar that houses up to four real ales at any one time. Ales are on a constant rotation so there is always something new to try. Simon also stocks an impressive collection of wines and spirits to compliment any meal, or to simply be enjoyed for their own merit. Guests can dine or drink throughout the inn, where bold designs and clever colour schemes draw the eye in to some of the pack Horse's more traditional features, such as the grand stone fire place in the bar. The stylish mismatching of furniture and boutique feel allows guests to enjoy a more contemporary atmosphere, whilst still appreciating the traditions that all good country inns embody.

The main attraction here of course is the food. Kurt manages a team of seven other professional chefs who produce arguably the most mouth-watering food in the area. Guests can choose from a variety of creative menus. The lounge and bar menu offers a tantalising selection of light bites, sandwiches, mains and salads to choose from. The regularly changing menu, focuses on freshly prepared meat dishes (using produce from a local award winning butcher), a selection of fresh fish dishes and a daily specials board. The desserts are all homemade fresh and range from Eton Mess, to Tipsy Cherry Trifle and the irresistible 'Sharing Chocolate Fondue.' Cheese lovers will not be disappointed either as Kurt provides his own hand picked cheese menu for those after dinner moments. Children are welcome to dine and dishes can be prepared to suit individual taste.

The Pack Horse also hires out the talents of its culinary team, which can be combined to create the perfect buffet for any event. A function room above the restaurant has capacity for a forty person sit down meal, or buffet for a hundred people. This room is as unique and quirky as the rest of the Pack Horse, allowing any event to be made that little bit more special. Please call for details.

12 DUKE OF YORK

Stockport Road, Romiley, Stockport SK6 3AN
Tel: 01614 302806
e-mail: mail@dukeofyorkromiley.co.uk
website: www.dukeofyorkromiley.co.uk

The **Duke of York** pub is found just a two minute walk from the Peak Forest Canal. Its pretty location means it sees many visitors who are no doubt also attracted by the inn's wholesome pub attitude. Landlord Jim Grindrod has been here many years and feels it is important to uphold traditional pub values. He says that dirty boots, mucky clothing and dogs are all welcomed into his pub, as are lovers of good food, ale and conversation.

Jim has won awards for the quality of his ales and keeps up to seven hand pumped ales to a cask marque approved standards. Each year he holds a popular beer festival towards the end of the summer when guests can enjoy a more al fresco experience when a large garden marquee is erected.

The inn is also popular for food, but its menu veers away from the traditional and is completely Mediterranean. Gino's Ristorante-Pizzeria (as it's titled) claims to offer the best pizza in town, alongside a whole host of chicken, meat, fish and pasta mains – all freshly prepared using Mediterranean flavours and techniques. Special lunch deals run throughout the year; please see website for details.

13 THE STAR INN

2 Howard Street, Glossop, Derbyshire SK13 7DD
Tel: 01457 853072

The **Star Inn** is a traditional street-corner inn, close to the centre of Glossop in Derbyshire's High Peak district. Hosts Paul and Vivien focus on what they do well, and that's making sure there's a wide range of real ales and ciders, perfectly kept in their cellar. The couple have been here seven years now, and are still discovering new beers and ciders to showcase.

For cider-lovers who often get left out in even the best of pubs, the Star Inn offers a real cider, Old Rosie. There are always several bitters to choose from, with Black Sheep being the regular "house beer". There are guest ales too, with as many as thirty available for sampling over the course of a month.

Accommodation is also available if booked in advance. There are two ensuite bedrooms, one double and one twin, which are usually let on a room only basis.

14 REVIVE COFFEE LOUNGE

55 High Street West, Glossop, Derbyshire SK13 8AZ
Tel: 01457 855116
website: www.revivecoffee.co.uk

Known across the country as the gateway to the Peak District National Park, the small market town of Glossop is a convenient and charming place to spend an afternoon. Nestled on the banks of Glossop Brook about fifteen miles east of Manchester, its pretty location is never too far from the big cities, but far enough away to allow its visitors to enjoy a certain countryside tranquillity. Within its heart on the winding high street is **Revive Coffee Lounge**.

The coffee lounge only opened in April 2010, but since that day its business has built steadily and now features prominently in the lives of most in Glossop. It's owned and run by mother and daughter team Barbara and Jo who keep their guests revived with not only coffee but their sparky personalities. Their relaxed and friendly approach to their customers immediately puts a smile on their faces, who enjoy the warm welcome they receive every time they step over the threshold.

The lounge is open seven days a week; from 8am-6pm Monday to Saturday and from 10am-5pm on Sundays and is usually busy with a pleasant mixture of locals and visitors.

Jo and Barbara specialise in teas and coffees and serve a mind boggling array of varieties to suit everyone from the coffee connoisseur to the coffee virgin. Guests can enjoy their coffee in a laid back environment, filled with squashy sofas, coffee tables and the pleasant chatter of friends.

Jo and Barbara also offer an exciting selection of snacks and main meals to accompany any drink here whether its tea, coffee or a soft drink. They are both excellent cooks and are supported by a team of hardworking and skilled local women from around the Glossop area who delight in baking a variety of homemade treats for Revive. The cakes are particularly popular and often include carrot cake, ginger cake and sumptuous chocolate orange cake. A delicious range of sweet and savoury scones are also available alongside the main menu which offers a few larger choices for hungrier customers. Choices range from simple sandwiches, to chunky toasties and other interesting varieties including hummus and roasted vegetables or chorizo, jalapeño and cheddar melts. A small range of salads and platters are also available alongside the specials menu which changes regularly to reflect the best in local produce. Children are welcome to dine at Revive at any time.

15 THE FLEECE INN

The Village, Holme, Holmfirth HD9 2QG
Tel: 01484 683449 Fax: 01484 683449
e-mail: shirley.amesbury@lineone.net

The Fleece Inn is found within the magnificent countryside of the Peak District National Park in the delightful village of Holme. Just a stone's throw from the better known town of Holmfirth, the inn attracts a steady clientele of walkers, cyclists and shoppers from the nearby town in search of a wholesome country meal and unbeatable hospitality. The inn is perfect for reservoir walks and exploring the trails through Yateholme Woods as both are within easy walking distance.

The inn is owned and run by Shirley Amesbury, who took over the inn thirteen years ago. She has created somewhat of a

destination inn, specialising in real ales, quality cuisine and entertainment. Shirley also endeavours to ensure that the inn has a real place in the hearts of the Holme community and regularly holds themed evenings and events for all at the inn. Recent evenings include bonfire night, tapas night, curry night, quiz night, afternoon teas and jazz evenings.

Apart from bank holidays, Shirley closes the inn on Mondays, but opens every other session throughout the rest of the week and all day on Saturdays. She keeps the homely bar well stocked at all times with a selection of three real ales on rotation and a good range of wines, beers and spirits.

Guests are welcome to dine throughout the inn and are also invited to enjoy the sunshine of the beer garden in the summer months. There are various lunch, evening and snack menus to choose from on top of a special Sunday lunch menu which offers a traditional home cooked roast with starters, desserts and a tempting array of alternative options. For something light, popular sandwiches include the camembert melt with roasted peppers sandwich, hot roast pork with stuffing and apple sauce and the Fleece Platter which includes a sandwich of choice and a bowl of Shirley's homemade soup. Main meals include sizzling chicken fajitas, creamy Moules frites, duck breast with spicy plum and noodle timbale and Shirley's famous steak and ale pie. The Fleece is also known for its fish dishes which include smoked haddock bake, prawn Waldorf and a fillet of roasted sea bass on a bed of creamed vegetables. These are showcased on the last Friday of every month when it's 'Fish Night' at the inn. Children are welcome to dine, all major credit cards accepted.

16 YE OLDE CHESHIRE CHEESE INN

How Lane, Castleton, Hope Valley, Derbyshire S33 8WJ
Tel: 01433 620330 Fax: 01433 621847
e-mail: info@cheshirecheeseinn.co.uk
website: www.cheshirecheeseinn.co.uk

Ye Olde Cheshire Cheese Inn is a delightful 17th century free house offering three star bed and breakfast accommodation in the historic Peak District village of Castleton. A warm welcome awaits you at this traditional, family run 'proper' country pub. Karen and John McKeever have been running the inn for the past four years along with the help of their excellent managers Catherine and Gary. Together with their hardworking team of staff comprising Chefs Guy, Dave and Chris, barman Neil and housekeepers Alex

and Graham, they ensure that the inn retains a real flavour of days gone by and a relaxed and friendly atmosphere that is sure to refresh visitors no matter how short their stay.

To maintain the traditional and welcoming ambience they have become known for, guests will not find any pool tables or duke boxes inside. Instead guests are free to sit undisturbed beside the fires in the heavily beamed, cosy bar area and enjoy a drink and a chat in quiet, relaxed surroundings. Karen and John keep a wide choice of award winning cask ales and also serve good, wholesome food in both the bar and restaurant.

Food is served from 12-9pm from Monday to Saturday and from 12-8:30pm on weekends. The menu at the inn is vast and varied with something for every appetite, children included. A starters and light bites menu comprises a selection of tasty soups, sandwiches and snacks including various sharing platters and tapas options. The main menu offers a treat for the taste buds with Ye Olde Cheshire Cheese's own special homemade favourites. Popular dishes include steak and ale pie, leek, potato and stilton crumble, roasted pork leg, spicy

meatballs, chorizo and mixed bean casserole, braised leg of duck and a moreish wild boar casserole. On Sundays a gargantuan roast dinner is added to the menu, hopefully leaving room for one of Catherine's homemade desserts.

Karen and John also offer guests the use of the restaurant as a function room with buffet style catering for a whole host of 'out of office' events, conferences and team building days.

The inn also offers ten tastefully decorated en suite bedrooms comprising two with four poster beds, six doubles, one twin and one single. Tariffs vary depending on season and length of stay, but always include a handsome Peak District English breakfast. Please call for details.

17 THE PEAKS INN

How Lane, Castleton,
Hope Valley, Derbyshire S33 8WJ
Tel: 01433 620247
e-mail: enquiry@peaksinn.com
website: www.peaksinn.com

Situated at the heart of the idyllic village of Castleton, **The Peaks Inn** is a quality inn surrounded by some of the country's most stunning scenery.

The Peaks Inn is an ideal base from which to explore the Peak District and it attracts plenty of walkers and cyclists keen to get out and about. The local area has some of the best walking and cycling trails in the UK. It really is a nature and outdoor enthusiast's paradise with fishing, climbing and horse riding all just minutes away.

This traditional country inn is extremely welcoming and log fires create a warm and cosy atmosphere. On warmer days many customers choose to chill out in the garden area, which provides a superb spot for dining or enjoying a refreshing tipple.

The well-stocked bar has something to suit all tastes with a fantastic range of premium brand lagers, cask ales, fine wines and malt whiskies.

The kitchen here is open throughout the day to serve up delicious meals and snacks and the chefs source as much of the produce they use from Derbyshire. The food here is particularly tempting and the traditional favourites on offer include meat & potato pie, sausage & mash, and fish & chips. For those with a lighter appetite there is a varied selection of filled sandwiches and jacket potatoes. All of the dishes here are reasonably priced and that definitely makes the already tempting desserts more tempting. Hot apple pie and chocolate fudge cake are some of the choices.

18 DENEWOOD

Buxton Road, Castleton, Hope Valley, Derbyshire S33 8WP
Tel: 01433 621595
Mobile: 07890 050196
e-mail: denewood.bandb@gmail.com
website: www.denewood.me.uk

Situated on the edge of the picturesque village of Castleton in glorious Hope Valley is **Denewood**. Emma and Jon Haddock offer luxury four star accommodation for guests looking to truly relax and enjoy all that Peak District has to offer.

Guests can choose from four affordable guest bedrooms, in twin/king size, family, double or single room sizes. Each room has full en suite facilities, TV Freeview, drink making facilities, plenty of storage and spectacular views across the Derbyshire hills. Rooms can also be adapted for families with extra beds, although larger families can opt to hire out all four rooms and have Denewood to themselves. All guests have full use of the guests lounge, where you can meet ner friends or just relax in front of the log burner. Off street parking is available.

Emma and Jon also work with other local bed and breakfasts and can accommodate larger groups if required. Denewood is also in partnership with **Chocolate Heaven** which offers innovative holiday experiences including **Cocoadance** Castleton's own chocolate factory. Guests can enjoy luxury

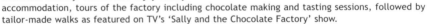

accommodation, tours of the factory including chocolate making and tasting sessions, followed by tailor-made walks as featured on TV's 'Sally and the Chocolate Factory' show.

There is also a holiday cottage available, sleeping up to 5 (1 double, 1 twin and 1 single). Situated in the heart of the village, both locations are ideal for exploring the surrounding countryside or just relaxing.

19 CAUSEWAY HOUSE

Back Street, Castleton, Hope Valley, Derbyshire S33 8WE
Tel: 01433 623291
e-mail: info@causewayhouse.co.uk
website: www.causewayhouse.co.uk

Nick and Janet Steynberg are your friendly hosts at their exceptional bed and breakfast, **Causeway House**. Their beautiful cottage with its original oak timbers may be as old as the 15th

century but Nick and Janet offer 21st-century comforts in their five guest bedrooms. There are three luxurious ensuite rooms, and two other rooms which share a bathroom. Guests with mobility restrictions are advised to phone ahead: the Garden Room is on the ground floor but with a couple of steps to access it. It offers access to the house's patio garden.

Star turn is the four-poster room, with a full four-poster canopy bed, plenty of space, a good-sized ensuite bathroom, TV, and tea and coffee facilities too. If you want to relax, this is the room for you. Even breakfasts are special at the Causeway, and Nick and Janet are proud that their extensive menu has won a Breakfast Award from the English Tourist Board. Derbyshire oatcakes, porridge, hash browns and black or white pudding all feature on the menu. All in all, there's no finer place to stay.

20 TREAK CLIFF CAVERN

Castleton, Hope valley, Derbyshire S33 8WP
Tel: 01433 620571
e-mail: treakcliff@bluejohnstone.com
website: www.bluejohnstone.com

Treak Cliff Cavern is an underground Wonderland of Stalactites, stalagmites, rocks, minerals and fossils. It is also home to Blue John Stone, a rare form of fluorite with beautiful colours. Popular as an ornamental stone and mined for 300 years, one of the largest pieces ever found, called The Pillar, is still in situ. The Blue John Stone in Treak Cliff Cavern can be seen all around the walls and roof of the Witch's Cave. The guided tour takes you deeper underground to see multi coloured flowstone adorning the walls of Aladdin's Cave, and further on you can experience the wonder of the stalactites and stalagmites in Fairyland and the Dream Cave. The most famous formation is 'The Stork', standing on one leg.

People of all ages can enjoy a visit to Treak Cliff Cavern (guided tours take about 40 minutes), and also experience special events held at certain times during the year. 'Polish your own' Blue John Stone is an activity usually available during most of the school holidays. Other events include an Easter Egg Hunt and. prior to Christmas. 'Carols By Candlelight' in the cavern.

21 THE OLD HALL HOTEL

Market Place, Hope, Hope Valley, Derbyshire S33 6RH
Tel: 01433 620160 Mobile: 07966 244364
e-mail: rickoldhallhotel@hotmail.co.uk
website: www.oldhallhotelhope.com

Experienced licensee Rick Ellison and Professional Chef Pascal took over **The Old Hall Hotel** in May 2010 and are enjoying their success already. Open all day every day, three real ales are available alongside a range of wines and spirits. Food is served daily from 12-3pm and 6-9pm in the winter and from 12-9pm in the summer months. Amongst the favourite dishes are roasted pork belly in cider apple sauce, the Sunday carvery and traditional Derbyshire pie stuffed with layers of venison, black pudding and mincemeat.

22 THE COURTYARD CAFÉ

8 Castleton Road, Hope, Hope Valley,
Derbyshire S33 6RD
Tel: 01433 623360

The pretty town of Hope within picturesque Hope Valley is home to **The Courtyard Café**. Nestled away in a hidden garden, this sun trap is a popular place for locals and visitors alike who enjoy the chilled out and refreshing ambience the café exudes. Dogs are also welcome and receive their own bowl of water on arrival!

The cafe is owned and run by Jason and Heather who have spent the last few months renovating the café to bring it back to its former glory. Clean cut lines, natural materials and neutral colours allow the light from the café's conservatory roof to fill the room, which overlooks the tranquil courtyard.

Jason and Heather have introduced premier home cooking here which stems from Jason's passion for food developed over twenty years as a professional chef. He serves up delicious homemade soups, freshly made sandwiches and takeaway style dishes which are all created using only the very best in locally sourced produce. Fair Trade coffee is also served with a selection of specialty teas. Visitors can also enjoy a mouth-watering range of homemade cakes and scones, prepared freshly each day by the local members of the Women's Institute.

23 YE OLDE BOWLING GREEN INN

Smalldale, Bradwell, Hope Valley, Derbyshire S33 9JQ
Tel: 01433 620450
e-mail: dalesinns@aol.co.uk
website: www.yeoldebowlinggreen.webs.com

When local resident Jez Warrington heard that his favourite pub was going to be sold, he was so keen to make sure it wasn't spoiled that he decided to buy it himself. Now Jez, his wife Karen and their daughter Carley find themselves running **Ye Olde Bowling Green Inn**, one of the most delightful inns in Derbyshire. The family's aim is to keep it that way.

Located in the picturesque hamlet of Smalldale, the Bowling Green was a former coaching inn and dates back to 1577. Much of its history and period atmosphere has been retained, with its bow windows, exposed stone walls, low-beamed ceilings, dark wood and open fireplaces. Outside there are colourful hanging flower baskets along the front of the whitewashed walls, and a patio area and a beer garden both with stunning panoramic views of the surrounding countryside and peaks.

Equally impressive for beer lovers is the view of the real ales in the bar. There are usually four to enjoy, with Black Sheep and a Copper Dragon brew being the regular resident ales.

The views are shared by the popular Garden Room Restaurant, where both Karen and Carly now cook, having freshened up the menu while maintaining their locally-sourced produce. There's a permanent printed menu and also a changing list of daily specials on the blackboard which might include such tasty dishes as Minted Lamb Shank, a Stilton and Broccoli Quiche, or for the really hungry a Desperate Dan Pie! The Sunday Carvery (from Oct-May) offers just about the best Carvery views in the county. You're well advised to book for this, and to dine on a Friday or Saturday night, and even on other evenings in the busy summer months. That's how popular this place is.

If those views tempt you to make your stay at Ye Olde Bowling Green a longer one, there are five ensuite guest bedrooms in an adjacent building, a converted barn that's not attached to the pub, ensuring peace and privacy. The rooms have a high 4-Star rating from the AA, so you know they're being regularly inspected and given a ranking that many hotels don't achieve.

Ye Olde Bowling Green is open every day and food is served Tue-Sat 12.30-2.30pm and 6-9pm, Sun 12.30-4pm. Children are welcome and major credit cards are accepted.

24 STONEY RIDGE

Granby Road, Bradwell,
Derbyshire S33 9HU
Tel: 01433 620538
e-mail: toneyridge@aol.com
website: www.stoneyridge.org.uk

Helen and Richard Plant are the proud owners of **Stoney Ridge** bed and breakfast, found in the village of Bradwell in a lofty position overlooking the idyllic Hope Valley. They are a local couple who have lived at Stoney Ridge for twenty-six years, providing high quality bed and breakfast services for the past twenty. They take real pride in their work and enjoy getting to know their guests whilst allowing them to take a relaxing break and enjoy the peace and quiet of Bradwell, the friendly village. Their experience serves them well and they see many repeat visitors year on year who commend their hospitality and unrivalled local knowledge which help to make any stay in this part of Derbyshire a restful one.

Guests can choose from four luxury bedrooms, each of which is carefully decorated with a vintage class not found in today's more contemporary guest houses. Three of the rooms have full en suite facilities whilst the other has its own private bathroom adjacent. The king size room has its own corner bath, perfect to unwind with a glass of wine and plenty of bubbles. Three of the rooms sport breathtaking views across Hope Valley, beautiful in any season with long rolling hills and nature's vibrant colours.

Helen and Richard also offer their guests a spa like experience at Stoney Ridge as they also have their own indoor heated

swimming pool which can be used before breakfast or after dinner every day. The pool itself is housed in a wonderfully bright room with high wood panelled ceilings and large French windows. Guests can enjoy Stoney Ridge's well established gardens which are also home to numerous wild birds.

Although lunch and evening meals are not available here Helen and Richard are pleased to point you in the direction of some of the area's finest restaurants and cosiest pubs depending on your mood. Breakfast however, is one of Helen's specialities and guests are indulged each morning with her generous cooked and continental breakfasts. Her breakfasts, served between 8:30-9am, are guaranteed to keep guests filled until dinner time, ensuring a full day of exploring the beautiful Derbyshire countryside is unhampered by hunger.

Helen and Richard also offer Christmas packages for small groups, couples and families, allowing the usual stresses of the holiday period to melt away completely, please call for details.

25 ELLIOTTS COFFEE SHOP & BISTRO

Station Road, Hathersage, Derbyshire. S32 1DD
Tel: 01433 659911
e-mail: michelle_elliott@live.co.uk

Elliotts Coffee Shop & Bistro was created by Stuart and Michelle in April 2009, transforming the garden centre previously there. This is their first venture into hospitality as Stuart was a vet for 32 years and Michelle a professional dancer and actress.

Michelle trained as a Barista learning roasting, frothing techniques and latte art. They specialise in freshly ground hand-poured coffee and loose-leaf speciality tea with customers travelling from miles around to sample the drinks. Elliotts offers a contemporary take on the European/Mediterranean bistro with elegant comfortable leather chairs, warm colours and a relaxed friendly atmosphere. They are fully licensed.

There are over 60 seats outside on three levels, and despite the stylish interior inside, muddy boots and dogs are made very welcome indeed, the latter getting a dog biscuit! You can choose from a delicious range of homemade food prepared and changing daily, all made from fresh ingredients including B.L.T's, fishcakes, sausage & mash, roasted stuffed aubergine, parsnip and apple soup, a choice of salads and quiches, and last but not least, their legendary venison burgers. There are many vegetarian and gluten free options available as well as dairy free. (Ring us if you would like to know the day's menu). Open daily from 10am everyday except tuesday.

Stuart and Michelle also offer two beautiful self catering cottages. One is adjacent to the Coffee Shop sleeping up to six, and the other in the beautiful village of Litton Mill, sleeping up to four guests.

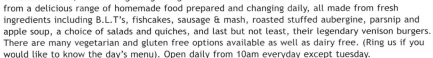

26 THE LITTLE JOHN INN

Station Road, Hathersage, Hope Valley,
Derbyshire S32 1DD
Tel: 01433 650225 Fax: 01433 659851
e-mail: littlejohnhotel@btconect.com
website: www.thelittlejohnhotel.co.uk

Stephanie and Andy have been running The Little John Inn since they first took it over in 1991. Like so many of their patrons they fell in love with the premises and were compelled to restore and grow the business. The inn is found in the well known village of Hathersage, nestled within the tranquil hills of Hope Valley.

Stephanie and Andy open all day every day to the public – luring many inside with the inn's own olde worlde poem; "Come in, through my roof beneath, and humble is my store, you can always depend, you'll meet with a friend, when you call at the Little John door." The poem accurately echoes Stephanie and Andy's feelings towards hospitality; they are both always happy to chat with old and new friends over the bar; an asset to newcomers as their knowledge of the local area is second to none.

The bar is kept well stocked and offers between three and five real ales a day depending on the time of year. Guests ales vary from local to national brews, but Easy Rider and Pride of Sheffield can usually be enjoyed here. Stephanie and Andy also have their own special ale brewed for them which is worth a taste if only for its name; Little John Smooth. On the second Saturday of every month the folk train arrives to entertain. It comprises a lively folk band who come to the Little John by train for dinner, drinks and to perform.

Food is available between Monday and Thursday from 12-2pm, on Saturdays from 12-10pm and on Sundays from 12-8:30pm. Options include starters, grills, vegetarian dishes, pasta and rice dishes, salads, snacks and sandwiches alongside a host of chicken and meat dishes. There is truly something for everyone, even children who have their own section on the menu. Amongst the favourites are the Robin Hood mixed grill, Irish stew and dumplings, BBQ ribs and spicy pepper marinated chicken wrap. Other dishes include sweet and sour chicken, chilli enchilada, and pan fried tuna steak in a ginger, lime and lemongrass sauce. Owing to popularity booking is recommended on Saturday nights. Pets are very welcome.

Stephanie and Andy also offer seven quality en suite guest bedrooms which are available throughout the year on a bed and breakfast basis. These rooms keep with the inn's traditional feel, without forgoing all today's modern comforts. If guests prefer to cater for themselves however, three self catering cottages are dotted around the inn's courtyard, ideal for families or couples on a longer stay away. Please call for details.

27 THE EATING HOUSE

The Derbyshire Craft Centre, Calver Bridge,
Hope Valley, Derbyshire S32 3XA
Tel: 01433 631583

People visiting the excellent Derbyshire Craft Centre in Calver Bridge often find themselves following their noses as the smell of home-baking lures them into the wonderful **Eating House** café-restaurant. Others come purely to sample the food at the Eating House and then find themselves lured by the beautiful range of arts and crafts on display. But as soon as you walk into

the Eating House you know you've come to the right place not only because of the tempting aromas and the queues of people, but also the ever-present smiles on the faces of the staff. One look tells you that they enjoy working here, and it shows in the results.

Katrina Leicke owns the Eating House and is responsible for the tasty array of cakes, of the old-fashioned kind where you feel yourself putting weight on just by looking at them. There's much more than just cakes, though, at this self-service restaurant. The ever-changing blackboards list the daily specials, with traditional dishes such as Ham and Poached Eggs, and Bubble and Squeak sitting alongside Salmon and Cream Cheese Bagels or a Jacket Potato with Apple, Celery and Ham. The old-fashioned puddings and desserts are naturally made to perfection, and if in doubt then try the classic Lemon Meringue Pie.

Snacks are available too, if you just want a bowl of homemade soup or a slice of the Eating House's own quiche. There is also a wide range of teas and coffees to choose from, if all you need is a drink and a sit-down. There's seating for 35 inside and a further 15 people outside, if the weather is fine. Children are made very welcome, and there is disabled access although not disabled toilet facilities. There is plenty of parking available at the Derbyshire Craft Centre, which is a popular attraction in its own right in the Peak District. It's on the A623 and is open every day of the year except Christmas Day, Boxing Day and New Year's Day. It's an attractive building of old stone, and the traditional interior has a contrasting contemporary design to it, along with the colourful work of local artists and craftspeople.

28 THE RYLES ARMS

Country Inn and Dining Rooms, Hollin Lane,
Higher Sutton, Macclesfield SK11 ONN
Tel: 01260 252244
e-mail: info@rylesarms.com
website: www.rylesarms.com

For centuries **The Ryles Arms** has been welcoming visitors through its doors. It is surrounded by hundreds of acres of picturesque countryside in Higher Sutton, within the Peak District National Park.

The Ryles Arms has recently been taken over by new owners Alex Diggory and Mark Taylor who have plenty of experience in the industry. There are six 4* en-suite rooms available here including a deluxe suite. The accommodation is absolutely superb and is available all year around. The reasonable tariff includes a fantastic full English breakfast, which will not disappoint.

The food here is a real winner and its reputation is growing daily. Offering a large and extensive menu from nibbles, starters, fresh fish, pasta, vegetarian, signature dishes and an wide selection from the grill. We pride ourselves on our grill selection. We cut our meat as thick as possible to ensure a superior juicy taste and texture. We age all our prime cuts of beef for no less than 21 days.

With daily specials creating additional options for diners and for those with lighter appetites there are a range of sandwiches and smaller dishes. A delicious roast dinner is served Sunday and breakfasts are available daily until noon with a selection of locally brewed real ales served every session.

30 THE HOLLY BUSH

75 Palmerston Street, Bollington,
Cheshire SK10 5PW
Tel: 01625 573073

The **Holly Bush** is a pub that's still the way pubs used to be. It's a handsome mock-Tudor building with an old-fashioned wood-panel interior, which adds to the cosiness and friendly atmosphere. The landlord, Andrew O'Shea, is rightly proud of his beers. He always has a range of Robinson's real ales from Stockport, including Unicorn, Hatters and their very popular Dizzy Blonde. On draught there's also Stella, Guinness and Strongbow, with a wide selection of bottled beers too.

Although the Holly Bush is open all day and every day, food is only served when they have one of their food-themed evenings, held once or twice a month. This might be a chilli night, or fish and chips, so ring to ask if you want to sample the fare. The fish and chip nights are always good, as the landlord has run a fish and chip shop for the last 26 years. At least once a month he also puts on a live music concert, usually on a Saturday night from 8.30pm, so phone to find out who's playing. In summer you can also enjoy the patio garden at the rear.

29 ADLINGTON HALL

Mill lane, Adlington, Macclesfield, Cheshire SK10 4LF
Tel: 01625 827 595 Fax: 01625 820 797
e-mail: enquiries@adlingtonhall.com
website: www.adlingtonhall.com

Adlington Hall, the home of the Leghs of Adlington from 1315 to the present day, was built on the site of a hunting lodge which stood in the Forest of Macclesfield in 1040. The Hall is a manor house, quadrangular in shape, and was at one time surrounded by a moat. Two sides of the courtyard and the east wing were built in 1581 in the typical 'black& white' Cheshire style. The south front and west wing were added between 1749 and 1757 and are built of red brick with a handsome stone portico with four Ionic columns.

Two oak trees, part of the original building, still remain with their roots in the ground and support the east end of the Great Hall, which was built between 1480 and 1505. Between the trees in the Great Hall stands an organ built in the style of 'Father' Bernard Smith (c 1670-80). Handel subsequently played on this instrument and, now fully restored, it is the largest 17th century organ in the country. At the west end of the Great Hall is a very fully developed canopy. This takes the form of a cove or quadrant and is divided into 60 panels containing armorial shields. The windows are on the south side so that the murals which adorn the north and west walls can be seen to advantage. Adlington Hall was a royalist garrison during the Civil War.

Adlington Hall is a great Cheshire garden set in the heart of the Cheshire Plain amidst some of England's finest countryside. The Estate, which is continually evolving, was landscaped in the 'Brownian' style during the 18th century, complete with a ha-ha. Earlier plantings are still in evidence, such as the ancient Lime Avenue dating from 1688 and the Wilderness with its myriad winding paths and open glades, also home to temples, bridges and follies. The large herbaceous border also along the North Drive is packed with interest from spring until late autumn and the woodland border offers exuberant displays of autumn colour. The path through the laburnum arcade leads into the formal Rose Garden which offers a feast of colour and fragrance all summer long. Pillars and rope swags frame the garden with a gazebo centrepiece providing a tranquil seating area. Carry on through the Rose Garden and you will discover a maze created from English yew.

Other features include rockeries, shrub borders and many fine specimen trees. The Father Tiber water garden, created in 2002, goes from strength to strength and offers a peaceful haven amongst ponds, rills, fountains and a water cascade.

The Hunting Lodge is part of the beautifully converted Georgian Mews adjacent to the black and white East Wing of Adlington Hall. The first floor banqueting suite is approached by a beautiful sweeping staircase (a lift is available if required).

The hunting Lodge is an ideal venue for wedding receptions, banquets, conferences or indeed any social or business occasion. For more information please contact The Hunting Lodge on 01625 827595.

31 THE CHURCH HOUSE INN

Church Street, Bollington, Macclesfield,
Cheshire SK10 5PY
Tel: 01625 574014
e-mail: info@thechurchhouseinn-bollington.co.uk
website: www.thechurchhouseinn-bollington.co.uk

The **Church House Inn** is on the edge of the Peak District National Park but its new reputation for fine food means that it is attracting food lovers from all over Derbyshire, Cheshire and even Manchester. One glance at the menus shows why, with starters like pan-fried scallops topped with pancetta and drizzled with a honey and mustard dressing, or mains including fillets of sea bass topped with a white wine, ginger and spring onion sauce.

The food is far from expensive, though, which is another reason for its popularity. There are also special menus for vegetarians and senior citizens, and a chance to cook your own steak exactly how you like it on a hot rock at your table. In addition to the top-quality dining, there are several real ales to enjoy, with Adnams from Suffolk and Sharp's Doom Bar Ale from Cornwall being local favourites. The Church House Inn also five tastefully-decorated ensuite guest bedrooms, and a 3-star rating from the AA. Food is available Mon-Sat lunch and dinner, and Sundays from noon-7.30pm.

32 FARMERS FEAST CAFE & BAR

Agricultural Business Centre, Agricultural Way, Bakewell,
Derbyshire DE45 1AH
Tel: 01629 815678

The **Farmers Feast Cafe and Bar** is always sure to be bustling with people enjoying a locally sourced traditional meal. With a cattle market located next door, owner David Nuttall doesn't have to look far for the very best quality meat and produce.

David has owned this popular cafe and bar since 2003 and for the past three years has been ably assisted by manageress and cook Sharon Jaggers. The cafe is located in a stylish building that is bright and airy with big glass walls and can be found within Bakewell's Agricultural Business Centre.

Farmers Feast Cafe and Bar is open every day between 9am and 3.30pm and seats up to 200 people in absolute comfort. Next door at the cattle market farmers buy and sell their animals at least twice a week and many of them come here to have a hearty meal.

There are plenty of dishes to choose from off the printed menu and specials board. The child and disabled friendly cafe and bar is renowned for its Sunday carvery and it is definitely an advantage to book early. There is plenty of quality meat to choose from such as topside of roast beef, leg of pork, roast turkey or roast lamb and the roast dinners are served with fresh local vegetables. The lunch menu includes a fine selection of traditional favourites including cottage pie, gammon steak, steak pie and a variety of steaks cooked to your liking. For those diners with a lighter appetite there is a range of filled jacket potatoes to choose from as well as quiche in various flavours.

Bakewell is famous for its Bakewell Tarts and at the Farmers Feast Cafe and Bar they now prepare and cook their own Bakewell puddings and Bakewell Tarts on the premises. They are extremely delicious – hence their popularity with customers, and highly recommended.

Situated next to the cafe is a smart licensed bar area offering a full range of draught beers, lagers etc. It is licensed from 11am until close.

If you are visiting Bakewell and have a gap to fill the Farmers Feast Cafe and Bar is well worth a visit.

33 BAKEWELL TART SHOP & COFFEE HOUSE

Matlock Street, Bakewell, Derbyshire DE45 1EE
Tel: 01629 814692
e-mail: orders@bakewelltartsshop.co.uk
websites: www.bakewelltartshop.co.uk
www.peakdistrictonline.co.uk
www.peakcottagesdirect.co.uk

In the heart of the Peak District, in the charming historic market town of Bakewell, is the award-winning **Bakewell Tart Shop and Coffee House**. On the main A6 Matlock Street, this popular shop has a little something for everyone with an impressive range of gifts and treats to suit every budget, appetite and taste.

The shop has been run by Zoe and David McBurnie since 2001, and they have created quite a following, not just locally, but globally with their online services. Customers are guaranteed to receive a friendly and warm welcome here. Most popular of course is the variety of Bakewell tarts on offer, from traditional to lemon flavoured, but the 'post-a-tart' scheme is fast becoming a popular gift idea. Customers can order a Bakewell tart, have their own message iced onto it and have it sent virtually anywhere in the world! Perfect for a variety of occasions like mother's day, valentines and much more. The shop is open daily from 8:30am-5:30pm (closing a little earlier between October and March), and also sells a variety of other homemade cakes, pies and preserves.

Bakewell itself is a lovely place to stroll around, and is ideal for a relaxed weekend away with easy access to acres of beautiful Derbyshire countryside.

To the rear of the shop is the Coffee House. Its classic coffee shop décor makes for a laid back and friendly atmosphere and is open to all throughout the day. Serving much more than just coffee, Zoe and David stock a wide range of speciality teas, coffees and hot chocolates, alongside a great menu which includes delicious homemade dishes such as cottage pie, fresh soup, and roast dinner, not to mention the award winning traditional pies. A good selection of breakfasts and sandwiches are also available, not forgetting the gluttonous selection of tarts, puddings and cakes.

Located above the shop, is Bloomfield House; a luxury conversion sleeping up to seven adults and one child. A variety of double and family rooms are available with options of either en suite facilities or the use of a large family sized bathroom. Each room is fresh and comfortable, with neutral colours and contemporary design. The accommodation is self catering and has the use of a modern, fully fitted kitchen. It is the ideal place to stay for a relaxing and stress free break. Great reviews and repeat guest bookings in just one year.

34 THE MANNERS HOTEL

Haddon Road, Bakewell,
Derbyshire DE45 1EP
Tel: 01629 812756

The Manners Hotel is a lovely little pub situated in the heart of Bakewell. It attracts an impressive base of clientele along with all the local regulars.

The hotel serves a full selection of draught beers, wines and spirits for your enjoyment. To stop all the guests from going hungry, a mouth-watering traditional pub grub menu is served every afternoon and evening and there is always an additional daily specials board to choose from. All of the dishes are reasonably priced and good portion sizes are welcomed by the customers here. Food is available every day between 11.30am and 3pm and 6pm - 8.30pm. For all those customers who feel they have had a bit too much to drink and cannot drive home there is cosy en-suite accommodation available.

Personally run by Richard Templeman, the hotel has two en-suite guest bedrooms, which are both doubles. The tariff includes a hearty breakfast, which sets guests up for exploring Bakewell and the surrounding area. Both of the guest rooms are located upstairs. Please call for more information or to make a booking.

35 HADDON HALL

Bakewell, Derbyshire DE45 1LA
Tel: 01629 812855 Fax: 01629 814379
e-mail: info@haddonhall.co.uk
website: www.haddonhall.co.uk

Only a mile to the south of Bakewell down the Matlock Road, on a bluff overlooking the Wye, the romantic **Haddon Hall** stands hidden from the road by a beech hedge. The Hall is thought by many to have been the first fortified house in the country, although the turrets and battlements were actually put on purely for show. The home of the Dukes of Rutland for over 800 years, the Hall has enjoyed a fairly peaceful existence, in part no doubt because it stood empty and neglected for nearly 300 years after 1640, when the family chose Belvoir Castle in Leicestershire as their main home. Examples of work from every century from the 12th to the 17th are here in this treasure trove.

Little construction work has been carried out on the Hall since the days of Henry VIII and it remains one of the best examples of a medieval and Tudor manor house. The 16th century terraced gardens are one of the chief delights of the Hall and are thought by many to be the most romantic in England. The Hall's splendour and charm have led it to be used as a backdrop to television and film productions including *Jane Eyre*, *Moll Flanders* and *The Prince and the Pauper*. Nikolaus Pevsner described the Hall as "The English castle par excellence, not the forbidding fortress on an unassailable crag, but the large, rambling, safe, grey, loveable house of knights and their ladies, the unreasonable dream-castle of those who think of the Middle Ages as a time of chivalry and valour and noble feelings. None other in England is so complete and convincing."

36 AVANT GARDE OF BASLOW

Hollingworth House, Calver Road, Baslow, Derbyshire DE45 1RD
Tel: 01246 583888

Avant Garde sells a stylish range of goods for the home and garden, and can be found a short drive from Chatsworth House. New owners Tracey Harrison and Gavin Thompson remain committed to scouring the UK and Europe for the latest trends.

Attention to detail is king at Avant Garde, and customers come first. Tracey and Gavin will happily try to track down that special item for you if they don't have it in stock. There's also a 'made to measure' service, so if you have an awkward corner or a particular spot to fill, Avante Garde will help you to define and then to design just what you want. They also offer a free local delivery service, with a nominal charge if you live slightly further afield.

Whether it's mirrors, cushions and throws from Sweden, wicker baskets, vases, silk flowers, books or gift wraps, there is sure to be something that will catch your eye. So well-designed and crafted are the objects that the shop has featured many times in national magazines. All the items are displayed on various pieces of furniture such as painted housekeepers' cupboards, painted dressers and old pine chests, accentuating that country look that is so admired nowadays. There's plenty of other furniture items for sale too, from wardrobes to wash stands, and everything in-between.

In addition there are many charming items for the garden, so you can personalise your outdoors as much as your home's interior. There's a range of French garden furniture, brightly painted bird houses, galvanised planters, sweet pea baskets, metal obelisks - Avant Garde has got them all, and more. Another section is called "Planted", where seasonal plants, bulbs and herbs are set in beautiful containers.

Those that visit this store just can't get enough, and their testimonials say it all:

"I could furnish my whole house from this shop" - Claire

"It's a lovely shop, with a great feel" - Jenny

Avant Garde of Baslow is a must-visit place for all your gift needs, and you can even buy Christmas gifts and decorations. It is open seven days a week from 10am to 5pm.

37 EYAM MUSEUM

Hawkhill Road, Eyam, Derbyshire S32 5QP
Tel: 01433 631371
website: www.eyam.org

Bubonic plague has been described as the 'most dangerous disease known to mankind' and has killed more souls than all the wars ever fought between all the nations of the world. Known as the Black death, the Great Plague entered London in the 17th Century and came to Eyam by the most unfortunate of mishaps - carried by fleas festering in a box of cloth brought from the capital for the village tailor. When the box was opened plague fleas were released. Between September 1665 and October 1666 260 people - perhaps a third of the population - met an awful, pained death. Only the intervention of two clergymen ensured that the village survived through the next terrible months. William Mompesson was newly appointed rector of Eyam - and he and his predecessor Thomas Stanley, persuaded the village to enter voluntary quarantine, to bury their own dead and even change their pattern of worship. Some had sent their children away, but most folk stayed in Eyam.

People in the surrounding area, especially the Earl of Devonshire, sent provisions to the people of Eyam so they would not starve, though careful precautions were taken to avoid infection. When the plague finally loosed its terrible grip on the village, it left a population of more than 400 people who, needing to make a living, returned to their traditional task of mining lead in the hills above the village. Smallholdings were tended again, a few sheep and cows helping provide some of the necessities of life. Cottages in the village, emptied by the plague, were filled again, often by growm-up sons and daughters who had once moved away. In this way Eyam prospered again. Visit **Eyam Museum** to experience the full story.

38 AISSEFORD TEA ROOM

Ashford-in-the-Water, Derbyshire DE45 1QB
Tel: 01629 812773
e-mail: rosylnM@aol.com
website: www.ashfordtearooms.co.uk

The picturesque village of Ashford-in-the-Water is famous for its colourful well-dressing ceremony but also among food-loving locals for the **Aisseford Tea Room**. Aisseford is simply the Saxon name for Ashford, and while the Tea Room isn't quite that old, the building does date back 400 years. It's a delightful place and has been very much a family affair since it opened in May 2008. Run by Dan McGoverne, his sister Elizabeth and their mum Roz, it isn't surprising that the food is delicious, home-cooked using fresh local produce as much as possible.

The Tea Room offers a warm welcome to everyone, including families, muddy-booted walkers and dog-lovers too. Open seven days a week, the day starts with a full Derbyshire Breakfast, with a wide choice of meals throughout the day. Even the sandwiches are prepared with loving care, with such tasty combinations as bacon, brie and cranberry, or local Stilton with green apple. You can indulge in a passion fruit tea or a goat's cheese and chutney panini, a simple scone or one of the really tasty daily specials like sea bass and lime fishcakes or sweet chilli chicken and mozzarella paninis. With arts and crafts for sale too, the Aisseford is much more than just the perfect tea room.

39 HORSE AND JOCKEY

Tideswell, Buxton, Derbyshire SK17 8JZ
Tel: 01298 872211
e-mail: horseandjockey2008@live.co.uk
website: www.horseandjockeyderbyshire.co.uk

The Horse and Jockey is an outstanding rural village in located in pleasant Tideswell between the A623 and A6 roads. The inn itself is an attractive building, full of the character and history of times gone by. Inside its walls are a pretty combination of old brick and stone, bedecked with a variety of brass memorabilia and china plates. The floors are old slate to match the gnarled oak beams that cover the ceilings, creating a real olde worlde atmosphere within. A wood burning stove is active during the winter months; the perfect spot to warm up in after a brisk walk around the peaks.

The inn is owned and run by Chris Flint and his family, who are born and bred in Tideswell. He's built up a solid reputation amongst the local community but also opens his doors to visitors from further afield every day.

Chris keeps the bar well stocked with three real ales on rotation from local breweries, alongside a host of choice wines and spirits. Food is served at the inn Monday to Friday from 12-2pm and 6-8:30pm and Saturday from 12-8:30pm and on Sundays 12-3pm. Chris creates his food using great locally sourced produce to make wholesome English dishes. The majority of vegetables used are home grown for that rustic taste. Dishes include steak, ale and mushroom short crust pastry pie, butterfly chicken served with creamy stilton and leek sauce, and a traditional braised lamb shank. A selection of succulent steaks also appear on the grill menu cooked to your liking. Fish and vegetarian dishes are also popular, with specials changing regularly. Throughout the day a range of light bites, starters, salads and sandwiches are also served. Special offers are made on weekday lunchtimes and Monday and Thursday evenings, making booking advisable.

Chris also offers his guests excellent bed and breakfast option with five en suite bedrooms to choose from. They come in a range of sizes, all decorated and furnished to a high standard to make each stay hassle free and comfortable. The inn makes a convenient base for exploring the area with historic market towns Buxton, Bakewell, Chatsworth and the Castleton Caverns all within easy reach.

40 THE GEORGE HOTEL

Commercial Road, Tideswell, Derbyshire SK17 8NU
Tel: 01298 871382
e-mail: simon@tght.co.uk
website: www.tght.co.uk

The George Hotel can be found lying in the impressive shadow of the famous 'Cathedral of the Peak.' Known as such for being the largest and most ornate church in the Peak District, Tideswell church draws many visitors, as does the town itself which holds much value for those interested in perusing its charming shops and winding streets which hark back to its status as an ancient market town.

The George Hotel itself is steeped in history, dating back to 1730 in parts. It was once visited by the Prince of Wales in 1806 before his coronation some years later in 1820, and the hotel was allowed to keep its namesake over all other 'George' named inns in the area because of its high standards.

The hotel's current owners Simon and Helen Easter strive to keep this tradition of high standards alive by offering all their guests, royal or not, the very best in hospitality. Together, the Easter's have over sixteen years experience in the licensing trade, meaning that their inn-keeping skills are second to none. They place much importance on retaining the character and history of the hotel which is proudly displayed throughout for interested visitors.

Simon and Helen offer four en suite guest bedrooms, available throughout the year for short breaks and holidays. Rooms come in a range of sizes and combine the hotel's traditional feel with modern comforts seamlessly. Guests are offered a delicious breakfast, taken downstairs.

Both residents and non-residents are welcomed to enjoy the hotel's bar and restaurant which opens throughout the week from Tuesday to Sunday. The bar is always kept fully stocked and houses a number of fine wines and spirits alongside a prized collection of real ales.

Food is available between 12-2:30pm and 6-9pm Tuesday to Saturday and from 12-2:30pm on Sundays. Simon is the chef and has dedicated his time to creating an excellent English menu, full of elegant presentations of traditional pub fayre. Guests can choose from a large variety of filled sandwiches with choices ranging from simple ham salad to bacon and brie or spicy meatballs. A good range of burgers are also on offer, made using only 100% beef and 100% chicken fillets with many varieties and options for vegetarians and others like the wild salmon burger. Simon's stone baked pizzas are also popular choices with toppings for all from Hawaiian to goat's cheese and the classic 'meat feast.' For those with a real taste for meat, something from the grill will be hard to resist. Grills are served on 'Black Rock' - a smooth slab of volcanic rock heated to 440 degrees, twice as hot as a conventional oven to truly sear the meat and trap in all that flavour. Children are more than welcome to dine and have their own menu to choose from. On Sundays a traditional English roast is served, but owing to popularity booking is recommended, as is the rest of the weekend.

41 OLD SMITHY TEAROOMS

Monyash, near Bakewell, Derbyshire DE45 1JH
Tel: 01629 810190
e-mail: smithy@monyash.com
website: www.oldsmithymonyash.co.uk

Beautifully located at the head of the Lathkill Dale nature
reserve, **The Old Smithy Tearooms** is hard to define but very
easy to enjoy. It's a combination café/bar/bistro/restaurant,
and welcomes anyone from wet walkers and weary cyclists seeking a mug of hot tea or a pint of
real ale to someone wanting a more substantial Smithy's Breakfast or Cornish pasty and chips.
Dine inside or out, seven days a week, in this characterful 250-year-old building.

43 THE PACK HORSE INN

Crowdecote, nr Buxton, Derbyshire SK17 0DB
Tel: 01298 83618
e-mail: thepack-horse@btconnect.com

The Pack Horse Inn is one of the most picturesque
hostelries in the Peak District. Nestling in the hillside of
the Upper Dovedale Valley, the historic public house,
built with limestone, dates back to the 16th century.

The inn was a former stop off point for the packhorse
trail from Newcastle Under Lyme to Hassop and is run
by Mick & Sharon who extend a warm welcome to all
including dogs. This traditionally furnished inn boasts
views looking across rolling countryside towards the
village of Longnor from both inside and the large rear
beer garden.

The Couple have been running the pub since mid
August 2010 and are building on the trade by using
locally brewed real ales and locally sourced produce.
The Pack Horse Inn is closed on Monday and Tuesdays
(except Bank Holidays), but it is open every other session with food served between 12pm and
2.30pm, and 6pm – 9pm Wednesday – Sunday. Professional chef Michael Claye has a glowing
reputation and his dishes live up to expectation. Dishes are listed daily on a big blackboard and
favourites include braised lamb shank slowly cooked in red wine gravy served with creamed mash
and seasonal vegetables.

42 THE DUKE OF YORK

Ashbourne Road, Pomeroy, nr Flagg, Buxton, Derbyshire SK17 9QQ
Tel: 01298 83345
e-mail: thedukeofyorkpomeroy@btconnect.com
website: www.thedukeofyorkpub.co.uk

Dating back to the 17th century, **The Duke of York** used to attract plenty of highwaymen through its doors. These days it draws many locals, tourists and visitors to the hamlet of Pomeroy to take in the atmosphere and enjoy the three real ales and wide range of food on offer.

The Duke of York is steeped in history and is outstanding in every department and has an extremely improved reputation since experienced licensees Derek and Cathryn took over in August 2009. Having been in the trade since 1988 they had a lot of ideas for this place and through their experience and hard work The Duke of York is now a popular place to socialise, drink and dine in the area. It offers the very best in ale, food, hospitality and has a picturesque setting, with a caravan and camping site housed to the rear of the main building.

The campsite is an ideal base for visitors to the area and its beautiful surroundings is perhaps why so many people camp here. The site has toilets, a shower and running water and facilities within the pub are available for campers to use. Ring for details.

This family friendly pub is open all day every day and food is available seven days a week between 12pm and 8.30pm. Such is the popularity of this fine establishment it is advisable to book at weekends. Professional chefs Kevin and Steve are employed here and they offer a tasty and extensive menu. Starters include black pudding in Dijon mustard sauce and homemade soup of the day. Traditional favourites litter the main menu with a good selection of pies as well as lasagne, steak, and sausages in rich onion gravy.

For those with a lighter appetite a delicious list of hot baguettes, sandwiches and jacket potatoes are available from the bar. There are specially adapted menus for vegetarians and children and for OAPs there is a meal deal on offer Mon - Fri.

If you have room left for dessert, you are likely to be tempted by the reasonably priced puddings. Hot chocolate fudge cake with double cream vanilla bean ice cream is one of the most popular here, with other choices including fruit crumble of the day with cream or custard, and apricot and ginger brulee torte.

44 THE WHITWORTH PARK HOTEL

Dale Road North, Darley Dale, Matlock, Derbyshire DE4 2FT
Tel: 01629 733111   Fax: 01629 735222
e-mail: info@whitworthparkhotel.co.uk
website: www.whitworthparkhotel.co.uk

The Whitworth Park Hotel is one of the most popular places to dine in Derbyshire. It is ideally located adjacent to the main A6 in Darley Dale, so a great base for visitors touring The Peak District.

Owners Robert Barrington-Evans and his daughter Katie have been in charge here for the past six years and are ably assisted by head chef Andy Whittaker, who is very confident in the kitchen. You only have to taste his food to discover why. He uses as much local produce as possible to create some fantastic dishes.

To start there is a wide selection of tempting dishes on offer such as oak smoked duck breast on a mango chutney finished with fresh rocket, tomato and parma harm bruschetta, and Irish blue cheese in herb infused breadcrumbs on a bed of endive with a sweet raspberry puree. For main course there is a good choice of dishes including medallions of pork fillet with spiced pan roasted apples & pears, finished with calvados baby onions & cream. Pan fried salmon topped with coriander, lime, chilli & ginger on a fluffy coconut basmati rice finished with fried rocket is another option and there are also several vegetarian options, for those diners who prefer not to eat meat. It is definitely advisable to leave room for a dessert to complete your meal with

chocolate fudge cake, treacle sponge and fruits of the forest sherry trifle all available. These dishes are from the current menu & the menus change regularly.

The well-stocked bar has everything you could possibly want to accompany your meal including a choice of rotating real ales.

After all of that, many guests like to retire to their rooms. There are five en-suite rooms available all year round and all of the guest rooms are located upstairs. They all vary in size and the excellent tariff includes a hearty breakfast served between 8am and 9am.

Food is served noon until 3 and 6pm – 9pm (closed Monday lunch times) and a fine roast dinner is served every Sunday between noon and 7pm. Booking is recommended to avoid disappointment.

The hotel hosts a range of entertainment with live music every Friday between 9.30pm and 11.30pm. Ring for details.

45 TALL TREES COFFEE SHOP & RESTAURANT

Oddford Lane, Two Dales, Matlock,
Derbyshire DE4 2EX
Tel: 01629 732932

You'll find **The Tall Trees Coffee Shop and Restaurant** in the Forest Garden Centre in Two Dales, and it's well worth finding. You don't have to be a gardener to enjoy the home-cooking, and the cakes and scones here are especially light and delicious. There's much more on offer than tasty treats, though, as Tall Trees produces a daily selection of hot meals including quiches, tarts and salads, and all at affordable prices.

46 RED LION INN

Main Street, Birchover, Derbyshire DE4 2BN
Tel: 01629 650363 e-mail: red.lion@live.co.uk
website: www.birchoverredlion.com

Dating back to the late 17th century, the **Red Lion Inn** can be found in the picturesque hamlet of Birchover. This stone built public house is one of Derbyshire's most popular destination pubs for lovers of fine food and excellent ales. Professional chef Matteo and his wife Alyson have been here for more than four years and have built a fantastic reputation. They have won numerous awards for their cuisine and ale, which attracts plenty of locals and visitors. The child-friendly inn plays host to a yearly beer festival where almost 20 real ales can be sampled.

48 HEIGHTS OF ABRAHAM

Matlock Bath, Derbyshire DE4 3PD
Tel: 01629 582365 Fax 01629 580279
e-mail: office@heightsofabraham.com
website: www.heightsofabraham.com

Featuring steep rocky gorges, vast caverns, fast running rivers, wide panoramic views and a cable car, it is easy to understand why the Victorian's called Matlock Bath "Little Switzerland"; however, the **Heights of Abraham Country Park and Caverns** overlooks the famous spa town, and provides a unique aspect to a day out or holiday in the Derbyshire Dales and Peak District.

The journey to the summit of the country park is easily made by taking the cable car, adjacent to Matlock Bath railway station and car park. The cable car ticket includes all the attractions in the grounds, as well as the two spectacular underground caverns. Tours throughout the day allow you to experience the exciting underground world within the hillside, with the "miner's tale' in the Great Rutland Cavern Nestus Mine, and the multivision presentation of the "story in the rock" at the Masson Cavern Pavilion.

The sixty-acre country park also features woodland walks, the Owl Maze, the Explorers Challenge, play and picnic areas, Victoria Prospect Tower, plus the High Falls Rocks & Fossils Shop featuring Ichthyosaur remains. When you have worked up an appetite, why not relax with a drink on the terrace and take in the views, or enjoy a snack in the Coffee Shop or a meal in the Woodlanders Restaurant. So next time you are planning a trip to the mountains, remember The Heights of Abraham at Matlock Bath "Little Switzerland" is nearer than you think.

47 RIVERSIDE TEA ROOM & OLD BANK CAFE BAR

44-48 North Parade, Matlock Bath, Derbyshire DE4 3NS
Tel: 01629 55550

The Riverside Tea Room and Old Bank Café Bar in the historic village of Matlock Bath attracts plenty of visitors who come here to enjoy a moment of unique atmosphere. The village can be very busy or very calm, but either way, The Riverside Tea Room and Old Bank Café Bar have an ambience all of their own - a sanctuary from the busy, bustling weekend days of the summer, and warm and friendly when Matlock Bath seems to have fallen asleep.

Paul and Jayne have owned these wonderful establishments for three years now and have built a solid reputation in the area. The Riverside Tea Room and Old Bank Cafe Bar draws in locals and visitors and it is extremely rare that anyone ever leaves here disappointed.

A visit to Matlock Bath can be very rewarding - whatever time of year you choose and whatever the weather. It lies in a beautiful gorge, running alongside the Derwent River. The river runs past the child friendly tea rooms and cafe and beyond the river is the rising tree-covered cliff-face of the gorge. Its spectacular views are what are most admired, as anyone who has gazed at the view from a good vantage point on either side of the narrow gorge can confirm.

It isn't just tea they serve here. Cakes, snacks and a fine selection of other food items can be enjoyed and there is a wide range of drinks to choose from.

Next door in the licensed Old Bank Café you can indulge in a full meal with a glass of wine. The menus feature a range of homemade treats. Jayne is your chef here and serves everything including starters, soups, mains, roast dinners, steaks, fresh fish, omelettes, sandwiches, paninis, jacket potatoes and salads. The roast dinners and full breakfasts are particular favourites. Both establishments offer al-fresco dining in the summer months with tables out the front. Children are more than welcome. Matlock Bath Illuminations and Venetian Nights are events that should not be missed! Ring for details.

Old Bank Cafe Bar is open daily from 9am until around 9pm. The Riverside Tea Room is open daily from 9am – 6pm and seats around 30 customers inside, 35 on the rear patio and 30 outside the front of the establishment.

49 THE PEAK DISTRICT MINING MUSEUM

The Pavilion, Matlock Bath, Derbyshire DE4 3NR
Tel: 01629 583834
e-mail: mail@peakmines.co.uk
website: www.peakmines.co.uk

Visit a hands-on museum where you can experience and wonder at the almost forgotten world of a Derbyshire lead miner. For centuries men have toiled underground in cramped and hazardous conditions to earn a meagre living by extracting the mineral *galena*, lead ore.

See the tools they used and the clothes they wore and encounter the problems that the miner overcame - flooding, explosions and roof falls. Experience the maze of twisting tunnels and shafts and observe the advances in technology and the great importance of lead in our modern day lives. Refresh yourself in the cafe and browse in the well-stocked shop. See the magnificent water pressure engine that was rescued from deep down in a local lead mine.

You can find out what "nicking" means and discover for yourself the amazing network of tunnels that exist under your feet and wonder at the crystals glistening in the walls. This two-man, working lead and fluorspar mine will give you an authentic insight into life underground and the tools and equipment involved. Gold! Gold! The magic word in mining. Stand in a real gold strike, then try your hand at panning for "gold" - but you won't get rich quick with the sort of gold that you recover! Don't think that the museum is a dry-as-dust, wet weather activity. The average family will be enthralled by the many hands-on, interactive and novel opportunities.

50 THE BOAT INN

Scarthon, Cromford, Derbyshire DE4 3QF
Tel: 01629 823282

The Boat Inn's new hosts, Maggie and Richard Geldard, only took over this charming village inn in May 2010 but have already given the pub a new lease of life. This is due in no small way to Maggie's skills in the kitchen, where her talents as a chef really shine. When you dine at the Boat Inn you know that all the food is home-cooked, and 95% of the produce is sourced locally. This is Derbyshire food at its finest, with daily specials as well as the regular menus, with dishes like Poached Salmon with New Potatoes, Homemade Beef and Guinness Pie, pt Pork Fillet in a Creamy Cider Sauce. On Sundays the traditional Sunday Roasts are added to the menus.

One of the Boat Inn's secret attractions is its beautiful rear 'hidden garden', the first place regulars head when the weather is fine. Abbot Ale is the regular beer, and there are also up to four changing guest real ales to enjoy too. The pub is open daily, with food available Tue-Sun noon-2pm and 6-9pm, but no food on Mondays.

51 RED LION HOTEL

Market Place, Wirksworth, Matlock, Derbyshire DE4 4ET
Tel: 01629 822214
e-mail: info@theredlionhotelwirksworth.co.uk
website: www.theredlionhotelwirksworth.co.uk

Originally a coaching inn built in the late 18th century, the **Red Lion Hotel** still welcomes locals and visitors alike, but in 21st-century style. For those wanting to stay in the heart of Wirksworth, whether for business or pleasure, the Red Lion has six ensuite guest bedrooms, all tastefully decorated and offering modern furnishings, free wireless internet, digital TV, complimentary toiletries, hot and cold drinks facilities, good off-road parking, and rounded off with a hearty English breakfast.

Like all good hoteliers – and owners Peter and Christine have years of experience in the trade – at the Red Lion they know that you have to satisfy the local regulars as well as the visiting tourists. That's why you'll find a constantly changing range of national and local ales in the bar, though Marston's Pedigree is always available. London Pride and Bass are other favourites, but chances are you'll find something new to slake your thirst if you've been out walking for the day.

While they're rightly proud of their bar and their beers, Peter and Christine know that today's travellers have discerning palates and expect top-class cuisine. New head chef Lee Mallinson is bringing his extensive catering knowledge to the Red Lion and will be introducing a full range of quality dishes using local produce. From traditional fish and chips, wonderful Sunday roast to more elaborate fish and game dishes he will also be accommodating

vegan, vegetarian and coeliac choices. If you want to stay or dine at the weekends booking is highly recommended.

The Red Lion boasts one of the most elegant function rooms in the area for weddings, parties, acoustic nights and other celebrations and the comments on their website from previous guests show that they know exactly what they're doing – 'From the moment we arrived... we were impressed' and 'We've just returned from a night at the Red Lion where we were made to feel extremely welcome and relaxed. Lovely, spacious room, cosy fires in the bars, fantastic breakfast and a friendly, efficient staff. '

Comments like these speak for themselves, and let you know that the Red Lion may well be in business for another 200 years or so at least.

52 THE COACH AND HORSES

27 Dig Street, Ashbourne, Derbyshire DE6 1GF
Tel: 01335 346818

Dating back in parts to the 18th century, **The Coach and Horses** is situated in the popular market town of Ashbourne. Located on one of the town's main roads, this fine public house was once a coaching inn, which had stables to the rear where horses were kept.

Larraine Clarke and her daughter Charlotte were born and bred in the town and took over at The Coach and Horses six months ago. They have totally refurbished the establishment and many locals agree they have given it a new lease of life. Being so well known in the town has helped attract more people through the doors of the pub and Larraine's charm, character and enthusiasm has ensured visitors and locals return.

The facilities here are fantastic and the bar is well stocked with two real ales that can be enjoyed – Marstons Pedigree is the regular.

The aroma of home cooked food is hard to resist. A variety of dishes are available daily, which can be chosen from the printed menu or specials board. Larraine is in charge of the kitchen here and the dishes she creates are delicious. Liver and onion; scampi, chips and peas; and shepherd's pie are among the most popular with diners and the succulent Sunday roasts are always a favourite. Meals can be enjoyed at one of the wooden tables in the dining area, which has a lovely atmosphere.

Outside you will discover a wonderful hidden beer garden to the rear of The Coach and Horses. It is a delightful place to enjoy refreshments or dine al fresco style on warmer days.

Entertainment is put on each week here, with a disco from 8pm – 2am every Saturday and a traditional pub games night until 2am on a Friday.

Open all day every day, hot drinks are served daily at this child and pet friendly establishment.

Disabled access is not a problem.

53 WHITE HART HOTEL

10 Church Street, Ashbourne,
Derbyshire DE6 1AE
Tel: 01335 344711
e-mail: whitehart.ashbourne@hotmail.co.uk
website: www.ashbournewhitehart.co.uk

The historic **White Hart Hotel** is right in the centre of Ashbourne, the Gateway to Dovedale. With four ensuite rooms to rent, guests have all the amenities of the town with the beautiful Derbyshire countryside a few minutes drive away. It's always been a popular local, but new owners Paul Attewell and his son Daniel are set to make it even more popular with Sunday lunches and specialty food nights. Monday sees a steak menu, Wednesday is ribs and Mexican cuisine, while Friday is for traditional fish and chips.

If you just want a drink then Marston's Pedigree is the regular real ale, with changing guest ales also available and naturally a choice of wines and other drinks too. It's the intention of Paul and Daniel to make their prices as appetising as their dishes, and entertainment is also available on different nights of the week. There are pub quizzes, bingo and killer pool nights, so ring for details of what's on when, as the pub is otherwise open all day, every day.

54 YE OLDE VAULTS

21 Market Place, Ashbourne,
Derbyshire DE6 1EU
Tel: 01335 346127

Even a good and popular place like **Ye Olde Vaults** can get better, and regulars are now raving about the food here since owner Stella Critchlow found a new and talented chef. The food is all home-made, with the pies proving especially popular – choose from the meat and potato, the cottage pie, or the steak and ale. There are also daily specials, with one dish always on offer at a very special price, and regular menu items include vegetable lasagne, rump steak and home-made chilli.

There are soups of the day, OAP specials and sandwiches, and of course a choice if real ales, all to be enjoyed in the historic surrounds of Ye Olde Vaults. And Ye Olde Vaults really is old, the building going back to about 1620 and it has been a pub since the late 18th century. Today there are four guest bedrooms, all ensuite, with tea- and coffee-making facilities, colour TVs and a full English breakfast. It may look small on the outside, but there's a big welcome and lots to enjoy at Ye Olde Vaults in the very centre of Ashbourne.

55 THE FLOWER CAFÉ

5 The Market Place, Ashbourne, Derbyshire DE6 1EU
Tel: 01335 344090
e-mail: theflowercafe@ntlworld.com
website: www.theflowercafe.co.uk

The Flower Café is always packed with local people. The home-cooking is unbeatable, and there's seating inside and out. Honey is from the family's own bee-keeper, eggs from local free-range hens, and all produce bought locally where possible. Dishes are cooked to order, and as well as a dish of the day, tasty cakes and specialty teas and coffees, there are choices like homemade quiche, jacket potatoes, grilled paninis and many more.

56 CHIMES CAFÉ

48 St John Street, Ashbourne, Derbyshire DE6 1GH
Tel: 01335 300220
e-mail: info@chimes-cafe.co.uk
website: www.chimes-cafe.co.uk

Chimes Café is a new and unique spot in Ashbourne, as it combines the family business of clock and watch making and repairing with a marvellous place to eat or drink. Robert and Alison James have run a clockmaker's business in Tutbury for over 20 years, but recently branched out to create the charming – and chiming! – Chimes Café.

The menu ranges from café-style dishes during the day to gourmet meals on a Friday and Saturday night – when it's definitely a good idea to book. The Café Menu offers sandwiches, salads, soups and jacket potatoes, while the Table d'Hote Menu appears at the weekends when you can choose from the 2-course or 3-course fixed price options.

Starters might include garlic mushrooms or a melon and grape cocktail, with main courses providing a wide range of tasty options such as mixed grill, chicken chasseur, Greek salad, salmon steak or chilli con carne. Wind it up, so to speak, with ice cream, waffles or jam roly poly and custard.

57 SARACEN'S HEAD

Church Lane, Shirley, nr Ashbourne, Derbyshire DE6 3AS
Tel: 01335 360330
e-mail: info@saracens-head-shirley.co.uk
website: www.saracens-head-shirley.co.uk

Although this historic inn dates back to 1791, the **Saracen's Head** definitely moves with the times. It is now one of the best gastro-pubs not just in Derbyshire but in the whole of England. A lot of

the credit obviously goes to its award-winning chef Robin Hunter, who not only runs the pub with his wife Terri but also takes charge of the kitchen with a team of professional chefs. Everything on the menus at the Saracen's Head is made on the premises, from the bread to the ice-cream, and Robin believes that any chef is only as good as the last meal he cooked.

Some visitors are happy just to have a snack and a drink in the bar, as even the quick bites at the Saracen's Head are exceptionally good. So too are the beers, with a range of real ales available on tap, though this is a pub which welcomes all, and you can pop in for a cup of tea or coffee and a slice of home-made cake, if that's all you want. The choice here will be equally aide, from jasmine and peppermint tea, green tea or camomile, with coffees including espresso, Americano, cappuccino, macchiato, latte or just regular filtered coffee, freshly brewed every time.

One look at the dishes on the blackboard, though, and you might find yourself hungrier than you thought. Starters might include fresh cod and coriander fishcakes served with a chilli syrup, or field mushrooms baked with goats cheese, garlic and a herb crust. All starters are served with their home-made bread. Main courses usually include the ever-popular large battered haddock with chips and mushy peas, to more elaborate dishes such as a roasted asparagus tart with mustard cream, soft poached eggs and a Mozzarella trellis. Whether your taste is for fish, meat, or vegetarian food, there's always a good choice on every menu.

Desserts are where the kitchen really shines, though, with a lengthy menu of fresh-made temptations that make you wish you had room for every one. From a double-cream rice pudding served with Victoria Plum jam or a strawberry pavlova through to real English puddings like steamed syrup sponge or sticky toffee pudding, every meal at the Saracen's Head ends on a highlight. Be sure to book, though.

58 SHOULDER OF MUTTON

Osmaston, Ashbourne, Derbyshire DE6 1LW
Tel: 01335 342371
e-mail: paulcranstone@btinternet.com

Hosts Tina and Paul welcome visitors to their popular **Shoulder of Mutton** pub in the beautiful village of Osmaston. It's the archetypal English village, with its duck pond, church and thatched cottages, and, of course, the perfect village pub. The Shoulder of Mutton is built of the same red brick as many of the village's other buildings, and though no-one knows for sure how long there's been a pub here, there is a date stone of 1803 showing it to be over 200 years old. Tina and Paul have been here for the last 17 of those years, turning it into one of the most popular pubs for miles around.

Once inside it's easy to see why from the cosy and friendly atmosphere. The customer is king here, and the standards of service are high, with a strong emphasis on giving good value for money, too.

There's no scrimping on quality, however, as the dishes from the pub's kitchen prove. They buy only the freshest and finest of local produce, and provide varied menus that combine the best of English home cooking with influences from abroad too. You can eat in the restaurant, the lounge, the bar or outdoors as well in the summer months.

There are two regular real ales, Bass and Marston's Pedigree, plus occasional guest ales and a comprehensive range of keg bitters, mild, cider and lager, along with whiskies, wines, liqueurs, brandies, and soft drinks too. As well as finding time to run the adjacent village shop and post office, Paul and Tina keep themselves busy by doing outside catering, including providing your own personal outside bar.

Being on the edge of the Peak District there is plenty to see and do in the area, including watching motor cycle racing at Darley Moor or visiting Alton Towers, just a few miles away. In short, the Shoulder of

Mutton is a good, old-fashioned English pub of the finest kind, with a friendly welcome and good food and ale.

The Shoulder of Mutton is open every day, and open all day on Saturdays and Sundays all year round, and on Fridays, Saturdays, Sundays and Bank Holidays in summer. Food is served every day from 12-2pm and 6-9pm. There are no bookings, so get there early or be ready to wait for a table.

59 THE BLACK HORSE INN

Hulland Ward, Ashbourne, Derbyshire DE6 3EE
Tel: 01335 370206

The Black Horse Inn is so old no-one knows for sure how old it is, but it dates back to at least the 1690s. What is sure is that it has lost none of the 'olde worlde' charm that it has built up over the centuries, and it is worth visiting for the décor alone. Owner and host Muriel Edwin has built up a fine gallery of colourful paintings, an enjoyable and fun collection of black and white cows, and other memorabilia – including a gallows hanging over the front door to welcome their guests.

The four ensuite guestrooms also keep up the historic feel as they all have four-poster beds but otherwise all the modern amenities you expect in accommodation these days. Muriel is in charge of the kitchens, where game is one speciality. Their venison comes from Lincolnshire, but otherwise everything is sourced locally wherever possible, and vegetarians are equally well catered for.

Beer is nothing but the best, too. The Black Horse is a regular in the Good Beer Guide, and always has several real ales on tap, and they change constantly but with Wadsworth 6X the regular. Food is served Mon-Sat noon-2pm and 6-9pm, Sun noon-2pm with the Carvery and 7-9pm in the evenings.

60 THE RED LION INN

Main Road, Hognaston, Derbyshire DE6 1PR
Tel: 01335 370396
e-mail: redlion@w3z.co.uk
website: www.redlionhognaston.co.uk

Situated in the picturesque village of Hognaston, **The Red Lion Inn** is a traditional seventeenth century, family-run public house. Tony and Jenny Waterall have been here for more than five and a half years and their chef son Jason works in the kitchen.

This olde worlde public house is nestled in a stunning location on the edge of the Peak District National Park. It overlooks the popular tourist destination of Carsington Water, making it the ideal place for visitors to the area to stay. There are three guest rooms available here, all with en-suite facilities, and were once frequented by John F Kennedy Jr and his wife Carolyn Bessette.

The Red Lion Inn is renowned for the fine food it serves and has been mentioned by Derbyshire Life, the Daily Mail, the Daily Telegraph and The Observer. In the kitchen James and his colleagues use only the very best produce and the succulent Sunday roast dinners are extremely popular.

This popular village inn is open every session serving four real ales and food times are 12pm - 2.30pm and 6pm - 9pm all week.

61 MAINSAIL RESTAURANT

Carsington Water Visitor Centre, Ashbourne, Derbyshire DE6 1ST
Tel: 01629 540363
e-mail: enquiries@newleafcatering.co.uk

There are many reasons for visiting the Mainsail Restaurant at Carsington Water, not least being the views you get of the reservoir and the surrounding, stunning scenery.

You can work up an appetite by walking, sailing, fishing and shopping at Carsington Water, then simply sit back in the relaxing atmosphere of the Mainsail and take in the views. If you wish to enjoy the glorious, fresh air and sunshine then the decked balcony area provides the perfect area to relax and enjoy lunch.

Many people visit Carsington purely to sample the food at the Mainsail. As a member of Peak District Cuisine, the restaurant ensures that as much of the produce as possible is sourced locally.

Opening at 10.00 am and with breakfasts served from 10.30am this is a great start to the day. Whilst lunch is served from 11.30am to 2.30pm with a great selection of specials, a fantastic range of speciality sandwiches, regular sandwiches, mouthwatering salads and light bites, cakes and desserts are also available throughout the day, all of which can be complimented with superb wines available from the comprehensive wine list.

For children there is a fantastic selection of dishes prepared using natural, local products wherever possible. Also available is the Lunch4kids counter where children can create their own lunchbox.

Of course you may just want to pop in for a coffee made with dark, roasted Arabica beans or a cup of English Breakfast tea, but whatever you choose you will always receive a warm welcome at the Mainsail Restaurant.

If you really can't pull yourselves away from the gorgeous views and wonderful food, then the Mainsail offers three self-catering cottages which make an ideal base from which to explore the Peak District. Two of the cottages sleep 17 and one sleeps 9, representing amazing value for money.

The Mainsail is open every day of the year, except Christmas Day, but please ring for detailed opening hours.

62 BRACKENDALE RESTAURANT & FUNCTION ROOM

Knockerdown Farm, B5035, nr Carsington Water,
Ashbourne, Derbyshire DE6 1NQ
Tel: 01629 540880 / 07891839151
e-mail: margaret@mchamberlain6.wanadoo.co.uk

Renowned for its delicious cuisine, **Brackendale Restaurant and Function Room** is talked about all over the county. It has been owned and personally run by Margaret Chamberlain for the past five years and is extremely popular with locals and visitors.

Inside, there is room for around 50 diners and it is definitely an advantage to book, but essential on a Sunday when a divine roast dinner is served. Local produce is used where possible and the dishes available are listed daily on a blackboard. They are all homemade and cooked to order and favourites include salmon in cucumber and dill sauce, chicken in stilton sauce, three cheese pasta bake, lamb casserole and beef lasagne.

Brackendale Restaurant and Function Room is child friendly and popular with families in the area and there is disabled access throughout. It can be found just off the A5035 within the grounds of Knockerdown Farm and close to the well known Carsington Water.

63 BENTLEY BROOK INN

Fenny Bentley, Ashbourne,
Derbyshire DE6 1LF
Tel: 01335 350278
e-mail: all@bentleybrookinn.co.uk
website: www.bentleybrookinn.co.uk

The Bentley Brook Inn in the Peak District National Park is far from being just another pub. It is also a historic landmark, which oozes history as it began life as a medieval farmhouse.

History alone doesn't make for a good hostelry, of course, and the General Manager Wendy Payne and her team work hard to ensure the food, the drink and the atmosphere is as good as it gets. Most of the produce used in the kitchen is local, organic and gluten-free. The homemade Steak and Ale Suet Pie is always popular, and Craig produces his own homemade curries and lasagnes too.

There are always at least two real ales to sample, alongside the resident Marston's Pedigree. Also always available is a fine beer called Leatherbritches, which used to be made here at the inn but is now brewed in nearby Ashbourne. For those wanting to stay and enjoy the scenery there are 11 ensuite guest bedrooms superbly maintained by our longstanding housekeeper Edna Stanley, rated 3-Star by the English Tourist Board, and a beautiful garden to enjoy. The Bentley Brook is open daily, with food available Mon-Fri noon-3pm and 6-9pm, Sat-Sun noon-8.30pm, with a Sunday Carvery noon-3pm.

64 TISSINGTON HALL

The Estate Office, Tissington, Ashbourne,
Derbyshire DE6 1RA
Tel: 01335 352200

The Estate came into the hands of the FitzHerbert
family as the result of Nicholas FitzHerbert
marrying the heiress Cicely Francis in the late 15th
century. The family originally came to England
with William the Conqueror and settled in
Derbyshire when William FitzHerbert was granted
the Manor of Norbury in 1125.

The baronetcy was conferred on William FitzHerbert by George III in 1784 for acting as Minister
for Woods and Rivers and for his role as a Gentleman Usher to the King. He divided his time between
London and Derbyshire and was succeeded by his eldest son, Anthony, in 1791. His brother Henry
inherited as a minor in 1798 and built extensively in and around the village during his 60 year
tenure. Successive baronets have tended diligently to the estate and village although the total
acreage has shrunk from about 4,000 acres at its peak in 1850, to 2,400 acres today. The sales were
mainly enforced by twentieth century death duties and the cost of Sir Hugo's divorce in 1922.

Tissington Hall was originally built in the early 17th century, a top floor was added around 1700
and then the well-known Derby architect Joseph Pickford remodelled the west aspect around 1780
by adding a projecting central bay and open arcading on the ground floor.

The Hall and Gardens are open to the public on 28 advertised days per year. Groups, parties
and societies are very welcome by arrangement throughout the year.

65 THE SOUTH PEAK ESTATE

The National Trust, South Peak Estate, Ham Hall,
Ilam, Ashbourne, Derbyshire DE6 2AZ
Tel: 01335 350503
e-mail: john.malley@nationaltrust.org.uk
website: www.nationaltrust.org.uk

The South Peak Estate lying within what is called the White Peak
area of the Peak District extends to approximately 4,000 acres.
Located to the north of the market town of Ashbourne the main
bulk of the estate is located within the two river valleys of the
Dove and Manifold. Within the property are popular visitor
attractions such as Dovedale and Ham Park.

The Estate is centred on Ham Park which contains Ham Hall

(now a Youth Hostel), together with the National Trust's
visitor facilities. To the north-west lies the Hamps and
Manifold Valleys and to the north- east lies Dovedale
stretching 7 miles to the north towards Hartington. Some
of the finest Peak District limestone grasslands and dales
woodland lie within these two valleys under Trust
management which are soon to be designated as Special
Areas of Conservation under European leglislation. Access
to the estate is available to the public all year round and
visitor numbers are very high with an estimated 2 million
visitors a year to Dovedale alone.

66 BERESFORD TEA ROOMS

Market Place, Hartington, Buxton, Derbyshire SK17 0AL
Tel: 01298 84418

Tea rooms are often countryside oasis' which conjure up thoughts of home-made food and pots of tea - and this is exactly what you can expect at Beresford Tea Rooms. What could be better after you've completed some of the best walks in the Peak District than a refreshing cup of tea, or coffee if that is your preference, and a freshly prepared traditional sandwich?

Here you're in for a real treat; this friendly place is great for light bites and tasty snacks or a more filling meal. It is all home-cooking here and it is that homely aroma that draws so many people in from the streets. The cakes are absolutely delicious as are the range of Derbyshire filled oat cakes and omelettes.

The Georgian town of Buxton rivals Ambleside for the title of the highest town in England and is surrounded by some of the most glorious of the Peak District countryside. Visitors to the largest settlement in the Peak District National Park often visit Hartington and it is hard not to take a closer look at this delightful tea room.

Seating 26 customers inside and a further eight outside on warmer days, this bustling tearoom is also the award winning village post office -providing a focus for the community and an opportunity to meet friends. Sue Bruce has owned the Beresford Tea Rooms for the past 25 years and the village post office within the tea rooms for the past decade.

For those with a sweet tooth the dessert menu is extremely tempting. Syrup sponge, sticky toffee pudding, Jam Roly Poly, Bakewell tart and treacle tart are among the favourites from the extensive selection. Diners can also browse, and purchase, local crafts, paintings, prints and produce displayed around the tea rooms.

The Tea Room is open daily from March to November between 9.30am and 5pm and in winter from 10am to 4pm.

67 BIGGIN HALL COUNTRY HOUSE HOTEL

Biggin-by-Hartington, near Buxton, Derbyshire SK17 ODH
Tel: 01298 84451
e-mail: enquiries@bigginhall.co.uk
website: www.bigginhall.co.uk

Biggin Hall is a grand country house that dates back to the 17th century, situated in the tranquil countryside of the Peak District National Park. Its lofty position 1,000 feet above sea level commands stunning views across the surrounding area – a photographer's paradise in any season. Derbyshire's ever changing landscape offers much for the walker or cyclist and Biggin makes the perfect place to stay for just such a holiday. An exhilarating stroll can offer dry-stone walling, deep wooded valleys, heather clad moorlands, and a charming selection of timeless market towns and villages. Throughout the year Biggin Hall offers a selection of special offer short and long breaks, all of which include a stay in the handsome manor house, a daunting grade II listed building filled with interesting nooks, crannies and original features including a large stone fireplace in the lounge which bears the inscription 1672. Despite the antiquity of the manor's appearance, it is fully equipped with all mod cons including free wifi access, and all twenty rooms have full en suite facilities.

Biggin Hall remains run and owned by Steve Williams, who has painstakingly restored the manor and its grounds to its former glory since his arrival. A true labour of love, guests now have the option of enjoying two large lounges, one with a roaring fire and one with a guest library. A private dining room is also available in which guests can be served an elegant dinner from the restaurant.

The restaurant itself is bedecked with glorious oak beamed ceilings, fine wooden furniture, cosy candlelight and unrivalled views across the gardens. Its menu champions local produce and seasonal goods, sourced from within the local area to serve up a selection of rustic and hearty modern English dishes. Chefs Mark Wilton and Carol Worall have a fine reputation for excellence in their cooking, focusing on simplicity and taste; dishes are freshly prepared and imaginatively planned. Throughout the day guests can choose from breakfast, lunch and dinner menus including sandwich menus and afternoon tea. An attractive selection of fine wines has been listed to accompany each menu, alongside a range of real ales and guest beers. Hot chocolates, speciality teas and coffees are also served throughout the day as the manor also finds itself a popular resort for non-residents.

Biggin is also an understandably popular place for weddings. With stunning scenery, regal dining halls and four poster bedrooms – alongside a bespoke wedding planning service with as little or as much intervention as is needed. Please see website for details.

68 THE CROWN INN

Riggs Lane, Marston Montgomery,
Ashbourne, Derbyshire DE6 2FF
Tel: 01889 591430
e-mail: esa@thecrowninnderbyshire.co.uk
website: www.thecrowninnderbyshire.co.uk

A new owner and a new talented chef have recently transformed the **Crown Inn** in the picture-postcard Derbyshire village of Marston Montgomery. Owner Esa Ruotsalainen and chef Ross Colledge have given this village inn a new lease of life, and provided quality accommodation, great menus and a wide range of wines, beers and other drinks that now bring in the crowds. It's certainly wise to book for a Friday or Saturday night.

On the bar side there are always three real ales available, often from local micro-breweries. In addition to the wine list there's a wide choice of whiskies too, not just from Scotland but from all over the world. It's reading the menus, though, when mouths really start to water. Start with the soup of the day, or perhaps pan-seared scallops with a pea purée, smoked bacon and a herb oil. Main courses always include vegetarian options, like a flavour-filled wild mushroom, spinach and ricotta saffron risotto, while fish and meat-eaters can enjoy dishes such as herb-crusted cod with a seafood broth or Gressingham duck breast with a redcurrant sauce.

69 THE SWAN

2 St Edward Street, Leek, Staffordshire ST13 5DS
Tel: 01538 382081
e-mail: nikki_lou@hotmail.co.uk

Located in the heart of the historic market town of Leek, **The Swan** is the town's oldest hostelry with a history dating back to the 15th century.

The child friendly, family run pub is run by Barry and Tina Birch, daughters Nikki and Carrie, son Mark and barmaid Paula.

The Swan is open all day every day and attracts a wide range of customers who are all warmly welcomed. Real ale lovers are in their element here with five real ales to enjoy with Bombadier, Hobgoblin, Abbot and Speckled Hen the regulars.

Quality homemade food can be ordered daily between 12 noon and 3pm and on Sunday there is an excellent carvery. Customers are invited to choose from a list of delicious dishes from the printed menu or specials board, including home cooked ham. It is hoped that in the future food will be available throughout the day. Ring for details.

A comfortable self catering apartment is available all year round. It sleeps up to three guests and breakfast can be arranged. Ring for details.

70 RAYMONDO'S

1-5 Russell Street, Leek, Staffordshire ST13 5JF
Tel: 01538 381190
e-mail: enquiries@raymondos.co.uk
website: www.raymondos.co.uk

Raymondo's has been an award-winning family-run restaurant ever since it first opened its doors in 1981. Centrally located in Leek, it oozes atmosphere thanks to its origins as three late 19th-century cottages knocked together. It's the food that counts, though, and there is a wide choice of superb tasty dishes such as Chicken Tarragon, Game mix en Croûte, Fillet of Salmon with a Lemon and Dill Dressing, juicy steaks, desserts like Treacle Pudding and vegetarian options also available.

71 THE THREE HORSESHOES

Long Lane, Dalbury Lees,
Ashbourne, Derbyshire DE6 5BJ
Tel: 01332 824481
Mobile: 07977 244184
e-mail: bar-2-u@hotmail.co.uk

The idyllic hamlet of Long Lane in the heart of the Derbyshire countryside is home to the traditional English inn of **The Three Horseshoes**. The inn itself dates back to 1750 and thanks to its landlord, Chris Peach, has retained much of that original eighteenth century charm. Real log fires, low oak beamed ceilings and brick facades all combine to create a cosy and atmospheric inn. Full of traditional furniture and memorabilia from the inn's history, guests are offered a sense of nostalgia without forgoing any of the modern comforts that make eating out easy.

In the winter months guests can warm themselves before the fire with a fine glass of real ale, whilst in the summer months the inn's attractive rear beer garden provides a happy respite for families. Owing to its location, the inn is also popular with hikers and cyclists who find the inn within easy stopping distance of some of the area's most beautiful walks.

A professional chef creates the menu here offering a range of hearty treats befitting the best of country inns. Chris also offers a hireable bar and hog roast service to give any event a deliciously earthy feel. The hog roast also makes occasional appearances at the inn's regular acoustic music evenings, usually on Fridays, please call for details.

Chris plans to create some accommodation at the inn over the coming months.

72 THE SWAN

Draycott-in-the-Clay, Ashbourne,
Derbyshire   DE6 5GZ
Tel: 01283 820031

Offering the very best in hospitality, food and
drink, **The Swan** is a quality, traditional village
pub. It can be found adjacent to the A515, a
couple miles south of its junction with the A50 in
Draycott In The Clay.

Martin and Trudy have been here for more than three
years, but became the leaseholders in January 2010. Food
can be enjoyed in the comfort of the dining area or
outside in the beer garden, which overlooks the
countryside, on warmer days.

The food is extremely popular and you will need to
book on Saturday evenings to avoid disappointment.
There is something for everyone on the extensive printed
menu with a range of burgers, pies, steaks and fish
dishes. A lot of the produce is sourced locally and all of the dishes are freshly prepared and
cooked to order. Freshly carved ham served with two eggs and chips, Lasagne, and grilled chicken
breast served with a barbeque dip are favourites among diners. For those with a lighter appetite
there is a fine selection of fresh salads, omelettes, filled jacket potatoes or hot sandwiches.
There is also a daily specials board offering additional choices and roast dinners are added to the
menu for Sunday lunch. Thursday steak nights are popular here.

73 THE ROEBUCK INN

Draycott-in-the-Clay, Ashbourne,
Derbyshire   DE6 5BT
Tel: 01283 820973
e-mail: theroebuckinndraycott@hotmail.com

The Roebuck Inn is a superb public house located in
Draycott-in-the-Clay. Business partners Amy McAllister
and Steve Wild have been here for four years and Amy is
the chef.

Visitors and locals flock to The Roebuck Inn for its delicious
food, which can be enjoyed in the bright and pleasant dining
area. There is seating room for 42 diners on an average day,
but when functions are held the inn caters for 50 people.
Ring for details.

Diners can choose from a varied selection of dishes which
are listed on a printed menu and food is served daily. Amy
tries to source as much of the produce she uses locally to
ensure the highest standard of cuisine. Additional options are
available from the daily specials board. Such is the popularity of eating at this child-friendly inn
Sundays need to be booked. Roast dinners are served between noon and 4pm and the full menu is
served Monday – Saturday between noon and 3pm and 6pm - 9pm.

Real ales are served at the well-stocked bar with Marstons Pedigree the regular. There is also a
good range of lagers, wines, spirits and soft drinks.

74 THE MASONS ARMS

1 Etwall Road, Mickleover, Derbyshire DE3 0DL
Tel: 01332 513156
e-mail: masons_arms@btopenworld.com

On the edge of Derby in the busy village of Mickleover is the also busy **Masons Arms**, which has been around since the 1700s. Hosts Nadine and Trevor Price have been running the pub successfully for the last ten years, with Nadine being a local girl.

With its exposed beams and old-fashioned atmosphere, the Masons Arms is everything a good pub should be. There are always four real ales to enjoy, with the regulars being Old Speckled Hen, Harvey's Pale and Marston's Pedigree. In addition there's also always guest ale too.

Nadine is in charge of the kitchen, and buys as much of her produce as possible from within Derbyshire. All dishes are home-cooked to order, with a printed menu and a board showing tempting daily specials like Homemade Beef Lasagne, Brewer's beef Casserole or Mushroom Stroganoff. On Sundays roasts are added to the menu too.

Many of the local regulars come for the combination of tasty food and good value, and when the regulars are happy then visitors know they're going to be happy as well. The Masons Arms is open daily. Food is available Mon-Fri 12-2pm and 5.30-8pm, Sat 12-2pm and 6-9pm, Sun 12-4pm.

75 THE SALT BOX CAFE

Derby Road, Hatton, South Derbyshire DE65 5PT
Tel: 01283 813189
e-mail: saltboxcafe@gmail.com

Attracting an impressive range of customers, **The Salt Box Cafe** has been welcoming customers for decades. Owned by John and Bobbie Yasin since August 2009 it can be found adjacent to the A511 at Hatton.

It is always bustling with a good mix of customers such as tourists, locals, businessmen and lorry drivers who come here eager to satisfy their varying appetites. Customers rarely leave disappointed because there is an extensive range of dishes on the menu, from toast to steak, all of which are freshly cooked to order. The produce is sourced locally ensuring a high standard of food and The Salt Box Cafe is well known for its generous portion sizes. People never leave feeling hungry - only eager to return.

This popular child-friendly cafe is open seven days a week and has room for 120 diners. Food is served 7am – 7pm every week day, 7am – 2pm on Saturday and 8am – 2pm on Sunday.

There is good access for disabled customers. Cash and card only.

76 NUMBER 10 CAFE BAR RESTAURANT

10 Belmont Street, Swadlincote, Derbyshire DE11 8JU
Tel: 01283 522811
e-mail: info@number10bar.com
website: www.number10bar.com

This fine establishment has recently undergone a major refurbishment transforming it into the hub of Swadlincote. **Number 10 Cafe Bar Restaurant** can be found at the heart of the town and is enjoyed by people of all ages.

It is very much a family-run venue owned by Jeff and Melanie Dixon and their son Jak. Open seven days a week from noon until close, Number 10 is spread across two floors. Bar food is available downstairs from noon until 6pm and from 7pm customers can dine in the beautifully renovated restaurant, which can seat around 50 diners.

There is a varied selection of dishes listed on the menu with a range of meat, fish and vegetarian options. All are reasonably priced and favourites include duck breast served with classic black cherry sauce and orange sauce; cod, mussels, leek and cider pie; and a choice of steaks and burgers. It is definitely a good idea to leave room for one of the tempting desserts like chocolate orange brownie, warm white chocolate sauce and orange sorbet, and all almond lemon Bakewell tart served with an English custard sauce.

77 THE BAY TREE RESTAURANT

4 Potter Street, Melbourne, Derbyshire DE73 8HW
Tel: 01332 863358
e-mail: enquiries@baytreerestaurant.com
website: www.baytreerestaurant.com

The Bay Tree Restaurant in the heart of Melbourne is one of the best-known and best-loved restaurants in Derbyshire. It has been in the same hands for over 20 years, and during that time its reputation has been built on good, honest cooking, fresh local ingredients and a combination of imagination and flair. Co-owners Vicki Talbott and chef Rex Howell are determined not only to maintain the high standards they have set but improve even further on them as well.

The restaurant is housed in a warm, old building of red brick that dates back to 1790, and which still retains many of its original features. The Bay Tree is recommended in all the best food guides, and behind the 18th-century brick frontage the 70-seat restaurant has been refurbished in a cool contemporary style by designer David Wrigglesworth.

The menu changes regularly in this award-winning establishment, but always boasts the best of New World cuisine. The owners like to take classic British dishes and ingredients and re-invent them using influences from around the world. The dinner menu might include such mouthwatering plates as griddled fillet of prime English beef 'paillard' on a rösti potato with a red pepper confit and pan-fried foie gras, or West Country mussels served Belgian-style, with French fries and mayonnaise.

Their Champagne Breakfasts have become so popular they're now held five days a week. Favourites here include the English breakfast grill, English hot smoked trout fillet, and the hard-to-resist Canadian pancakes served with fresh strawberries or crispy bacon rashers. Dishes always vary, though, according to what is fresh and in season.

Champagne Breakfasts are served from Tuesday to Friday from 10.30am to 11.45pm, and Saturday from 10.30am to 2pm. Lunches are served from noon until 2.30pm, with dinners being from 7pm onwards. The Sunday hours are from 12.30pm until 4.30pm, and the restaurant is closed on Mondays.

The wine list has been carefully chosen to reflect the cooking in the Bay Tree, so there is sure to be something that will suit your dinner perfectly. And someone is always on hand to help you choose just the right wine.

There are various menus, including set price dinner menus, set-price lunch menus and à la carte menus. Children are most welcome, and all major credit cards are taken.

78 PUMPKINS CAFÉ BAR

12-14 Derby Road, Melbourne, Derbyshire DE73 8FE
Tel: 01332 864836
website: www.pumpkinsbistro.com

The pretty town of Melbourne is home to **Pumpkins Café Bar**. It's been up and running since 2006 under the watchful eye of Sam and her husband Matt who have lived in the area all their lives. Pumpkins is their venture into the hospitality trade and they have made quite the success of it. The couple are both charming and friendly individuals who have developed a real passion for their work. They open Tuesday to Saturday from 9am-4pm however they are planning to open in the evenings over the coming months.

Pumpkins specialises in delicious home cooking, using only the freshest local produce in their dishes. The menu samples a variety of delights including main meals, sandwiches, soups and light bites, and a handsome array of baked goods. Sam does the majority of cooking here and her culinary skills are evident. Her homemade cakes are raved about by whoever tries them, as are her cream teas which are fast becoming a local delicacy.

Sam and Matt stock a range of teas, coffees and hot chocolates, along with various juices and soft drinks. They also have a license so dining guests can enjoy a glass of wine or bottle of beer with their meal. Children are welcome at all times. Cash only please.

79 YE OLDE PACKHORSE

Pack Horse Road, Kings Newton, Melbourne,
Derbyshire DE73 8BZ
Tel: 01332 862 767
e-mail: info@yeoldepackhorse.com
website: www.yeoldepackhorse.com

Ye Olde Packhorse is a superb country inn offering the very best in olde worlde hospitality, well-kept ales and quality cuisine. You can find it at the heart of the delightful village of Kings Newton, which is just a short drive away from Melbourne.

Chris Baggott is in charge here and he is also firmly in charge of the kitchen, with 20 years experience as a chef under his belt. Using local produce is important to Chris and this helps him maintain the high standard of pub grub served here. There is a fine selection of sandwiches, melts,

pittas, jacket potatoes and salads to choose from as well as a range of char grills. Main meals include traditional pub favourites such as beer battered fish, chips and mushy peas, and lasagne.

Ye Olde Packhorse is open all day every day for ale and food is served between noon and 3pm and 6pm – 9pm Monday – Saturday. On Saturdays the pub opens for breakfast between 9am and noon. Food is served between noon and 8pm on Sundays and it is definitely advisable to book at weekends.

Two beer festivals are held each year and a quiz is held once a month. Ring for details.

80 IVY HOUSE FARM B&B & WOODLAND HILLS COURT

Stanton-by-bridge, Derby, Derbyshire DE73 7HT
Tel: 01332 863152 / 01332 694606
e-mail: mary@guesthouse.fsbusiness.co.uk
website: www.ivy-house-farm.com
or www.woodlandhillscourt.co.uk

Ivy House Farm B&B and Holiday Cottages offer the very best in guest house and self-catering accommodation to discerning holidaymakers. Set on a working arable farm in the quiet village of Stanton-by-Bridge, Derbyshire, Ivy House Farm offers guests the chance to experience a traditional farmhouse stay.

Dating back to the 17th Century and converted at the turn of the Millennium, the rooms are aptly named after their former occupation on the farm, including the Cow Shed, Sheep Shed, Pig Sty and Stable. The four diamonds rated accommodation offers excellent amenities, with en-suite bathrooms, tea and coffee making facilities and televisions. A traditional décor adds to the natural charm and character of the rooms. A hearty breakfast is included in the tariff, and children are most welcome.

The homely dining room lets guests enjoy the delicious full English breakfast in comfort. Proprietors Mary and David Kidd cater for the preferences and tastes of all diets, with local produce and homemade bread contributing to an excellent standard of food.

Within the adjacent courtyard is Woodlands Hill Court, five ground floor, self-catering cottages, one of which is suitable for the disabled. They have been furnished, decorated and fitted out to an exceptional standard, and

sleep three to four. They come fully equipped, and the price is all-inclusive with the exception of electricity. People should phone first for details of availability. Local tearooms and cafés at Melbourne Hall, Calke Abbey and Staunton Harold provide quick snacks with hearty meals found in pubs and restaurants a short drive away.

There is so much to do and see in the area around Ivy House Farm. Stanton-by-Bridge is a sleepy, typically English village famous for its Swarkeston Bridge and Stanton Causeway. It was here, in 1745, that Bonnie Prince Charlie abandoned his march south to take London for the Jacobites. Derby is only a few miles away, as is East Midlands Airport and Castle Donnington Race Track. Visitors are assured of a warm welcome on arrival and a comfortable base to enjoy this beautiful area in the heart of England.

Whether you are visiting Ivy Farm House for an unwinding break or are travelling for a night due to work, the idyllic scenery and laid back atmosphere ensure a relaxing time for all.

81 THE SWALLOW'S REST

29 High Street, Repton, Derbyshire DE65 6GD
Tel: 01283 702389

The success of **The Swallow's Rest** bed and breakfast speaks for itself, as most of their visitors are repeat customers who appreciate the combination of top quality and value for money. They also appreciate the gardens in which the Old Coach House stands, which is where the two ensuite guest bedrooms are located in this building set apart from the main house. The rooms (one twin, one double) both have superb quality furnishings and decor, and it's best to book well ahead if you want to stay in one of the best b&bs in Repton.

82 THE UNICORN INN

Repton Road, Newton Solney,
Derbyshire DE15 0SG
Tel: 01283 703324
e-mail: info@unicorn-inn.co.uk
website: www.unicorn-inn.co.uk

This outstanding village inn can be found in the picturesque village of Newton Solney and is definitely worth a look. Paul Needham is the man in charge at **The Unicorn Inn** and he is ably assisted by head chef Jacob Grant who serves up a high standard of pub grub in the kitchen.

The former coaching inn can be found a short drive south west of Repton on the B5008. With eight comfortable en-suite guest rooms available, it provides an ideal place to stay for visitors to Derbyshire or for users of nearby East Midlands Airport. Four of the rooms are located on the ground floor making them more accessible for disabled guests and there is a mix of double and twin rooms. The tariff includes a hearty breakfast and excellent wholesome food is available daily between noon and 3pm and 6pm – 10pm.

The evening menu offers plenty of choice with starters including marinated olives with balsamic and olive oil, and sautéed spicy tiger prawns. There is a good range of main courses on the menu with several traditional favourites as well as more contemporary cuisine such as roasted breast of duck with fondant potatoes, wild mushrooms and butternut squash puree.

www.findSOMEWHERE.co.uk
For people who want to explore the United Kingdom

Places to Stay

83 THE PLOUGH INN

68 Main Street, Rosliston, Swadlincote,
Derbyshire DE12 8JL
Tel: 01283 761354

This pretty village inn dates back some 400 years and is full of character with a lot of traditional features. **The Plough Inn** can be found south of Burton-upon-Trent in the picturesque village of Rosliston.

Lorraine and Ian Bedworth-Griffiths have been in charge here for the past four years and their hospitality is second to none. It goes hand in hand with the well-kept ales and Lorraine's superb cooking. All of the dishes are freshly prepared and home-cooked by Lorraine, and many return time again to sample the delicious pub grub on offer.

Food is served between noon and 2.30pm and 5pm – 8.30pm Tuesday, Wednesday and Thursday. On Fridays orders can be placed between noon and 2.30pm and 5pm – 9pm and on Saturday between 12pm and 9.30pm. A succulent carvery is served between 12pm and 4pm every Sunday and booking is recommended to avoid disappointment.

The roaring fire at The Plough Inn is always very welcome on colder days and gives a real cosy feel. Whether you are out for a family meal, meal for two or a drink with friends The Plough Inn is definitely a good place to start.

84 THE NAVIGATION INN

Spring Cottage Road, Overseal,
Derbyshire DE12 6ND
Tel: 01283 760493
e-mail: thenavigationinn@yahoo.co.uk

Ruth and Steve Lewis took over **The Navigation Inn** in May 2010 and have established themselves yet another fine reputation for quality services. This charming and enthusiastic couple have devoted their lives to the running of hostelries, taking real pride in building up businesses from the ground for their communities. They have transformed fifty-three establishments during their time in the trade and have done a fine job with this inn too.

The inn is now a real local attraction for lovers of fine food and ale, with excellent bed and breakfast accommodation. There are four beautifully decorated en suite bedrooms available in a mixture of sizes, all of which come with a hearty English breakfast.

Food at the inn is equally delicious, served between 12-8pm daily. All dishes are freshly prepared and home cooked to perfection. The menus focus on producing wholesome traditional English food, renowned locally for its quality. On Sundays a popular carvery is offered with a choice three meats. Children and families are welcome and Steve has even created a 'Whacky Warehouse' inside for the kids and also an outdoor play area for sunnier weather.

85 THE SHOULDER OF MUTTON

6 Chapel Street, Oakthorpe, nr Swadlincote, Derbyshire DE12 7QT
Tel: 01530 270436
website: www.scragfolk.co.uk

Julie Mole and her mother Brenda have been
running **The Shoulder of Mutton** successfully now
for the last 18 years. Never content to rest on their
laurels, however, Julie and Brenda are always
looking for new ways to make the pub more
appealing. The latest addition is their link-up with
the Scrag End Folk Club, who meet in the Lounge
Bar every Sunday evening from 8.30pm.

Folk music and good ale have always gone
together, of course, so it's little surprise that the
club opted for the Shoulder of Mutton as their
permanent home. There are always two real ales on offer,
with Marston's Pedigree the regular, alongside one guest ale.

Food is available Tue-Sun noon-2pm and Tue-Sat 6-9pm,
with booking essential at the weekend for their 45-seat
restaurant. Starters usually include the home-made soup of
the day alongside several more options, such as spicy crab
cakes. Mains include salmon fillet covered in lemon butter,
and a range of steaks, while vegetarians have their choice of
dishes too, like a brie and courgette crumble.

87 CRICH TRAMWAY VILLAGE

Crich Tramway Village, Nr Matlock, Derbyshire DE4 5DP
Tel: 01773 854321
e-mail: enquiries@tramway.co.uk
website: www.tramway.co.uk

Crich Tramway Village offers a family day out in the relaxing atmosphere of a bygone era. Explore
the re-created period street with its genuine buildings and features, fascinating exhibitions and
most importantly, its trams. Unlimited tram rides are free with your entry fee, giving you the
opportunity to fully appreciate the Village and surrounding countryside.

Journey on one of the many
beautifully restored vintage
trams, as they rumble through the
cobbled street past a traditional
police telephone known as the
'TARDIS', the Red Lion Pub &
Restaurant, exhibition hall,
workshops, children's play and
picnic area, before passing
beneath the magnificent Bowes
Lyon Bridge. Next it's past the
bandstand, through the woods,
and then on to Glory Mine taking
in spectacular views of the
Derwent Valley.

86 THE DEVONSHIRE ARMS

137 Market Street, South Normanton, Alfreton, Derbyshire DE55 2AA
Tel: 01773 810748
e-mail: tricia333v@aol.com
website: www.the-devonshire-arms.co.uk

It's no surprise that long-time favourite the **Devonshire Arms** is featured in the Good Beer Guide.
Landlords Tricia and Bill Henry keep their cellar in prime condition, and always have several guest real ales on tap, and one real cider. Local beers like Sarah Hughes Dark Ruby are as popular with visitors as they are with the many regulars, and other brews on offer include John Smiths, Mansfield original, Stones and Manns Chestnut. As well as the guest cider there are always Strongbow and Old Rosie, while lager-lovers have their own wide range including Stella, Fosters, Fosters Super Chilled and Carling.

The food at the Devonshire Arms is as tasty and as varied as the list of beers. No-one ever got bored by the menus at this delightful pub in peaceful South Normanton. There are full menus on their website, and daily specials too, but the Homemade Pies are always favourites. They include Meat and Potato, Steak and Kidney, and a Steak and Ale Pie topped with a rich short-crust pastry and served with homemade chips or potatoes, vegetables and gravy. Other favourites include deep-fried Scampi in Breadcrumbs and the ever-popular Fish and Chips: Battered or Breaded Cod served with chips, tartare sauce and mushy or garden peas.

As well as catering for their regulars and visitors, Tricia and Bill and their team of trained and friendly staff also host birthday parties, anniversaries, engagements and other special occasions. Hot and cold buffets and refreshments are available, and the inn has ample car parking at the rear of the property, and good disabled access. Major credit and debit cards are accepted, and special diets can also be catered for.

Located just one mile from Junction 28 on the M1, the Devonshire Arms is within easy reach of Mansfield, Derby and Chesterfield. At the gateway to the Peak District, here you can enjoy a drink with friends, a family meal or host an organised function, for business or pleasure. Food is available Mon-Sat noon-8pm, and on Sunday from noon-3pm when they have one of the best Carveries for miles around. Children under-16 are welcome until 9pm.

88 EAGLE TAVERN

94 Ripley Road, Heage, Derbyshire DE56 2HU
Tel: 01773 857235
e-mail: theeagletavern@talktalkbusiness.net

The popular **Eagle Tavern** offers the very best in real
ales, freshly cooked food and top quality service. It has
been family run for the past four and a half years by
Stephen Alford, his mum Alma, his sisters Jane and
Denise, his daughters Kelly and Kymberley and his son
Bradley.

Stephen, Alma, Jane and Denise are in charge of the
cooking here and delicious home cooked food is available
daily. The printed menu offers an extensive choice of
traditional favourites and the specials board has daily
alternatives. All of the dishes are cooked to order using
fresh local produce and so fine is the food here that
locals and visitors return time again.

There are three real ales to enjoy here with Marstons
Pedigree the regular and a national and local rotating
guest ale. The bar is well stocked with wines, lagers,
spirits and more and if it is a relaxing evening you are after the child-friendly Eagle Tavern
located in Heage is definitely worth a visit.

89 HEAGE WINDMILL

Chesterfield Road, Heage, Belper,
Derbyshire DE56 2BH
Tel: 01773 853579
website: www.heagewindmill.co.uk

Heage Windmill stands in a very striking position
overlooking the village of Nether Heage. A Grade
11* listed building, she is the only working, stone-
towered windmill with six sails in England and the
only working windmill in Derbyshire. She started
grinding corn in 1797 and prior to her restoration,
was last worked by miller, Thomas Shore in 1919.

The mill has much of her old wooden mechanism
in place which drives one of her two pairs of
millstones. Work is in hand to enable the mill to
produce flour again in the near future.

In the basement, the interpretation centre tells
the story of Heage Windmill. The adjacent kiln has
been restored as a reception centre with toilets
and a shop selling flour, souvenirs and
refreshments. There is wheelchair access to the ground floor of the windmill, the interpretation
centre and the reception centre.

There is a large car park on site.

90 THE RAILWAY TEA ROOMS

3 Midland View, Belper, Derbyshire DE56 1QB
Tel: 01773 823561

In the centre of Belper in the Amber Valley stands the
Railway Tea Rooms. Some might come for the view it gives
of the main Derby-Sheffield railway line, but most people
come for the truly delicious home baking and home-cooked
food. It's the kind of place where the smell of fresh baking
lifts your spirits as you walk through the door.

Created by business partners June and Wendy seven
years ago, the unusual Railway Tea Rooms has been a
runaway success. This is due, of course, to the quality of
the food and the friendliness of the service, both of which
bring visitors back time and time again. All the cooking is
done on the premises by June and Wendy themselves, from
the breakfasts to the Derbyshire Cream Teas.

For those with a lighter appetite they offer a range of
sandwiches, like Corned beef, BLT and Salmon and
Cucumber, and there are Baguettes, Jacket potatoes and
other snacks too. The Railway Tea Rooms is open Mon-Sat
9am-4pm.

91 THE CROSS KEYS

35 The Market Place, Belper,
Derbyshire DE56 1FZ
Tel: 01773 599191

Visitors who find themselves near the market place in the
bustling town of Belper will do well to make a rest stop at
The Cross Keys. This handsome local inn is a perfect
respite from the busy town where good old fashioned
conversation can be enjoyed in traditional surroundings,
befitting any English inn.

The Cross Keys is run by Anita and John who have been
working together for four years. They took over the inn in
July 2009 and haven't looked back. Here they fulfil their
passion for hospitality by offering their guests a warm and
welcoming service that focuses on providing quality drink.

Although the inn stocks a good range of soft drinks, its
speciality is real ale. Attracting ale lovers from the local area and further afield the inn is proud
to hold up to five real ales at any one point. All ales are on constant rotation ensuring that there
is always something new to sample. Cider lovers will not be disappointed either with two real
ciders also available including Weston's Perry and a traditional West Country Scrumpy. Anita and
John showcase their wares each year with a beer festival held in the last weekend of October
during the town's 'Fair Week.' Smaller beer festival events are also held throughout the week and
are supplemented by a variety of local musicians and bands that often grace the inn's
performance area on weekend evenings from 8:30pm, please call or check facebook for details.

92 THE TAVERN

11 Derby Road, Belper, Derbyshire DE56 1UU
Tel: 01773 826956
website: www.thetavernbelper.co.uk

The Tavern is found on the edge of bustling Belper town on the main A6 road through to Derby. This quality free house is run by Nicola and Peter Foster who took the helm three years ago. They are a local couple and have brought many friends in amongst the usual clientele, adding a very laid back and jovial feel to any evening spent here.

The inn is opened from 4pm until close Monday to Thursday, from noon until close Fridays and Saturdays and noon until 10:30pm on Sundays. It's renowned for its collection of real ales and pulls in a steady crowd of ale lovers. Four real brews are available to try at any one time including an ale brewed especially for the inn called 'Tavern Top Notch.' Throughout the month ales are on rotation, allowing guests to sample something new every time they return. In May and August each year Nicola and Peter hold beer festivals which always prompt an impressive turnout. At these times a further nine ales are on offer along with two real ciders and the usual wine and spirit selection. Throughout the week sports fans will be well looked after as the Tavern has a full Sky Sports package with ESPN available for whichever sporting event customers want to see.

93 ANGELO'S RESTAURANT

The New Inn, Hopping Hill, Milford, Derbyshire DE56 0RL
Tel: 01773 822338 e-mail: info@angelosthenewinn.com
website: www.angelosthenewinn.com

Angelo's Restaurant offers beautifully intimate candlelit dining with the finest foods, prepared by Angelo and his brother Mario, the chefs. There is naturally plenty of Italian fare but also the best French and English cuisine too. Start with the home-made soup of the day, or perhaps fresh asparagus spears grilled with garlic butter and parmesan cheese. There's always a fresh fish of the day, and a range of steaks, but the extensive menu also includes dishes such as Gressingham duck breast in an orange and Grand Marnier sauce or pan-fried salmon steak served in a lobster sauce.

www.findSOMEWHERE.co.uk
For people who want to explore the United Kingdom

Places to Stay

94 THE SPOTTED COW INN

12 Town Street, Holbrook, Derbyshire DE56 OTA
Tel: 01332 881200
e-mail: info@thespottedcow.co.uk
website: www.thespottedcow.co.uk

Situated just five minutes from Derby city centre in the village of Holbrook is the Spotted Cow Inn. This popular village inn regularly draws in the crowds to experience affordable, fine dining at its best. The inn dates back to 1820 when it was originally an Alehouse, acquiring its liquor license in 1840. Today, its owners Andrew and Fiona West-Hunt still ensure that a healthy selection of real ales, lagers and spirits are available alongside a handsome wine list which can be enjoyed all day every day.

The inn is full of character and retains some beautiful old features such as oak beams, wooden floors and brick walling. These features are complimented by an interesting selection of memorabilia and traditional farm house décor, which creates a warm and friendly feel. Although popular for drinks, the inn is best known for its food. Head Chef Robert Baker has been here for almost three years and has dedicated himself to providing guests with a their perfect meal. Robert's menus are classically English, but have a modern twist to excite the palette. He places much emphasis on using only the best in fresh local produce, and is always happy to cater for any special dietary requirements such as gluten or dairy free diets. All dishes and sauces are cooked fresh to order on the premises so most dislikes can also be catered for with the omission or replacement of various ingredients where possible. Guests can choose from a variety of delicious choices from rump steak with peppercorn sauce, salmon fillet in a pool of plum jus, spicy chicken wraps and homemade pie of the day. A wide range of hot baguettes, jackets and salads are also available, with plenty of children's and vegetarian options too. Throughout the week the team offer a variety of offers such as complementary supper at the Tuesday night quiz, free soup or coffee with every meal, children eat free on Thursdays, and a free bottle of wine with steaks on Wednesday's Steak night. Robert also caters for a variety of special occasions, please ring for details.

Andrew and Fiona also offer two luxury bedrooms and one suite, all of which are lavishly styled with sumptuous linens, scatter cushions and modern art. Conveniently located to many of Derby's best attractions, the Spotted Cow is ideal for a fantastic weekend away.

95 THE COFFEE HOUSE

2 Station Road, Ilkeston, Derbyshire DE7 5LD
Tel: 01159 306668

The Coffee House sits in the heart of Ilkeston on Station Road and has a bright and cheerful red exterior, with the welcome inside being every bit as cheerful. The café is a family-run business where Rebecca Simpson and her mother Cynthia have been providing satisfied customers with the best home-cooking for five years now. It's a winning formula, and all meals are cooked to order, from the very popular breakfasts onwards. The Tuesday and Thursday roast dinners are also very much in demand and served from 11am. Both hot and cold dishes are available and the menus include jacket potatoes with a range of fillings, various toasties, a separate kids menu and those

extra-special filling breakfasts with, for the hungry, sausage, bacon, eggs, mushrooms, hash brown, black pudding and toast.

On warmer days there's a rear patio to enjoy, with seating for 12 people, and you're welcome to just have a tea, coffee and a cake of you wish. The Coffee House is open Mon-Sat from 7am, with food served till 2pm, and drinks available till 2.30pm.

96 ALL SAINTS CHURCH

Dale Abbey, Stanton by Dale, Derbyshire DE7 4PN
Tel: 01159 324584

All Saints Church, Dale Abbey is the only church in England which shares its roof with a farm. Apart from electrics and some old radiators the interior has not been altered since around 1650 and retains its box pews. There is a medieval wall painting and a leaning pulpit dated 1634. The communion table, actually a Jacobean cupboard, is in front of the reading desk, whereas normally it should be behind and there is in effect a three-decker pulpit arrangement. In about 1485 the building next door to the church became the infirmary for the nearby abbey and the church became the infirmary chapel, the sick being brought through doors both downstairs and on the gallery where they could see the service from the low balcony.

More recently the adjoining building became the Blue Ball Inn. Clergy would robe in the inn and enter the church through the downstairs door, blocked up in the 1820's but still clearly visible.

Dale Abbey used to be a 'peculiar' and did not come under the authority of the Diocesan Bishop. It had its own Lay bishop, Lord Stanhope, whose Episcopal throne is in the church. It was thus Derbyshire's first cathedral.. There was a court at Dale with the authority to issue licences for weddings, which meant that banns did not have to read and so Dale became the Gretna Green of the Midlands in the seventeenth and eigthteenth centuries, with many weddings being performed. There is a plaque in the church describing one of the Lay Bishops. It is said to be the smallest Anglican church in England still in regular use.

97 THE OLD SCHOOLHOUSE DELI

School Lane, Stanton by Dale, Derbyshire DE7 4QJ
Tel: 01159 305699
e-mail: alison.lycett@sky.com
website: www.theoldschoolhouse.moonfruit.com

Visit **The Old Schoolhouse Deli** and you can sample cakes fit for a Prime Minister. Baker Aly Lycett, known as the Cake Sculptor (www.thecakesculptor.co.uk), has made cakes for everyone from David Cameron to Katie Price, who ordered a fairy-tale fantasy castle cake for her 30th birthday. Now with the help of her mum and dad, Val and Ray, she also runs this deli and café in the picturesque village of Stanton by Dale.

Drawing on the rich diversity of local food producers, the Old Schoolhouse offers much more than just Aly's sensational cakes. The changing menu is very wide-ranging, and seasonal depending on what's available, but you'll find dishes as creative as any of Aly's cakes: chicken and chorizo paella, porcini and parmesan risotto, home-made curries or beef and red wine lasagne. Don't leave without trying one of their signature cupcakes or brownies - or both! The local produce is also for sale in the deli, including gourmet preserves, scones, cakes, pies and quiches, but also basic groceries like milk and bread so it remains very much a community centre too. Open Tue-Sat 10-3.

99 THE OLD CROWN INN

Cavendish Bridge, Shardlow, Derbyshire DE72 2HL
Tel: 01332 792392
e-mail: the.oldcrowninn@btconnect.com

Once a coaching inn, **The Old Crown Inn** goes back to the late 17th-century, and as soon as you walk in you appreciate the historic feel. This is a pub the way pubs used to be, beautifully located on the banks of the River Trent in the hamlet of Cavendish Bridge. Inside there's a cosy atmosphere, with low beams and a host of memorabilia from a bygone age.

James and Monique are your hosts here, and as well as maintaining the traditional feel of the place are intent on keeping its excellent reputation for real ales. Up to nine real ales are available at any given time, with a range of regular and guest ales that include Marston's Old Empire, Marston's Pedigree, Jennings Cumberland Ale and Cock a Hoop. The inn also holds beer festivals in March and September every year when over 20 real ales are brought in to sample.

Guests also come to the Crown for its delicious home cooked food, ranging from simple sandwiches and baked potatoes to steak and ale pie, chicken pasta Leonardo, rump steak and mushroom and red pepper stroganoff.

98 THE SEVEN OAKS INN AND RESTAURANT

Lows Lane, Stanton by Dale, Ilkeston, Derbyshire DE7 4QU
Tel: 01159 323189

Dating back in parts to the 18th Century, **The Seven Oaks Inn and Restaurant** is a charming child-friendly establishment located on the outskirts of the small village of Stanton-By-Dale. Owned by Ryan and Kelly it was originally built as a farmhouse before becoming an alehouse. The first landlord came from Sevenoaks in Kent, hence the rather unusual name.

Ryan and Kelly are both chefs and have been here for six years. The food served is extremely popular and it is best to phone and book to guarantee yourself a table, especially on Sunday when a succulent roast dinner is available. There is a wide variety of dishes listed on the printed menu and additional options can be found on the daily specials board. Food times are 12pm – 2pm and 5pm – 8.30pm Tuesday, Wednesday and Thursday; and 12pm – 9pm Friday, Saturday and Sunday.

There are four real ales to enjoy here, with brews from the Blue Monkey brewery (micro) and Theakston ranges, plus Marstons Pedigree and a rotating guest ale. The well stocked bar has an extensive range of wines, spirits, lagers and soft drinks.

The Seven Oaks Inn and Restaurant has superb gardens and a patio area and there is a marquee, which caters for 300 people, available for hire. Ring for details.

This public house is well-known for the entertainment it offers, which is welcome to all. You can enjoy Bingo from 9pm on Tuesday, a general knowledge quiz from 9pm on Wednesday, a music quiz on the first Friday of the month, and karaoke on the second Friday of the month. There is also regular live entertainment.

It is closed on Mondays (except Bank Holidays) and is open every other session and all day on Friday, Saturday and Sunday.

For a closer look at this fine public house you can check out its Facebook page.

100 THE CROSS KEYS

90 Bondgate, Castle Donington, Derbyshire DE74 2NR
Tel: 01332-812214
e-mail: thecrosskeys@ntlworld.com
website: www.thecrosskeyspub.com

From the moment you walk through the doors at
The Cross Keys you can feel the warmth and
hospitality at this welcoming, friendly pub in the
heart of Castle Donington. It's been here
welcoming travellers and serving locals for the
last few hundred years, and is as popular today
as it's ever been. It's known for having a sporty
feel with three teams attached to the pub - a
rugby team, a cricket team and a football team.

Hosts Donna and Andy Moon, have been in
charge for six years now, and have built up a
solid reputation for combining a great
atmosphere with excellent drink and good-value
filling snacks. Benefiting from a recent
refurbishment, the exterior is very attractive, and
well-proportioned, and has colourful hanging baskets
that add to its appeal. Inside the spacious pub,
evidence of the refurbishment continues with smart
new toilets, newly decorated interior and a flat
screen television, making it everything a good
English pub should be.

The Cross Keys has been given a Cask Marque for
their ales and serves three regular ales plus a
special guest ale, the regulars being Deuchars IPA,
Sharps Doom Bar and Marston's Pedigree. Beyond
these there is a wide range of other beers, lagers,
cider, spirits, wines and soft drinks should you be
driving.

Snack food is available lunchtimes and early
evenings, and if you're short of time you can
telephone your food order in by calling ahead on
01332 812214. The local favourite is the traditional
'hand-raised' Pork Pies - where you can help yourself
to pickles, condiments and home made chutneys, all
for a very reasonable price. Other snacks include
various Pies, Peppered Steak Slice, Cornish Pasties,
Small and Large portions of chips, and a Chip Cob
with Melted Cheese to name but a few!

In the winter months there is a quiz every other
Wednesday night from 8.30pm onwards, with free food for all quiz participants, and everyone is
welcome (ring for details). There is plenty of outdoor seating in the courtyard, and ample parking
spaces.

Donington Park racetrack is nearby and also houses the largest collection of Grand Prix cars in
the world. It is only 4 miles from both the East Midlands Airport and the M1 motorway, making it
an excellent location in which to stay when entering the county.

101 THE JOLLY SAILOR

Main Street, Hemington, Derbyshire DE74 2RB
Tel: 01332-810448

Parts of **The Jolly Sailor** date back to the 17th century, and what is now the village pub was once a set of weavers' cottages in one of the most picturesque villages in this part of Derbyshire. Hemington is a quiet place that not too many people know about, though the Jolly Sailor is renowned for its open fires and fine ales.

You'll find the Jolly Sailor in the Good Pub Guide, which isn't surprising as hosts Martin and Caroline keep eight real ales on tap. These include Abbot Ale, Timothy Taylor Landlord, Bass, Ruddles County, Greene King, Greene King IPA, Greene King XX Mild and St Edmond's.

Martin has 20 years experience in the catering trade, and since they arrived at the Jolly Sailor a year ago, he and Caroline have started to build up the food side and their new Steakhouse Restaurant is now open. The kitchens use all local produce and there are daily specials, featuring such dishes as pork and cider strips on tarragon mash, home-made fishcakes or salsa-baked cod fillet. The Jolly Sailor is open every day, with food available Thurs - Sat evenings 6pm - 9pm.

102 COCK AND MAGPIE

2 Church Street North, Old Whittington, Chesterfield, Derbyshire S41 9QW
Tel: 01246 454453
e-mail: janice.w@virgin.net

The Cock and Magpie is a warm, friendly, family-run pub. The front bar has low-beamed ceilings, cubbyholes and arches, plus paintings of animals and of the pub making it a cosy place to enjoy a convivial pint.

The town in which it stands, Old Whittington, is most famous for its Revolution House, now a thatched cottage, but it once was the 'Cock & Pynot Inn' (Pynot is an old dialectic colloquialism for a 'Magpie'). Today it takes its name from the 'Glorious Revolution' that totally changed the face of English history. The national importance of the 16th century former 'Cock & Pynot Inn' is signified both by its Museum status and its designation by English Heritage as a Grade 1 listed building. Nearby and on the corner of Church Street North stands its late-Georgian successor, the Cock & Magpie, erected around 1790 and taking over trade from the former alehouse.

The picturesque pub has been run by Neville and Janice Watson for the past three years. Customers can choose from a full selection of draught beer, wine and spirits along with a range of soft drinks. Two real ales are served with Cock a Hoop the regular.

If you fancy a bite to eat, an excellent traditional home cooked pub menu is available, served in the lovely 80-seat restaurant or throughout the pub. The new 'snug' area has now been opened giving more dining room and on sunnier days the beautiful rear garden is often bustling with people.

The main menu has every base covered: there are steaks and grills, vegetarian dishes, pasta dishes, fish dishes and meat dishes, though not forgetting starters, sandwiches, 'Cock & Magpie' cobs, salads, jacket potatoes and a 'miscellaneous' section, which features cheese burgers, hot beef cob with gravy plus many more. You really are spoilt for choice and such is its popularity it is advisable to book at all times. Thursday night is pie night and a two course Sunday lunch special is very popular.

If you require something in the way of amusement, then they have that too. There is always something going on at the child friendly pub, from quizzes to live entertainment. Ring for details.

103 THE WHITE HORSE

High Street, Old Whittington, Chesterfield, Derbyshire S41 9LQ
Tel: 01246 450414
e-mail: white-horse@talktalk.net
website: www.whitehorsechesterfield.co.uk

The White Horse's new hosts, Richard and Becky van Wyk, have been getting rave reviews since they arrived at the already well-established inn in 2010. They have added an international flavour to the menus, with Portuguese, Spanish and South African influences on the food with dishes like seafood paella, Boerewors South African sausages made by the chef, and a delicious Cape Malay

Sosatie or South African Kebab, which is a mild and fruity curry-flavoured pork dish, served on a skewer with apricots, prunes and peppers. From Portugal comes the Steak Trenchada, which are tender strips of rump steak sautéed with onion, tomato, peppers, garlic and the White Horse's own secret Portuguese spices.

There's also a less expensive and more extensive bar menu, as well. Dishes like steak, egg and chips may sound straightforward but here at the White Horse the steaks are marinated in their own secret mixture of herbs and spices, the chips are home-made, and the egg is a free-range duck egg. On the bar menu you'll also find dishes like a steak salad, a tapas platter, a rather different salmon and mushroom omelette, with popular desserts such as sticky toffee pudding or ice cream with strawberries.

Even the special children's menu has had an international make-over, and young ones can also enjoy their own Boerewors sausage, which is meaty but preservative-free and served with fried egg and chips. Spare ribs and home-made chicken goujons are also available in child-size portions.

To go with the excellent food the White Horse also offers an extensive range of beers, wine, spirits and cocktails. These too have an international look to them, including South African Castle Lager and Klipdrift brandy, but beer lovers shouldn't worry as the best of British real ales are also available. There are always two on offer, with Bombadier being the regular ale plus one changing guest ale.

Richard and Becky are encouraging special events at the new improved White Horse too, with everything from bungee jumping to a charity Tramps and Tarts fancy dress and live music night, so phone or check their website for the latest on what's happening. Some things at the White Horse are kept traditional, of course, like the popular Sunday lunch. Food is served Monday-Saturday from noon-9pm and on Sundays from noon-5.30pm.

104 THE VICTORIA INN

Lowgates, Staveley, Chesterfield, Derbyshire S43 3TR
Tel: 01246-472458

Tucked away in the north-east corner of Derbyshire, the **Victoria Inn** has recently been given a new lease of life with the arrival of new hosts Samantha and Adam, their daughters Emily and Aimee, and their son Bailey. Together they're transforming this traditional pub, and naturally being a family-run place it's very much a family-friendly establishment with children being more than welcome. Samantha has worked in the trade for ten years, so knows what she's doing, and is determined to make the Victoria Inn a shining example of a good British pub.

Built of red brick and standing proudly on a corner near the town centre, the inn is already attracting an increasing number of locals. Visitors to the area too are starting to discover the warm welcome that the family go out of their way to provide. Staveley is only five miles north-east of Chesterfield, and three miles from Junction 30 of the M1. Attractions nearby include the Poolsbrook Country Park, with walking and cycling trails, and Staveley Hall, an early 17th-century Grade II listed building.

Whether you're local or visiting the area's attractions you'll also discover the real ales that are available at the old-fashioned bar in the Victoria. There are two different rotating guest ales at present, but the hosts plan to increase the choice as time goes by. The same goes for the food, which is currently available only on Sunday lunchtimes. Because of this, it's advisable to book for a meal as word is getting out about Samantha's skills in the kitchen. She cooks the Sunday lunches herself, offering a good choice of dishes all kept at very reasonable prices.

Other features of the Victoria include a pool table, and a karaoke night every Friday from 8.30pm. Here too Samantha and Adam plan to add to the entertainment available, with live music on a Saturday evening before too long. Ring the pub to check the latest news. The Victoria Inn is open all day, every day, with food available on Sundays from 12-3pm.

Since this guide has been published, the inn has undergone a refurbishment.

105 THE HARDWICK INN

Hardwick Park, Chesterfield S44 5QJ
Tel: 01246 850245
e-mail: batty@hardwickinn.co.uk
website: www.hardwickinn.co.uk

The picturesque **Hardwick Inn** dates back to the 15th century and has been in the hands of the same family now since 1928. Peter and Pauline Batty are the third generation, running the inn now with their daughters Jenny and Sarah. It's close to Hardwick Hall, and both places are owned by the National Trust, showing the historic importance of the Hardwick Inn.

Long-time chef Paul Booth is another reason the inn has become known as one of the best dining and drinking pubs in Derbyshire. His skills range from superb versions of old favourites to imaginative new dishes, some of which you'll see in the extensive regular menu and others on the board of daily specials. The Carvery Restaurant has lovely views as well as good food, with the carvery itself offering a daily choice of three of the following, all sourced locally: Roast Topside of Beef, Roast Leg of Pork, Roast Turkey, Roast Leg of Lamb or Honey-Roast Gammon. Choosing from the main menu there are starters like Grilled Black Pudding smothered with Stilton Mushroom Sauce, while the mouthwatering choice of main courses include several traditional pot roasts and casseroles, and a range of homemade pies such as Homemade Steak & Kidney Pie, or Steak and Stilton Pie.

Outside the gardens are almost as extensive and well looked-after as those of the nearby stately homes, while inside the historic bar you'll find a choice of over 200 malt whiskies and five real ales, such as Old Peculier, Black Sheep, Bombardier and Theakston's XB. In addition the inn sells a local real ale especially brewed for them: Bess of Hardwick. There's also a good choice of wines with an emphasis on affordability, including house wines at under £10 a bottle, while the Bar Menu offers tempting seasonal choices like lamb from the Chatsworth Estate and everything from the restaurant menu too.

The Bar menu is available Mon-Sat 11.30am-9.30pm, Sun 12-9pm, while the Carvery Restaurant is open Mon-Sat 12-2pm and 6.30-8.30pm, and on Sundays for two sittings at 12-1pm and 4pm-5.30pm. It is essential to book ahead at weekends for the restaurant, and advisable during the week too. No bookings are taken for the bar. Children welcome and all major credit cards accepted.

106 THE FAMOUS SHOULDER

Hardstoft, Chesterfield, Derbyshire S45 8AF
Tel: 01246 850276
e-mail: info@thefamousshoulder.co.uk

The Famous Shoulder is an ancient inn, a 300-year-old country local in the little hamlet of Hardstoft. The surrounding beautiful Derbyshire countryside is where the patron and chef Simon Johnson gets most of the produce for his menus, with food being one of the Famous Shoulder's prime attractions.

Simon prides himself on producing good food at affordable prices. The Bar Menu includes inventive sandwich options such as Tiger Prawn and Rocket Aioli with Salad and Parsnip Crisps, while the Grill Menu is a carnivore's delight. All meat is sourced locally and hung for 28 days for maximum flavour, and as well as the steak selection there are seasonal game offerings such as Guinea Fowl, and creative dishes like Gammon Steak, Chilli and Pineapple Jam. Other mouth-watering options include Venison and Thyme Pie, or the popular 12-hour Belly of Pork.

The bar offers 5-6 real ales at any one time, always changing and chosen from both local and national brewers. One way to really appreciate the quality and variety of the food and is to stay for a few days, and there are four ensuite rooms with free wifi and a home-cooked Derbyshire breakfast. The Famous Shoulder is open all day, every day, with food served Mon-Sat 12-9pm, Sun 12-5pm. Booking essential for the weekends.

108 THE BARLEY MOW INN

Langer lane, Wingerworth, Chesterfield,
Derbyshire S42 6TX
Tel: 01246 541771

A few miles south for Chesterfield in the village of Wingerworth stands the traditional **Barley Mow Inn**. New hosts Anthony and Janice Quigley are building on those traditions, concentrating on the food, drink and friendly atmosphere that make the pub what it is. On the drink side, their regular real ales are London Pride and Adnams, but there's always something new to try too.

The same goes for the food prepared by their team of professional chefs, who cook all meals to order using local produce as much as possible. As well as the regular menu you can choose from the daily specials on the blackboard. Here there's a mix of pub favourites, like Sizzling Sirloin Steak that's served on a hot skillet, or you might try their Fresh Rainbow Trout or something more elaborate such as Stuffed Chicken with Mango.

Outside is a pleasant beer garden while inside is the cosy atmosphere of the best kind of British pub. The Barley Mow is open all day, every day, and food is served Mon-Sat 12-8.30pm, Sun 12-5pm.

107 TELMERE LODGE

Mansfield Road, Hasland, Chesterfield S41 OJH
Tel: 01246 206847

With superb gardens, children's play area, well rested ales and delicious food on offer, The **Telmere Lodge** is not to be missed. This popular establishment is situated just a short drive from the centre of Chesterfield in the village of Hasland. The impressive premises had been shut for over a year before Andy, Helen and Helen's mother Mary took over as new tenants, and the Telmere Lodge continues to go from strength to strength. Andy, Helen and Mary are very hands on, they are always striving to make sure that each visit is one to remember by ensuring that the gardens are kept, the ales well rested and the food lovingly prepared. It is this attitude that has the locals flooding back and visitors arriving in droves.

The bar is well stocked with Black Sheep the regular ale with three or four rotating guest ales available. Customers can relax and enjoy their drinks and/or food in the comfortable beer garden in summer months.

The main draw of the pub though, has to be the food. Mary is "Queen of the Kitchen" and utilises the local produce to great effect and has created a mouth-watering menu and daily specials, which depend on what meat is delivered from nearby Darley Dale. The menu includes a submenu from `The Pie Shop' featuring; Steak & Kidney, Chicken, Ham & Mushroom, Suet Pudding and Steak & Stilton, all of which sound sumptuous in their descriptions. There is such choice though; the starter menu holds tempting dishes like BBQ Spare Ribs, Smoked Salmon Wrap and the Telmere Special, which is a combination of Prawns and Crab Meat. The grill offers fresh meat daily and there are four cuts of meats from which to choose. Ever popular roast dinners are served on Sundays. Food is served between 12pm - 3pm & 5pm - 9pm Monday - Friday and from 12pm

- 9pm on Saturday and Sunday. Such is the popularity of this place it is recommended that guests reserve tables for the weekend.

Thursday nights are special nights, known locally as Pie Night, the pub lays on a menu of home-cooked pies and follows it up with a quiz evening. The pub has extensive parking, a newly refurbished function suite available for weddings, corporate events and the suchlike and full disabled access. Ring for details.

109 THE WHITE HORSE

Badger Lane, Woolley Moor, Alfreston,
Derbyshire DE55 6FG
Tel: 01246 590319
e-mail: via website
website: www.thewhitehorsewoolleymoor.co.uk

You know the **White Horse** is good from the fact that you have to book ahead to be sure of getting a table on Saturday nights, and it's a good idea for other nights of the week too. Owners David and Melanie Boulby and their talented chefs Craig and James produce real quality gastropub fare, which brings people in from miles around.

Many come just to taste the mouth-watering specialty of Crispy Belly Pork with Spring Onion Mash and Smoked Bacon Sauce, though the very reasonably-priced menu ranges from traditional Cod in Beer Batter with Chips and Mushy Peas to more complex creations such as Barbary Duck Breast with Potato Rosti and Black Cherry Jus. There are daily specials too, like Bakewell Best Sausages with Mash and Gravy, or a Mixed-Bean Cassoulet.

David and Melanie take as much care with their beers as they do with their food, and only serve locally-brewed real ales. There are up to three available at any one time, with Bakewell Best being the regular, brewed by Peak Ales on the Chatsworth Estate. The White Horse is open Mon-Sat 12-3pm and 6-11pm, and Sun 12-3pm. Food served Mon-Sat 12-1.45pm and 5.30-8.45pm, Sun 12-2.30pm.

111 THE PEACOCK INN

School Hill, Cutthorpe, Chesterfield,
Derbyshire S42 7AS
Tel: 01246 232834
e-mail: info@thepeacockpub.com
website: www.thepeacockpub.com

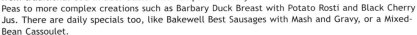

The Peacock Inn stands in its own picturesque grounds on the edge of the equally picturesque village of Cutthorpe. It's a historic stone-built former coaching inn, dating back to the 17th century. New tenants Louise and Chris, together with their experienced Head Chef Tom Alberts, have transformed the food and drink available while losing none of the inn's historic charm.

Tom's dishes are very varied, offering something for everyone. Traditionalists enjoy perfect plates of dishes like plaice and handmade chips, or sirloin steak, but for the more adventurous Tom cooks his own curries, jerk chicken, and vegetarian options such as halloumi cheese bake. There are Lite Bites too, if you just fancy the homemade soup of the day, while desserts include a cheesecake of the day and old favourites like bread and butter pudding.

There are wines by the glass and the bottle, and the two resident ales are Black Sheep and Young's Special. In addition there's a caravan and camping park behind the inn, available all year round. The Peacock Inn is open all day, every day, with food available Mon-Sat 12-9pm, and Sundays 12-6pm when there is also a carvery.

110 KELSTEDGE INN

Matlock Road, Kelstedge, Ashover, Derbyshire S45 0DX
Tel 1: 01246 590448 Tel 2: 01246 590305

The pleasant village of Kelstedge is found just north of Matlock on the way to Chesterfield. It's very much a traditional English village, and the **Kelstedge Inn** follows suit. It is everything a Derbyshire inn should be, with great quality home cooked food, real ales and good old fashioned values.

The inn itself dates back to 1759, built in traditional style with local stone and quaint leaded windows. It occupies an unrivalled location upon the crest of steep hill overlooking the village, affording guests with window seats handsome views across the English countryside. Inside the Kelstedge, guests can occupy a cosy environment with traditional furnishings and décor, befitting a country house.

The inn was taken over by Andrew and Lois in June 2010. The pair have worked tirelessly to return the inn to its full potential, using their experience and hospitality skills to create a place popular for both locals and visitors to the area alike. They open lunchtimes and evenings throughout the week, but open all day on Sundays. The bar is always kept well stocked with a range of fine wines, spirits and lagers, with a small selection of real ales also on rotation.

The inn is particularly popular for food, served daily from 12-2pm and 6.30-9pm Monday to Saturday and from 12-3pm (Traditional Sunday Lunch) 5-9pm Main Evening Menu. Traditional Sunday roasts such as Beef, Lamb, Pork and Chicken with all the trimmings and seasonal vegetables are available every Sunday until 7pm, after which the main menu is employed. Andrew and Lois' chef has devised interesting and varied menus for each session, with options for every budget and appetite. The lunch menu samples dishes like lemon and ginger salmon, homemade steak and ale pie, mushroom stroganoff and chickpea curry with pilau rice. The evening menu offers tantalising

treats like Mediterranean pasta, roasted sea bass, minted lamb shank, and chicken stuffed with chorizo and cream cheese. Light bites are also available with a wide range of hot and cold baguettes, toasties and jacket potatoes. Any meal here is complimented by a decadent dessert with hot chocolate fudge cake, tarte citron, raspberry roulade and cheeseboards all being popular choices. Owing the popularity of dining here, booking is advised over the weekends.

112 COFFEE CENTRAL

6 High Street, Dronfield, Derbyshire S18 1PY
Tel: 01246 418702
e-mail: pwattsthewatts@aol.com

The aroma of homemade cooking attracts plenty of passersby through the doors of **Coffee Central**. Located in the centre of the wonderful town of Dronfield, this popular coffee shop has a fantastic reputation for its superb coffee and homemade delights.

Coffee Central has been owned and personally run by Melanie Watts for the past three years. She has a wealth of experience in the catering trade and her hospitality is second to none.

Melanie prides herself on using produce sourced from local bakers and butchers. There is a varied selection of light snacks, pastries, toasted sandwiches, paninis, baguettes and jacket potatoes available. Salads, quiche, omelettes, and homemade soup can also be enjoyed here and they are all reasonably priced.

Whether it is lunch, a snack or a quick refreshment you are after, Coffee Central is the ideal place to relax. There is seating for 30 customers spreading two floors and children are welcomed. On warmer days some customers choose to sit outside in the eye-catching patio area. Daily specials are available and once a month there is a bistro style menu available and booking is required. Ring for details.

113 THE MANOR HOUSE

10-14 High Street, Dronfield,
Derbyshire S18 1PY
Tel: 01246 412119   Fax: 01246 418473
e-mail: marie@manor-house-hotel.co.uk
website: www.manorhouse-hotel.co.uk

Located in the busy market town of Dronfield, **The Manor House** is a delightful boutique hotel, cafe, restaurant and bar. Since its extensive refurbishment by the new owners in 2008 this fantastic hotel has come back to life.

The stunning 16th century Grade 2 listed building now offers eleven individually designed bedrooms, incorporating two luxury suites. The sympathetic renovation has made sure that the building has retained all of its original features and charm whilst giving it a more lively contemporary feel. The feel is relaxed and comfortable throughout.

Breakfast is served from 7am in the cafe bar which offers a range of meals and snacks throughout the day. In the evening the menu is varied based upon a tapas style with a twist. The two talented young chefs offer a variety of specials daily, catering for all tastes.

If you enjoy a hotel which is relaxed, comfortable, lively and a stones throw from The Peak District then The Manor House will not disappoint.

114 THE MINERS ARMS

115 Carr Lane, Dronfield Woodhouse,
Derbyshire S18 8XF
Tel: 01142 891407
e-mail: miners_arms1@btconnect.com

Dronfield Woodhouse is a pretty Derbyshire village that's well worth a visit, with **The Miners Arms** as an extra treat to enjoy when you get there. Hosts Jenny and Mark Bingham recently refurbished this former estate pub, where over the years they have built a solid reputation for both fine food and exceptionally good beer. The local ale Easy Rider is just one of the three real ales available, alongside Clack Sheep and Greene King IPA.

The kitchen draws visitors here too, using as it does only the best of local meat and vegetables to produce pub food that combines top quality with value for money. Pub favourites include sausage and mash, fish, chips and peas, and a warning steak and Guinness pie. Jenny and Mark are known for their curries, too, with dishes such as chicken korma, beef madras and chicken tikka masala, but there are plenty of vegetarian dishes as well, including a sweet potato chick pea and spinach curry.

TOURIST INFORMATION CENTRES

Ashbourne

13 Market Place, Ashbourne, Derbyshire DE6 1EU
e-mail: ashbourneinfo@derbyshiredales.gov.uk
Tel: 01335 343666

Bakewell

Old Market Hall, Bridge Street, Bakewell,
Derbyshire DE45 1DS
e-mail: bakewell@peakdistrict.gov.uk
Tel: 01629 813227

Buxton

The Crescent, Buxton, Derbyshire SK17 6BQ
e-mail: tourism@highpeak.gov.uk
Tel: 01298 25106

Castleton

Buxton Road, Castleton, Hope Valley,
Derbyshire S33 8WN
e-mail: castleton@peakdistrict.gov.uk
Tel: 01629 816572

Chesterfield

Rykneld Square, Chesterfield, Derbyshire S40 1SB
e-mail: tourism@chesterfield.gov.uk
Tel: 01246 345777

Derby

Assembly Rooms, Market Place, Derby,
Derbyshire DE1 3AH
e-mail: tourism@derby.gov.uk
Tel: 01332 255802

Glossop

The Heritage Centre, Bank House, Henry Street,
Glossop, Derbyshire SK13 8BW
e-mail: info@glossoptouristcentre.co.uk
Tel: 01457 855920

Holmfirth

49-51 Huddersfield Road, Holmfirth,
West Yorkshire HD9 3JP
e-mail: holmfirth.tic@kirklees.gov.uk
Tel: 01484 222444

Leek

Stockwell Street, Leek, Staffordshire ST13 5HH
e-mail: tourism.services@staffsmoorlands.gov.uk
Tel: 01538 483741

Macclesfield

Town Hall, Macclesfield, Cheshire SK10 1DX
e-mail: macclesfieldtic@cheshireeast.gov.uk
Tel: 01625 504114

Matlock

Crown Square, Matlock, Derbyshire DE4 3AT
e-mail: matlockinfo@derbyshiredales.gov.uk
Tel: 01629 583388

Sheffield

Visitor Information Point, 14 Norfolk Row,
Sheffield S1 2PA
e-mail: visitor@sheffield.gov.uk
Tel: 0114 2211900

Swadlincote

Sharpe's Pottery Museum, West Street,
Swadlincote, Derbyshire DE11 9DG
e-mail: tic@sharpespotterymuseum.org.uk
Tel: 01283 222848

IMAGE COPYRIGHT HOLDERS

Some images in this book have been supplied by **http://www.geograph.org.uk** and licensed under the Creative Commons Attribution-Share Alike 2.0 Generic License. To view a copy of this license, visit **http://creativecommons.org/licenses/by-sa/2.0/** or send a letter to Creative Commons, 171 Second Street, Suite 300, San Francisco, California, 94105, USA.

COPYRIGHT HOLDERS ARE AS FOLLOWS:

IMAGE COPYRIGHT HOLDERS

Brassington, Brassington   © Alan Heardman pg 69
Dressing of Hall Well, Tissington
  © Mick Lobb   pg 71
Viator's bridge, Milldale   © Alan Heardman pg 72
Ilam Hall, Ilam   © Hall Family   pg 74
Thor's Cave, Waterhouses   © Val Vannet pg 74
Hanson Grange, Alstonefield
  © Tim Marshall   pg 76
Hartington Hall, Hartington
  © Alan Heardman   pg 78
Nicholson Institute, Leek   © Martyn Davies pg 79
The Roaches, Leek   © Bob Jones   pg 80
Tittesworth Reservoir, Leek   © Row17 pg 80
Dinghy Racing on Rudyard Lake, Rudyard
  © Jane Andrews   pg 81
Gresley Wood, Church Gresley   © Sue Adair pg 83
Pickford's House Museum,, Derby   © J147 pg 84
Allestree Hall, Allestree Park, Derby
  © Eamon Curry   pg 86
River Derwent , Darely Abbey
  © Stephen McKay   pg 87
Mackworth Castle, Mackworth
  © Stephen G Taylor   pg 87
Kedleston Hall, Kedleston   © Jthomas pg 88
Entrance Drive to Edneston Manor, Edneston
  © Mike Bardill   pg 89
Longford Hall, Longford   © David Stowell pg 90
Sudbury hall, Sudbury   © Jthomas   pg 91
Well Dressing, Etwall   © John M   pg 92
Calke Abbey, Calke   © Mark Anderson pg 94
Swarkestone Bridge, Swarkstone
  © Jerry Evans   pg 95
Foremark Hall, Repton   © Phil Myott pg 97
Moira Furnace, Moira   © Chris Allen pg 99
Amber Valley,   © Nikki Mahadevan pg 101
Wingfield Manor, South Wingfield
  © Sam Styles   pg 103
Crich Stand, Crich   © Garth Newton pg 104

Fritchley Windmill, Fritchley
  © Alan Murray-Rust   pg 105
Parish Church of St Andrew, Swanick
  © Alan Heardman   pg 106
Heage Windmill, Heage
  © Alan Murray-Rust   pg 108
Codnor Castle, Codnor   © Alan Murray-Rust pg 109
East and North Mill, Belper   © Chris Allen pg 111
Nutbrook Canal, Mapperley   © David Lally pg 114
Middlemore Almshouses, Stanton by Dale
  © Garth Newton   pg 116
All Saints Church, Risley   © Oxymoron pg 116
Victoria Mill, Draycott   © Oxymoron pg 118
Elvaston Castle, Elvaston   © Jthomas pg 118
Canal Moorings, Shardlow   © Roger Kidd pg 119
Trent Lock, Long Eaton   © Stephen McKay pg 121
Ashover Show, Ashover   © Alan Heardman pg 123
Chesterfield Canal, Chesterfield
  © Richard Croft   pg 125
Renishaw Hall & Gardens, Renishaw
  © Dennis Thorley   pg 126
Cresswell Crags, Cresswell
  © Alan Heardman   pg 128
Bolsover Castle, Bolsover   © Galatas pg 129
Poulter Country Park, Scarcliffe   © Ann B pg 129
Sutton Scarsdale Hall, Heath
  © Tony Bacon   pg 130
Hardwick Hall, Ault Hucknall
  © Trevor Rickard   pg 131
Tibshelf Ponds, Tibshelf   © Dave Bevis pg 133
Ogston Reservoir, Ogston
  © Trevor Rickard   pg 134
Ashover Village, Ashover
  © George Mahoney   pg 135
Chimney, Holymoorside
  © John Poyser   pg 135
Linacre Reservoir, Cutthorpe   © Peter Barr pg 136

ORDER FORM

To order any of our publications just fill in the payment details below and complete the order form. For orders of less than 4 copies please add £1 per book for postage and packing. Orders over 4 copies are P & P free.

Please Complete Either:
I enclose a cheque for £ [   ] made payable to Travel Publishing Ltd
Or:

CARD NO: [   ]   EXPIRY DATE: [   ]

SIGNATURE: [   ]

NAME: [   ]

ADDRESS: [   ]

TEL NO: [   ]

Please either send, telephone, fax or e-mail your order to:
Travel Publishing Ltd, Airport Business Centre, 10 Thornbury Road, Estover, Plymouth PL6 7PP
Tel: 01752 697280   Fax: 01752 697299   e-mail: info@travelpublishing.co.uk

	PRICE	QUANTITY		PRICE	QUANTITY
HIDDEN PLACES REGIONAL TITLES			**COUNTRY LIVING RURAL GUIDES**		
Cornwall	£8.99	....	East Anglia	£10.99	....
Devon	£8.99	....	Heart of England	£10.99	....
Dorset, Hants & Isle of Wight	£8.99	....	Ireland	£11.99	....
East Anglia	£8.99	....	North East of England	£10.99	....
Lake District & Cumbria	£8.99	....	North West of England	£10.99	....
Lancashire & Cheshire	£8.99	....	Scotland	£11.99	....
Northumberland & Durham	£8.99	....	South of England	£10.99	....
Peak District and Derbyshire	£8.99	....	South East of England	£10.99	....
Yorkshire	£8.99	....	Wales	£11.99	....
HIDDEN PLACES NATIONAL TITLES			West Country	£10.99	....
England	£11.99	....			
Ireland	£11.99	....			
Scotland	£11.99	....			
Wales	£11.99	....	**TOTAL QUANTITY**		
OTHER TITLES					
Off The Motorway	£11.99	....	**TOTAL VALUE**		
Garden Centres and Nurseries of Britain	£11.99	....			

READER REACTION FORM

The *Travel Publishing* research team would like to receive readers' comments on any visitor attractions or places reviewed in the book and also recommendations for suitable entries to be included in the next edition. This will help ensure that the *Hidden Places series of Travel Guides* continues to provide its readers with useful information on the more interesting, unusual or unique features of each attraction or place ensuring that their visit to the local area is an enjoyable and stimulating experience. To provide your comments or recommendations would you please complete the forms below and overleaf as indicated and send to:

The Research Department, Travel Publishing Ltd, Airport Business Centre, 10 Thornbury Road, Estover, Plymouth PL6 7PP

YOUR NAME:

YOUR ADDRESS:

YOUR TEL NO:

Please tick as appropriate: COMMENTS ☐   RECOMMENDATION ☐

ESTABLISHMENT:

ADDRESS:

TEL NO:

CONTACT NAME:

PLEASE COMPLETE FORM OVERLEAF

READER REACTION FORM

COMMENT OR REASON FOR RECOMMENDATION:

READER REACTION FORM

The *Travel Publishing* research team would like to receive readers' comments on any visitor attractions or places reviewed in the book and also recommendations for suitable entries to be included in the next edition. This will help ensure that the *Hidden Places series of Travel Guides* continues to provide its readers with useful information on the more interesting, unusual or unique features of each attraction or place ensuring that their visit to the local area is an enjoyable and stimulating experience. To provide your comments or recommendations would you please complete the forms below and overleaf as indicated and send to:

The Research Department, Travel Publishing Ltd, Airport Business Centre, 10 Thornbury Road, Estover, Plymouth PL6 7PP

YOUR NAME:

YOUR ADDRESS:

YOUR TEL NO:

Please tick as appropriate: COMMENTS ☐   RECOMMENDATION ☐

ESTABLISHMENT:

ADDRESS:

TEL NO:

CONTACT NAME:

PLEASE COMPLETE FORM OVERLEAF

READER REACTION FORM

COMMENT OR REASON FOR RECOMMENDATION:

....
....
....
....
....
....
....
....
....
....
....
....
....
....
....

READER REACTION FORM

The *Travel Publishing* research team would like to receive readers' comments on any visitor attractions or places reviewed in the book and also recommendations for suitable entries to be included in the next edition. This will help ensure that the *Hidden Places series of Travel Guides* continues to provide its readers with useful information on the more interesting, unusual or unique features of each attraction or place ensuring that their visit to the local area is an enjoyable and stimulating experience. To provide your comments or recommendations would you please complete the forms below and overleaf as indicated and send to:

The Research Department, Travel Publishing Ltd, Airport Business Centre, 10 Thornbury Road, Estover, Plymouth PL6 7PP

YOUR NAME:

YOUR ADDRESS:

YOUR TEL NO:

Please tick as appropriate: COMMENTS ☐   RECOMMENDATION ☐

ESTABLISHMENT:

ADDRESS:

TEL NO:

CONTACT NAME:

PLEASE COMPLETE FORM OVERLEAF

READER REACTION FORM

COMMENT OR REASON FOR RECOMMENDATION:

....

....

....

....

....

....

....

....

....

....

....

....

....

....

....

....

INDEX OF TOWNS, VILLAGES AND PLACES OF INTEREST

INDEX OF TOWNS, VILLAGES AND PLACES OF INTEREST

INDEX OF TOWNS, VILLAGES AND PLACES OF INTEREST

INDEX OF TOWNS, VILLAGES AND PLACES OF INTEREST

INDEX OF TOWNS, VILLAGES AND PLACES OF INTEREST

ADVERTISERS

ADVERTISERS